Defending Probabilism

Defending Probabilism

The Moral Theology of Juan Caramuel

Julia A. Fleming

Georgetown University Press / Washington, D.C.

As of January 1, 2007, 13-digit ISBN numbers will replace the current 10-digit system.
Cloth: 978-1-58901-113-7

Georgetown University Press, Washington, D.C.

Library of Congress Cataloging-in-Publication Data
Fleming, Julia A.
    Defending probabilism: the moral theology of Juan Caramuel / Julia A. Fleming.
p. cm. — (Moral traditions series)
Includes bibliographical references (p.) and index.
    ISBN 1-58901-113-9 (alk. paper)
1. Caramuel Lobkowitz, Juan, 1606–1682. 2. Probabilism. 3. Christian ethics.
I. Title. II. Series.
    B4598.C344F54 2006
    241'.042092—dc22   2006003008

This book is printed on acid-free paper meeting the requirements of the American
National Standard for Permanence in Paper for Printed Library Materials.

13 12 11 10 09 08 07 06   9 8 7 6 5 4 3 2
First printing

Printed in the United States of America

This book is dedicated, with deepest gratitude, to the teachers who first inspired my interest in the history of moral theology, Charles E. Curran and Brian Johnstone, C.S.s.R. It was a privilege to study with you.

Contents

Foreword

WHY DO WE STUDY AND READ HISTORY? HISTORY HAS A VALUE AND, importance in itself. The pursuit of knowledge is a good in itself. History has become a very significant academic discipline in our world and history touches all aspects of our existence. Countries are proud of their histories; institutions want their histories written; historical figures play a significant role in the memories and lives of people. But history also has a more utilitarian role for all of us. We can and should learn from history. We can learn not to repeat the errors of the past and at the same time we can learn from what the past has accomplished. Yes, historical circumstances change and today's realities differ, sometimes considerably from those of a former era. But nonetheless, certain similarities remain.

The Roman Catholic Church and its theology have given great importance to history, primarily because of their emphasis on tradition. Tradition is the handing on (the transmission) of the life, doctrines, rituals, and the life of the church. The Catholic approach has recognized that one cannot just continue to cite the scriptures exactly as they were written. The church, through the gift of the Holy Spirit, must live, appropriate, and bear witness to the gospel message in light of the ongoing historical circumstances of time and place. Before Vatican II, many Catholic theologians spoke of scripture and tradition as two different sources of revelation. But Vatican II properly insisted on a closer and more reciprocal relationship between the two as forming the one deposit of faith.

As a result, the Catholic theological tradition has always paid great attention to history because the Church itself has developed in and through history. The councils of the Church form a very significant source of tradition because they involve the authoritative teaching of the Church as it responds to the requirements of the gospel message and the needs of the times. Catholic theology has paid significant attention not only to the historical development of official church teaching but also to its own history by studying great figures in the theological tradition such as St. Augustine, St. Thomas Aquinas, St. Bonaventure, St. Alphonsus Liguori, and Cardinal Newman among many others.

In this context, one would expect to find much written on the history of moral theology. But unfortunately, this is not the case. In fact, there does not exist today a definitive treatment of the historical development of moral theology. There have been some attempts at writing a general history, and some individual periods have been discussed. But the reality is that the discipline of moral theology as such lacks a standard history of its own development. What explains this seeming paradox? Despite the general Catholic emphasis on tradition and history, there is no definitive history of moral theology.

The nature of the development and discipline of moral theology partially helps to explain this paradox. For most of Christian history, ethical reflection was simply part of theology's general project. With Aquinas, for example, all theology is one. There is no distinction made between systematic theology and moral theology. In contemporary thought, on the other hand, moral theology is a separate discipline dealing primarily with the life of Christians as they try to respond to the call of God and the needs of the time. Moral theology came into existence as a separate discipline, primarily in the very practical role of preparing confessors for the sacrament of penance.

The fourteenth and fifteenth centuries saw precursors of later writings in the new discipline of moral theology with the penitential *summas* that catalogued penances according to the gravity of the sin. This was the period of the revival of private penance, and confessors had to be trained to know the appropriate penances to give for particular sins. Often the *summas* were arranged in alphabetical order and, therefore, did not involve any in-depth systematic understanding of the moral life. In the sixteenth and seventeenth centuries, with the beginning of seminaries and the need to train confessors for the sacrament of penance, the *Institutiones Morales* came into existence. These textbooks or manuals again had the practical aim of training future confessors to know the existence of sin and the gravity of sin. The more theoretical and systematic aspects of the moral life were developed only in a sketchy manner because the primary purpose of these manuals was the practical one of training confessors.

These manuals stayed in existence throughout the Catholic world until the Second Vatican Council. For most of its existence, the separate discipline of moral theology had a very pragmatic interest and was really not a systematic understanding and development of the whole moral life of the Christian. These manuals cite the opinions of older authors on subjects, but still the primary focus was the practical one of knowing the existence of sin and the gravity of sin for confessors in the present time. The authors of these manuals were not interested in the historical development of their own discipline.

The fact that moral theology emerged as a separate discipline primarily with the textbooks of moral theology in the early seventeenth century and the very practical orientation of the discipline helps to explain why there is no existing standard or definitive history of moral theology. But other factors also play a role. One of the major problems is that critical editions, or even reprint editions, do not exist for many moral works produced during the early modern period. In this book, Julia Fleming points out how difficult it is to work without a critical edition of Juan Caramuel's works. His books went through multiple editions and printings with a resulting significant variation with regard to the same works. Caramuel even complained that some printings of his works did not follow his own wishes. In studying Caramuel, one cannot find the vast majority of his works in libraries in the United States. The scholar has to work with microfilm facsimiles. Scholarly work in the history of moral theology is not easy.

Julia Fleming's book admirably achieves the two purposes of history mentioned above. First, her scholarly work contributes to a better understanding of the role of Juan Caramuel in Catholic moral theology. In light of the state of the history of moral theology today, this contribution is important in itself. One hopes that others might follow her example in studying other significant figures in the historical tradition.

The second purpose of history can be called utilitarian insofar as it can assist moral theologians today in dealing with the issues we face. This book analyzes Caramuel's role in the discussion over probabilism that consumed so much time and energy of moral theologians in the seventeenth and eighteenth centuries. The question of probabilism was deeply imbedded in the historical and cultural matrix of its own time, which is quite different from today. But we continue to face the same basic problem of how moral theology and the conscientious believer or any conscientious human person deals with the reality of provisional knowledge. Today people too often see moral reality only in terms of certitude or relativism. In reality, however, we often lack certitude and have to work on the basis of provisional moral knowledge and judgments. Consequently, this historical study makes some contribution to contemporary debates.

But Julia Fleming's book makes a third and even more significant contribution to the history of moral theology. She challenges the generally accepted judgment of Caramuel as a laxist. I was introduced to Caramuel as a laxist in the doctoral seminars of Louis Vereecke at the Academia Alphonsiana in Rome in 1960. Vereecke taught courses at the Alphonsiana in the history of moral theology beginning in 1950 and is now a professor emeritus. He is recognized today as the foremost contemporary authority on the history of moral theology. To help his students, Vereecke published in mimeographed form in the course of his long teaching career four volumes dealing with what he called the history of modern moral theology from 1300–1789. These volumes, however, were also sold to anyone who was interested in them, and people dealing with the history of moral theology today frequently refer to these notes in their publications.

Why did Vereecke never publish these four volumes in book form? From the outside one cannot know for sure why he never did so. But, in my judgment, he never published these notes as books because he realized they were not an authoritative and definitive history of modern moral theology. Too much work on individual authors has to be done before such an authoritative history can be written. Vereecke was well aware of the problems involved in writing such a definitive history. The manualists often merely copied what others said about their predecessors; for example, Alphonsus Liguori did not read the works of most of the authors he cited. It certainly was impossible for Vereecke himself to have read firsthand the works of all the theologians he discussed in these four mimeographed volumes. He obviously had to rely very often on the judgment of others.

The judgment about Caramuel, which I first learned from Vereecke, has been strengthened and solidified by every other thing I have read about Caramuel. The articles on Caramuel in theological encyclopedias in many different languages always describe him as a laxist and often as the prince of laxists. Contemporary moral theology seems to be in universal agreement that Caramuel is a laxist. The early commentators on Caramuel cite passages from his writings as proof of their judgment that he was a laxist. The judgment of Caramuel certainly received great support from Alphonsus Liguori's description of him as the prince of laxists.

But Julia Fleming examines the citations of Caramuel's words proposed by his critics and also discusses in detail some of Caramuel's later works where he gives a more systematic and sustained answer to the critics of probabilism. She concludes that Caramuel's approach to probabilism simply does not conform to the common portrait of him as a laxist. As any good book does, Fleming's work also raises many other questions. For example, what was the basis for St. Alphonsus's judgment about Caramuel as the prince of laxists? Why did so many people come to the judgment that he was a laxist? If the generally accepted understanding of Caramuel is not accurate, what does this say about the existing histories of this whole period of the discussion about probabilism in the seventeenth and eighteenth century?

These questions simply underscore the need for much more work to be done in the area of the history of moral theology. Julia Fleming's work is a step in this direction.

Charles E. Curran
Elizabeth Scurlock University Professor of Human Values
Southern Methodist University

Preface

IN 1663 JUAN CARAMUEL, THE BISHOP OF A POOR ITALIAN DIOCESE, responded to what he regarded as dangerous ethical innovations by defending in print a "most ancient and universal" Christian moral doctrine. Rejecting this tradition, he warned, would lead to dire consequences for the social order and for the Church itself. The title of his defensive little treatise (should one happen upon it accidentally in a library catalogue) suggests a scenario familiar to the modern world: a conservative ecclesiastic, a daring moral theory, and an almost inevitable collision of perspectives and concerns.

Yet Caramuel's *Apology for the Most Ancient and Universal Doctrine of Probability, Against the New, Individual, and Improbable Opinion of Lord Prospero Fagnani* is not at all what its title initially suggests.[1] Fagnani, Caramuel's opponent, was not a theologian but an extremely influential canonist, who published his "new" moral ideas within a Vatican-requested commentary on the decretals of Gregory IX.[2] Nor were Fagnani's moral views particularly liberal by the standards of his day. In the next century, Alphonsus Liguori, the patron saint of moral theologians, would dub him the "great prince of rigorists."[3]

One should also note the moral principle that Caramuel was defending from Fagnani's criticisms. It was not the Ten Commandments, the Evangelical Counsels, or the concept of Natural Law. The bishop called it *probability*, but within a decade of his death, another participant in the debate would speak of *probabilism,* the name familiar to Catholic ethicists today.[4] Modern scholars tend to agree with Fagnani that it was the brainchild of Bartolomé de Medina, a Spanish theologian whose groundbreaking thesis on probable opinion was published in 1577, less than thirty years before Caramuel was born.[5] In the centuries that followed, acceptance or rejection of probabilism became the major methodological dividing line for Catholic moral theologians. It was Caramuel, rather than Fagnani, who was championing the cutting-edge theory of his age against a conservative reaction.

In a sense, this is unsurprising, given the character of Caramuel himself. A Spanish Cistercian who left his native country as a young man, he spent the years preceding his episcopal consecration in a variety of places, including the Low Countries, Germany, Bohemia, and Rome. Caramuel served as an abbot, a preacher for the imperial court, and vicar general of Prague. As the leader of a group of hastily armed ecclesiastics, he helped to repel a Swiss surprise attack upon that city and received a gold medal from the emperor in consequence. Caramuel also played an extensive and controversial role in Counter-Reformation efforts in Bohemia and Moravia.[6] A few years later, he moved to Rome and briefly served as a consulter to the Congregation of Rites and even to the Holy Office.[7] When Rome faced a devastating bout of plague, he cared for its victims, and then urged his brother monks not to take advantage of a dispensation from fasting so that they might better express their gratitude for God's deliverance.[8] And through it all, Caramuel wrote tirelessly, producing over a hundred published and unpublished works on every subject under the sun, including astronomy, architecture, music, mathematics, linguistics, philosophy, politics, and of course, theology.[9] Even his enemies admired his erudition. In some circles, he was as famous (or infamous) as his dioceses were obscure. When he died, he was honored by memorial services at major universities, including Louvain, Paris, Salamanca, and Alcalá, in addition to the obsequies attended by the emperor in Vienna.[10] Yet today, moral theologians tend to know only Alphonsus Liguouri's characterization of him. If Fagnani was the "prince of rigorists," Bishop Juan Caramuel was called the "prince . . . of laxists."[11]

Caramuel's book did provoke a response from Church authorities, but not the one he had desired. Instead of acting on his concerns, Rome consigned his volume to the Index of Forbidden Books.[12] Ironically, this was the only one of his many controversial works that the Spanish theologian would see condemned.

Why Does It Matter Today?

Why, after more than three centuries, should moral theologians care about this obscure little volume, or indeed, about any of Caramuel's theories regarding probabilism? First, his analyses illuminate the history of our discipline. The controversy over probabilism was moral theology's central methodological debate during the Early Modern Period. As we shall see, Caramuel devoted great attention to the theoretical foundations of reliance upon probable opinion. His work—which has received insufficient consideration from his successors—thus sheds light on a conflict critical for the development of moral theology.

Moreover, while probabilism itself is now a part of history rather than of contemporary ethical theory, the issue that this moral approach sought to address is a perennial one. How can a person behave responsibly in a situation where the correct moral response is less than clear? Caramuel's theories address a problem that, if anything, has only become more serious with the passage of time. This shared challenge offers a second warrant for the claim that his legacy merits our attention. Caramuel's work highlights the value of provisional moral knowledge. In our search for moral truth, the theory of probable opinions reminds us that relativism is not the only alternative to certainty.

Finally, Caramuel saw more in the controversy regarding probabilism than a disagreement over ethical method. For him, the ultimate question behind these debates was theological, if one understands that term in the sense of "discourse about God." At root, it concerned the nature of God's dealings with humanity, especially the nature and scope of divine mercy. In Caramuel's view, this ethical problem—does probable opinion suffice for security of conscience?—was really a question about God's compassion toward finite creatures. Caramuel's work is thus a valuable reminder that theological ethics inevitably rests upon an understanding of God, and that Christian ethical theory is, in a sense, a proclamation about God. Reflecting upon his analysis can encourage us to examine the unexpressed theological foundations of our own methodological debates.

The Structure of the Present Work

The scope of the present discussion is necessarily limited. It does not reappraise the debate over probabilism or Caramuel's place within the history of moral theology, although both of those projects could be quite informative. Nor will it conduct a comprehensive review of Caramuel's writings on probability. The present analysis will focus on the *Apologema,* since that text is less available and more pastorally oriented than some of the author's other works. It will, however, devote significant attention to other texts that preceded and followed the *Apology* in order to trace the development of Caramuel's theory over time.

To understand the *Apologema,* one must place it in context. Accordingly, chapter 1 considers preliminary questions: What were the characteristics of seventeenth-century moral theology? What was probabilism? Who was Caramuel? Why is he such a valuable witness concerning this common moral method? Chapter 2 further develops the background by looking at two of Caramuel's early writings on probability, texts that are far better known than his mature works. In light of this, chapter 3 examines how Caramuel used probabilism, and discusses his resolution of one spectacular controversy in political ethics: the freedom of a Catholic prince to make peace with Protestants. All this sets the stage for the analysis of the *Apologema* in chapters 4 and 5, the first focused on its negative project (i.e., the response to criticism) and the second on its positive project (explaining the nature and proper use of probable opinions). Chapter 6 considers Caramuel's *Dialexis de Non-Certitudine,* a later work on probabilism, which refines his earlier theories and takes the argument in a new direction. The concluding section ("Afterword") addresses the contemporary significance of Caramuel's legacy. What, if anything, do these long-forgotten writings have to say to us today concerning the history of moral theology, the importance of provisional knowledge, and connection between ethical theory and one's concept of God?

Working with Late-Seventeenth-Century Texts and Ideas

The nature of Caramuel's writings poses some definite challenges for the modern interpreter. There are no critical editions of his theological works, and one most easily consults them (at least in the United States) via microfilm. To aid the reader, the notes to the present text eliminate most of the conventions of seventeenth-century printing, such as Latin abbreviations and the use of *f* for *s*. (I have not supplied modern quotation marks, however, for the quotations that appear within the early texts. Unless noted otherwise, I have retained all italics used in the original texts.) Scholars interested in a literal transcription of the text must consult the original volume. When translating passages from Caramuel, I have omitted the honorific title *D.* (*dominus*), although the word is cited in the Latin text that appears in the notes. All translations are my own work.

Several of Caramuel's books went through multiple editions and printings. Some of these reflect wide variations. This can create difficulties for the modern researcher because the volumes are not easily obtained. Page number references can prove very difficult to verify, if the volume to which one has access differs from the one available to a previous commentator. Accordingly, the notes to the present discussion utilize each volume's internal tract designations in addition to the page numbers (except where such designations are erroneous or missing). The penultimate number in a reference is usually the margin number, which often appears in Roman numerals in the original text; page numbers appear within parentheses. I hope that this system of citation, though very tedious, will give other researchers a fighting chance to find the passage in question, should their edition or printing of a given volume differ significantly from my own. I use this system consistently, except in reference to the *Apologema*. Ironically, because this banned work enjoyed only one edition, it is sufficient to rely upon page numbers.

It is easier to refer to *probabilism* than to *the legitimacy of relying upon probable opinions*; hence, the discussion that follows will often use the noun rather than the phrase. The reader must be aware, however, that this usage is anachronistic: neither Caramuel nor Fagnani ever uses the term *probabilism*. They describe the debate not in terms of competing systems (i.e., probabilism versus probabiliorism) but in terms of the answer to a question: Does reliance upon probable opinion suffice for security of conscience? To understand their arguments, it is helpful to keep this distinction in mind.

Finally, the reader should note that there was a great deal of intellectual borrowing, both documented and undocumented, in seventeenth-century theological literature. Caramuel is by no means the only author, for example, to appeal to Jesus' "easy yoke" as grounds for rejecting moral rigorism.[13] In reviewing the present discussion, the reader must distinguish claims of advocacy from claims of originality. One can reasonably assert that Caramuel provides a unique witness to probabilism without claiming that all of the arguments he espouses were exclusively his. Assessing the extent of his originality lies beyond the limited scope of the present discussion. This book analyzes what Caramuel wrote. It does not analyze his reliance upon the works of other moralists.

Acknowledgments

While the author bears responsibility for all errors and weaknesses in the present work, its production would have been impossible without the assistance of others, especially Charles E. Curran, who composed the foreword, James Keenan, S.J., and Richard Brown of Georgetown University Press. I owe many thanks to Martin Stone for his encouragement regarding the project. I also wish to acknowledge the useful comments of the anonymous reviewers who evaluated the draft. *Studia Moralia* graciously granted permission for the reprint of materials from my earlier article: "Juan Caramuel and the Nature of Extrinsic Probability" (vol. 42, 2004, pp. 337–59). Creighton University's College of Arts and Sciences provided financial support during my sabbatical. Special thanks are due to the libraries and librarians who helped to supply rare texts and references, especially Lynn Sherwood at Creighton University's Reinert Alumni Library, G. Brian Cardell at The Catholic University of America's division of Special Collections, and Brother Anthony Logalbo at St. Bonaventure University. Professional reproductions of Caramuel's texts came from the Bodleian Library and the British Library. I am particularly grateful to Professor Joseph Selling of the Katholieke Universiteit Leuven and to Etienne D'hondt and Franz Gistelinck of that institution's theological library for providing a photocopy of the *Apologema*. Finally, for their encouragement and their patience in answering questions and supplying references concerning the seventeenth century, I wish to thank my brother and sister-in-law, historians Donald F. Fleming and Janet Pope.

Situating Probabilism

The Ethical Theory and Its Significance for Caramuel

B ECAUSE TODAY NEITHER PROBABILISM NOR CARAMUEL HIMSELF IS
likely to be a popular topic of conversation, it would be a mistake to
wade into an analysis of his moral theory without clarifying its concepts
and outlining its historical context. Answers to the following questions
can make sense of a discussion that might otherwise prove unintelligible:
What were the characteristics of Roman Catholic moral theology in the
seventeenth century? What was probabilism? Who was Caramuel? How
did his understanding of the search for ethical knowledge affect his approach to probabilism? Finally, why is he such an important resource for
interpreting the history of this influential moral theory?

Moral Theology in the Seventeenth Century

Juan Caramuel was born near the beginning and died near the end of the
seventeenth century, a period of great significance for the history of Roman Catholic ethical thought. At the century's beginning, Louis Vereecke
explains, moral theology emerged as a distinct field of theological spe-
cialization, equipped with its own principles, methods, authorities, and
sources.[1] With the publication of Jesuit Juan Azor's *Institutiones Morales*,
the new discipline even produced a literary genre, a formula for ethical
exposition that would shape Catholic moral thought for centuries.[2] This
age witnessed a proliferation of publications in moral theology, including

both pastoral and academic works.[3] An attempt to account for this effusion must credit many influences, including the availability of the printing press, which enabled scholars like Caramuel to publish and to issue revised editions of their texts in relatively short order. Yet the central explanation for this growth in Catholic ethical literature lies in the Church's efforts to respond to the cultural, political, and religious challenges of the previous century.

Caramuel's birth in 1606 came less than 120 years after Columbus's initial voyage to the New World, and less than a century after the beginning of the Protestant Reformation. Copernicus's controversial treatise had passed its sixtieth anniversary of publication, and Rome's judgment that it should be consigned to the Index of Forbidden Books (until corrected) was still a decade away. It is not surprising that Caramuel's moral works contain references to Columbus, Luther, and Galileo.[4] Such political, religious, and scientific changes—or more accurately, revolutions—demanded that moralists consider their practical implications for the Christian life. How were individuals and communities to function when traditional religious and cultural unities, or time-honored presuppositions about the physical world, could no longer be taken for granted?

Ironically, Catholic moralists confronted these challenges at the same time that the competing churches of Western Europe were emphasizing mission and the communication of Christian doctrine to ordinary people.[5] Moral teaching played an important role in this catechesis. As Albert Jonsen and Stephen Toulmin point out: "To people of the sixteenth century, activities we now distinguish into different kinds—as political or economic, religious or social—were all 'moral' activities."[6] Every sphere, every facet of human existence posed some type of question for moral theology, especially because of its focus on the Sacrament of Penance. Any problem that a penitent might conceivably bring to his/her confessor became an appropriate subject for analysis.

In many ways, this emphasis upon confession in seventeenth-century Catholic moral thought reflected the legacy of the Council of Trent. In rebutting Protestant objections to Catholic penitential theology and practice, the Council had explicitly described confessors as judges and anathematized those who denied that sacramental absolution was a judicial act.[7] The Council had also insisted that penitents must confess each individual mortal sin they could remember, describing any circumstances that might affect its proper classification.[8] This mandate concerning confession of sins according to species (i.e., type) made it all the more important that confessors be able to identify and evaluate their penitents' acts correctly. To fulfill their juridical function, priests had to known how to classify sins—a task for which many were not adequately prepared. The new discipline of moral theology attempted to address these problems. One can reasonably argue that facilitating confession became its central organizing principle.

The emergence of moral theology as a specialized area of expertise, therefore, occurred in conjunction with the Church's efforts to develop a proper training system for its sacramental ministers. The Council of Trent had mandated the establishment of seminaries, schools devoted to the education of diocesan clergy. Such institutions provided a shorter, more practically oriented course of studies than the theological training that had long been available in the universities. Because preparing students to celebrate the sacraments was an important part of their raison d'être, the seminaries devoted great emphasis to casuistry, the resolution of cases of conscience, so that the future priests could draw upon this knowledge when hearing confessions. Religious orders such as the Jesuits also emphasized casuistry within their formation programs.[9] But the effect of this focus on casuistry was not limited to the young clerics who studied it, since a discipline is inevitably shaped by what its practitioners are called upon to teach. Seminaries and other houses of formation were not simply "seed beds" for clergy. On an intellectual level, such programs became greenhouses for the development of a moral theology devoted to the diagnosis of sins and the resolution of concrete moral dilemmas.[10]

Yet if the moral theology of Caramuel's age had evolved in response to the role of the confessor as judge, it had also inherited a benevolent medieval tradition that described the confessor as a physician, and the sacrament as a font of encouragement, consolation, and healing.[11] This longstanding emphasis on the confessor's need for compassion exercised a great influence upon Caramuel and many of his colleagues. They repeated their predecessors' warnings that a harsh confessor could drive a penitent to despair. The problem of the scrupulous conscience, excessively fearful of malfeasance and prone to dwell upon nonexistent faults, was all too familiar to the moralists of the seventeenth century.[12] They were very anxious to ensure that confessors could distinguish real guilt from imagined guilt, and that they were prepared to offer not only an accurate evaluation of acts but also a compassionate response to persons.

All of these factors—the focus upon confession, conscience, and casuistry, as well as the awareness that the world was changing and that a penitent's scruples could pose as many challenges for the confessor as moral carelessness—influenced the character of seventeenth-century moral theology. Not surprisingly, they also shaped its central methodological debate. The argument over probabilism—note again that use of this term in reference to the seventeenth century is anachronistic—concerned the prudent response (especially by a confessor) in the face of differing conclusions regarding moral obligation. At heart, it was a debate over the flexibility not only of sacramental practice but also of moral theology in an uncertain age.

Probabilism

For Roman Catholic moral theology, it is possible to evaluate a moral decision from two different perspectives: by focusing either upon the action or upon the person who performs it. While the first approach analyzes the behavior's content, the second assesses the agent's moral responsibility for his or her act. Inevitably, the second perspective confronts the problem of human limitations. The appropriate course of action is not always easy to discern. Despite their best efforts, finite human beings sometimes make ethical mistakes. In light of this risk, how can we avoid becoming paralyzed by the recognition of possible error? Is there a way to ensure that our choices will be responsible, even when gaps in knowledge limit our ability to identify appropriate options?

In the age of Early Modern Catholicism, the appeal to probable opinion offered one answer to this question. Probabilism was a method for ensuring moral responsibility in the absence of speculative moral certitude. It could also be described as a remedy for practical doubt. Catholic moral thought had long asserted that one must not act upon a doubtful conscience, i.e., with the reasonable fear (but no certain knowledge) that the action might be prohibited.[13] To risk committing sin, from this perspective, was sinful in its own right.[14] But that stricture created practical problems, especially when the limitations of human knowledge collided with the need for immediate action. Sometimes, persons do not have the luxury of postponing decisions until all uncertainties are resolved. Catholic ethics needed a way to give people confidence that they were acting responsibly, even if their choices might eventually prove to have been mistaken.

In time, moral theology would delineate a variety of moral systems that offered such ethical reassurance. Each provided a basic rule of thumb for making responsible decisions when identification of the correct choice was subject to debate. Tutiorism required selection of the "safer" course, i.e., the choice that best insured that the agent would avoid sin.[15] Probabiliorism (as it was eventually defined) allowed the agent to adopt a position in favor of liberty only if it was more probable (i.e., supported by stronger arguments, stronger authorities, or both) than the judgment that he or she was constrained by moral obligation.[16] A third method, eventually known as probabilism, offered the greatest latitude for moral choice. Under certain circumstances, it allowed the agent to follow a probable opinion, even if contrasting views were arguably stronger in some way.[17]

It is important to emphasize that such clear definitions of the various approaches did not exist in Caramuel's time. When he attacks those who insist upon adherence to the more probable opinion, for example, he is clearly referring to a position different from probabiliorism, as it would later be understood.[18] The seventeenth-century debate focused upon the adequacy of probable opinion for responsible action. There were those who believed that probable opinion sufficed for surety of conscience, and there were those who rejected this view.

In essence, the seventeenth-century debate was a reaction to the innovative thesis of Bartolomé de Medina. Medina, a Spanish Dominican and professor of theology at Salamanca, had formulated the conclusion that would become probabilism's central principle.[19] "It seems to me," argued Medina in his commentary on the *Prima Secundae*, "that if an opinion is probable, then one is permitted to follow it, even if the opposite [opinion] is more probable."[20] In contrast to his predecessors, Medina thus identified conformity with probable opinion as the rule of thumb for ensuring "the minimal standards of moral rectitude."[21]

Medina's commentary was published in 1577. His basic argument was quickly adopted, extended, and refined by others, especially the Jesuit Francisco Suarez, who drew upon principles from the theology of law to explain why one could rely upon probable opinion when the existence of a relevant precept was uncertain. Like St. Thomas Aquinas, Suarez insisted that promulgation (i.e., publication) was an essential characteristic of law. Hence, when the existence of a particular law was uncertain, one could argue that it had been insufficiently promulgated and did not bind the subject, who remained in possession of his or her liberty.[22] Through the efforts of Suarez and others, Medina's basic argument thus gave rise to increasingly complex ethical theories.

The appeal to probable opinion quickly became a popular method for resolving cases of conscience. University professors embraced it, as did the authors of practical and pastoral moral works. The list of probabilism's advocates also included seminary instructors.[23] In light of probabilism's rapid diffusion and widespread popularity, it is fair to say that, in the seventy-five years following its first expression, the theory enjoyed remarkable success.

Reactions against Medina's approach remained isolated until the second half of the seventeenth century. For the next hundred years, however, they proceeded with a vengeance. In 1747, the French Dominican Billuart claimed that, whereas there had been twenty probabiliorists for every probabilist in 1710, that ratio had now been extended to forty to one in favor of probabiliorism.[24] Although not absolutely eliminated, probabilism suffered a long period of decline.[25] It would require the efforts of Alphonsus Liguori in formulating a revised form of probabilism (i.e., equiprobabilism) before the theory regained widespread respectability.[26] Alphonsus's writings on the subject, however, began to appear only in the mid-eighteenth century, and his influence became widespread in the nineteenth, when he was canonized and eventually acclaimed as a doctor of the Church. In the seventeenth century, probabilism's meteoric rise was followed by an equally precipitous descent.

Why did probabilism's reputation fall so dramatically? To put the matter in simple terms, the reaction to probabilism was a storm falling on ground that had been scarred by other controversies, some long-existing, so that the cumulative effect of the disputes was like an avalanche. An unresolved debate over grace and recurrent attacks upon laxism (i.e., excessive leniency in moral theory) dovetailed into the Jansenist crisis, all of which shaped the discussion of probabilism.[27] These were theological disagreements, but politics, both civil and ecclesiastical, also played an important role. The debate over probabilism became a casualty of rivalries both within and between religious orders. It was marred by nationalistic prejudices and sucked into the ongoing battle for control of the French Church.[28] Finally, Vatican authorities' fear of scandal and desire for unity in the face of Reformation losses configured its outcome.[29] Formal Roman condemnations of two sets of laxist moral positions (in 1665–66 and 1679, respectively) proved particularly damaging for probabilism, since adherence to its principles was sometimes invoked as an explanation for such lapses.[30] These were not auspicious circumstances for a calm academic debate over moral theory. As we shall see, Juan Caramuel's most famous and most controversial work of moral theology first appeared just before the conflict reached a stage of crisis.

Caramuel's Life and Theology

Like probabilism, Juan Caramuel y Lobkowitz was a child of Spain, although his mother was from Bohemia and his father, an engineer and amateur astronomer, from Luxembourg. Born in Madrid in 1606, Caramuel was educated at a Jesuit school before moving on to more advanced studies at Alcalá. From there, he entered the Cistercian Order and eventually was sent to the University of Salamanca for training in theology.[31] By Caramuel's day, Salamanca's golden age as a theological center had passed, but he reveals that his training there greatly influenced his thinking about probabilism.[32] Years later, he would credit a "great man," the Cistercian scholar Angel Manrique, with teaching him to understand the essence of intrinsic probability.[33]

What formal level of academic achievement Caramuel obtained in Salamanca is unclear, as is the immediate course of his life after leaving the university. Eventually he settled in Louvain.[34] There he decided to supplement his academic credentials by applying for admission to the doctorate in theology. Although the evaluators of this prestigious university initially gave short shrift to his achievements at a Spanish institution, the faculty awarded him the degree in 1638.[35]

By joining the community of scholars at Louvain, Caramuel had entered an institution where longstanding disputes had created factions— factions that would, in the next decade, have an important impact upon the wider Church. One recurrent quarrel concerned the role of the Jesuits in Louvain, where the university resisted the Society's efforts to offer public instruction in philosophy and theology as an encroachment upon its privileges and a threat to its economic welfare.[36] (So bitter did this dispute become that a letter directed from Louvain to its fellow institution at Alcalá asserts: "Christianity is divided into two camps: the Company and the universities."[37]) Supplementing this educational turf war was a theological controversy concerning grace. From the Vatican's condemnation of a number of propositions attributed to Louvain's Michael Baius in 1567, through the faculty's 1587 censure of the views of Léonard Lessius (a Jesuit whose teachings have been described as diametrically opposed to those of Baius), the battle over grace shaped the history of Louvain.[38] As the dispute between the university and Lessius raged on, the nuncio of Cologne (at the behest of the pope) took action to quiet the controversy, eventually declaring that theologians enjoyed the liberty to defend either position and precluding the parties from censuring their adversaries.[39] Soon afterwards, however, another dispute about grace arose in Spain, this time primarily between by Jesuits and the Dominicans.[40] In 1607, Pope Paul V prohibited further publications on the subject without prior review. It was to this restriction that the Jesuits would appeal in 1640, to try to prevent the posthumous publication of Cornelius Jansen's *Augustinus*.[41]

From the time that he first applied for admission to the doctorate, Caramuel felt the influence of Louvain's controversies on his career. Before granting his degree, for example, the faculty required him to retract two propositions about grace and to promise to abstain from asserting them further among those studying at the university. Caramuel's views on grace, developed in the Spanish schools, were closer to Molina's approach than to the position of Bañez.[42] Caramuel's background, therefore, predisposed him to an alliance with the Jesuit faction at Louvain, a relationship that (as we shall see) was eventually realized during the initial phases of the Jansenist controversy. This alliance, moreover, associated him with a group that was attacked at Louvain not only for its theology of grace and its infringement upon university prerogatives, but also for its "laxism."[43]

At Louvain, according to Hugo Hurter's *Nomenclator Literarius Theologicae Catholicae*, Caramuel debated scripture with Professor Libert Froidmont regarding the safety of embracing probable opinions.[44] Without naming Froidmont, the *Theologia Regularis*, which contains the first of Caramuel's significant discussions of probabilism, responds to some of Froidmont's arguments.[45] As we shall see, the *Apologema* refers even more explicitly to the significance of the exchange with Froidmont.[46] Caramuel's role as a defender of recourse to probable opinion, therefore, was established very early in his theological career.

The period in Louvain also initiated several recurring patterns that would shape Caramuel's life for many years to come. The first was his scholarship on a wide variety of topics: during his years in the Low Countries, he published treatises on theology, astronomy, and philosophy, as well as political polemics and spiritual works.[47] The second pattern was his quest for academic or ecclesiastical preferment. For much of his life, Caramuel would succeed in obtaining only titular positions, for example, as abbot of monasteries long since emptied by the Reformation. But for our purposes, the most important development was his public involvement in the quarrel over Jansenism.

Before his short-lived elevation to the episcopacy, Cornelius Jansen had been associated with Louvain, twice as a student and then as a professor.[48] Jansen eventually became rector of the university and was nominated for the see of Ypres in 1636. Plague claimed him in 1638, the year that Caramuel received his doctorate. Two years later at Louvain, Jansen's literary executors Froidmont and Henri Calenus published his masterwork, the *Augustinus*, a product of over two decades of reflection on the bishop of Hippo's theology, especially the anti-Pelagian writings.[49] This work ignited the firestorm over what we now call Jansenism. At the urging of the Jesuits, the Vatican issued a bull (*In eminenti*) in response to the publication, without, however, expressly naming the author or the volume.[50] A decade later in 1653, the Holy See condemned five propositions purportedly drawn from the *Augustinus* concerning grace, human nature, human freedom, and the universal salvific will of God regarding Christ's sacrifice. For the present discussion, the most important of these propositions is the first: "Some precepts of God are impossible for just persons who wish and attempt [to fulfill them], according to the present powers that they have; [for] they also lack that grace, by which [their fulfillment] would become possible."[51]

Long before debate over these propositions had become a matter for the Church at large, however, acrimony concerning Jansen's legacy was swirling at Louvain, where it fed upon the earlier university disputes concerning the theology of grace and the teaching role of the Society of Jesus.[52]

In 1641, the Jesuits sponsored a public examination of Jansen's theology.[53] Caramuel supported the Jesuits' positions, and when the scholar presiding over the event suggested that Jansen might have erred "materially" through invincible ignorance, the Cistercian expressed incredulity that a learned theologian and professor at Louvain could fail to recognize heretical propositions in his own work. If this were true, how could any ordinary person commit formal heresy, given that he or she was far less learned in theology than Jansen? Either Jansen committed formal heresy, Caramuel argued, or virtually no one in Europe was doing so.[54]

Caramuel was quite proud of having been one of the first theologians outside of the Society of Jesus to confront Jansenism publicly. Not only did his statements earn him the gratitude of the Jesuits, but (through the Company's intervention) they also brought him to the notice of Fabio Chigi, at that time nuncio to Cologne, an ecclesiastic who was to exercise an enormous influence upon his career.[55] As Caramuel would learn, however, the Jansenists could make very dangerous enemies. In later years, his defense of probabilism would be closely tied to his opposition to Jansenism.

As previously mentioned, Caramuel's years at Louvain were literarily productive in science as well as in theology. He published works in mathematics and astronomy, corresponded with important scholars, and even experimented with a pendulum by hanging weights from a library roof.[56] Yet what he failed to do, despite his continued efforts, was to obtain a permanent academic or ecclesiastical position. Finally, at the end of 1643, an opportunity seemed to open elsewhere. Under the aegis of his occupying armies, Philip IV of Spain was seeking to revitalize Catholic ecclesiastical presence in Germany by reconstituting religious communities extinguished by the spread of Protestantism. Caramuel received an appointment as abbot of Disibodenberg, and in early 1644, set out upon his new mission.[57]

The result was another disappointment. In a letter to Chigi, Caramuel described what he found when he reached the monastery: crumbling stones (requiring a "great reformation") and committed Calvinists (already "too much reformed").[58] Nor was the military situation stable. Caramuel attempted to take part in missionary activities, but the ongoing violence forced him to move frequently.[59] Although he continued to write, even publishing his first systematic work in moral theology during this period, his situation remained difficult.[60] At last, however, the influence of Emperor

Ferdinand III obtained for Caramuel what his ecclesiastical connections had failed to provide: a secure position as abbot of two (Benedictine) monasteries, one in Vienna and the other in Prague.[61] By accepting these benefices, he effectively entered the imperial service.

Almost immediately, this decision brought him into conflict with his longtime patron. The emperor was in negotiation with the Protestants to end the Thirty Years War, and Chigi supported the arguments of a work with obvious political ramifications concerning this process, the Jesuit Heinrich Wangnereck's *Theological Judgment on the Question: Whether the Peace Such as the Protestants Desire Is Illicit in Itself?*[62] The author answered his own question in the affirmative. When Chigi asked for Caramuel's opinion, the new abbot responded that he was publishing his own work on the same question. Caramuel, in fact, invoked probabilism to reject Wangnereck's thesis, in defense of the emperor's policy.[63]

Such disloyalty infuriated Chigi. In a letter to the cardinal secretary of state, he felt it necessary to distance himself from Caramuel, whom he described as lacking prudence consonant with his intelligence.[64] "He was previously my friend," he wrote to the assessor of the Holy Office.[65] (It is quite interesting to compare Chigi's words to curial officials with his amicable statements to Caramuel himself.[66]) The breach between them required some time to heal, if indeed it was ever completely mended.

Caramuel was well aware of the risks of publishing the book and feared that it would draw condemnation from Rome. After the Vatican's formal disavowal of the Peace of Westphalia, the worried theologian wrote directly to Innocent X, arguing that the book contained a hypothetical argument rather than a judgment of fact.[67] Yet for all his professed willingness to see the book perish, if it displeased the pope, Caramuel's letter also asserted: "I think that there is nothing in that entire work that is not probable."[68] Far from consigning the volume's memory to oblivion, Caramuel explicitly cited it within his other works.[69] As we shall see, the text provides a particularly interesting application of his theories on probabilism.

For the next few years, Caramuel focused his practical energies on the revitalization of Catholicism in Bohemia and Moravia. As vicar general of Prague, he presided over a tribunal for the reform and reduction of heresy, using both educational and coercive means to restore dissenters to the Catholic fold. Caramuel proudly claimed to have returned thirty thousand souls to the faith, an assertion of achievement that would appear within his epitaph.[70] Yet busy as he was, these years also constituted one of the most productive literary periods of his life. During this time, he produced the first edition of his best-known moral work, the *Theologia Moralis Fundamentalis*, which historian of philosophy Dino Pastine describes as "one of the most significant seventeenth-century treatises on argument."[71] For the debate over probabilism, this volume would prove particularly influential.

Modern scholars posit diverse explanations for the next major development in Caramuel's career: his move from the imperial court to Rome. Pastine argues that Caramuel desired the change, not least because of a concern that his distance from the Holy Office was providing an opportunity for his enemies.[72] Alessandro Catalano, on the other hand, maintains that, even though Caramuel's position (especially as abbot) had become untenable, he deliberately delayed the journey out of fear of the Inquisition. The complaints of Caramuel's opponents in Bohemia (Catalano believes) had only increased Roman distrust of a theologian already suspect because of his writings on the Peace.[73] Whatever the truth of the matter, it is clear that Caramuel finally made the change after the election of his patron, Fabio Chigi, to the papacy (as Alexander VII) in April of 1655.[74]

In Rome, Caramuel served as a consulter to the Holy Office and to the Congregation of Rites, where he brought his scientific acumen to the analysis of apparent miracles.[75] He studied Chinese and put his knowledge of Arabic to use in an analysis of the famous engravings discovered in the catacombs of Granada in 1595.[76] During an outbreak of plague that claimed fifteen thousand lives, he exercised particular zeal in caring for the sick and ensuring the burial of the dead.[77] But Caramuel's residence in Rome was not destined to last long. In July 1657, he was consecrated bishop of Satriano/Campagna, a small, remote, plague-decimated, and very poor Italian diocese, much of it in an area beset by bandits.[78] When Caramuel eventually reached his see in 1659, he discovered that his residence was adjacent to a mill and that its noise made concentration difficult. In a play on words that exploited the similarity between the names of the Vatican tribunal (*Rota*) and the Italian word for wheel (*ruota*), he remarked, "I believed that the pope had made me a bishop, but now I find that he has made me Auditor of the wheel."[79]

Why his longtime patron awarded Caramuel this dubious promotion and whether it should be interpreted as a prize or an exile are matters of

some conjecture and argument.[80] Clearly, however, this appointment occurred at a time when there was much public discussion about the problem of novel and insufficiently stringent moral teaching. Criticism of Caramuel's work, especially the *Theologia Moralis Fundamentalis,* became part
of a broader church debate. It is certainly not unreasonable to interpret
Caramuel's appointment as a response to a dispute that, by the late 1650s,
was spreading well beyond the boundaries of the theological academy.

In 1654, we know that an assessor for the Congregation of the Index
passed judgment on twenty propositions from Caramuel's work.[81] In
general, they seem to have concerned his solutions to particular cases of
conscience.[82] Caramuel certainly feared that the *Theologia Moralis Fundamentalis* might be condemned and was anxious to defend it.[83] He was, in
fact, required to make corrections and issued a new edition of the work
in 1656. (The subtitle of this volume—which was dedicated to Alexander
VII—promises that it rejects many "extremely lax opinions," which neither truth nor theological prudence can accept.[84]) However, other theologians responded to the original edition, which continues to be the most
famous and widely disseminated text of the *Theologia Moralis Fundamentalis.* In 1656, for example, the Spanish Dominican Juan Martínez del
Prado published his *Observationes circa Theologiam Fundamentalem D.D.
Ioannis Caramuel.*[85] Over the next decade, there would be a number of such
critical theological responses to the new bishop's theological project.[86]

Caramuel's writings particularly outraged his Jansenist critics. Soon
Caramuel's longstanding feud with the Archbishop of Mechlin, Jacques
Boonen (whom our author described as the "prince of Jansenists") broke
out into open warfare.[87] In 1655, Boonen, who had long disapproved of
the theologian's ideas, forbade the sale, reading, or possession of any of
Caramuel's works—an enormously broad condemnation, considering the
range of subjects treated by the author.[88] Caramuel clearly interpreted this
act as retaliation for his publication, as vicar general of Prague, of the condemnation of the archbishop's *apologia* (i.e., for his failure to propagate
the first Roman bull issued in response to the *Augustinus*).[89] Caramuel ap-
pealed to the tribunal of the Inquisition, which, in October, ordered the
ban lifted. Yet the deaths of Boonen and then of his vicar general delayed
any action, as did resistance to the Roman order on the part of local officials.[90] The issuance of Jansenist responses to the *Theologia Moralis Fundamentalis,* was, in fact, far from over.[91]

With the protection of Alexander VII, Caramuel clearly weathered the initial storm over his controversial work.[92] (Chigi, while still a cardinal, had in fact, consulted Caramuel as a theological authority regarding Jansenism during the same year that the Congregation of the Index was evaluating his ideas).[93] More significant in the long run seems to have been the broader church reaction against "laxist" moral positions, especially the admonition to Dominican theologians inserted into the acts of the general chapter held in Rome in 1656. Exhorting Dominicans to remain faithful to the teaching of St. Thomas, this document warns them against embracing novel and dangerous moral positions.[94] According to Thomas Deman, the actions of the general chapter brought about the general detachment of the Dominican order from probabilism.[95] In addition to his other critics, Caramuel soon faced objections from a number of Dominicans.[96]

If the Dominicans sounded the theological warning bell against moral novelty, the *Provincial Letters* carried that warning into the court of public opinion. Repudiating laxism had been a Jansenist concern long before Caramuel's major works appeared, as an earlier Jansenist attack upon the moral theology of the Jesuits makes clear.[97] However, in the mid-1650s, laxism became the most effective counterargument for the beleaguered French Jansenists in their battle for survival. In January of 1656, their leader Antoine Arnauld was facing certain censure and expulsion from the Sorbonne.[98] In desperation, one of the lay adherents of the movement, Blaise Pascal, began to publish anonymously a series of short, satirical counterattacks against the enemies of Jansenism, especially the Jesuits. His arguments on grace had little effect. But when Pascal turned his attention to morality and to his enemies' theory of probable opinions, the scandal spread like wildfire.[99] As Jonsen and Toulmin explain, Pascal did not analyze probabilism's theoretical foundations; instead, he simply listed "the decisions that those casuists who had adopted probabilism rendered in particular cases."[100] In the *Provincial Letters*, probabilism appears not merely ridiculous but even sinister in light of the outrageous actions that its principles will justify. By circulating satires based on extracts from authors that he himself had never read, Pascal held probabilism up to public ridicule. Very persuasively, he suggested that it was the path to moral laxism.[101]

Perhaps because he was not a Jesuit, Caramuel was not a major target of the *Provincial Letters*, garnering only a few references in the original texts.[102] However, it seems likely that the satire's popularity affected

Roman attitudes toward the ongoing dispute regarding moral theory, and hence, toward Caramuel's contributions in this area. It is interesting to note certain parallels in the Roman condemnations of laxism and Jansenism: a year after the first proscriptions of laxist opinions, for example, the Holy Office issued a decree defending the liberty of scholars to argue in favor of attrition (which the Jansenists had long argued was insufficient for sacramental absolution).[103] Similarly, one month before the condemnations of 1679, the Congregation on the Council issued a decree defending the practice of frequent communion, another target of the Jansenist complaints concerning relaxed moral standards.[104] In their ongoing battle with Jansenism, central Church authorities could not risk appearing to be morally permissive, especially since their opponents had excoriated laxism so effectively. Perhaps scholars like Caramuel had become a liability for Church leaders who were trying to prove that they were no less strict than their opponents.[105]

In the first years following his appointment to the episcopacy, Caramuel published nothing. Whether pastoral responsibilities, the technical difficulties of his remote venue, or an uncharacteristic theological caution deterred him is unclear.[106] As a result, however, he was silent during the first years of the spreading reaction against probabilism. In 1663, he chose to re-enter the fray by responding to Prospero Fagnani and other critics in the *Apologema*.[107] Reaction was swift, with the book's consignment to the Index in January of the following year. Franz Reusch suggests that this condemnation was the result of an accusation of Jansenism that the book raises against Fagnani (although, as we shall see, Caramuel repeatedly emphasizes that he does not believe Fagnani is a Jansenist).[108] Caramuel did not again address the Roman canonist directly; yet Julius Velarde Lombraña reports that his unpublished writings preserved at Vigevano include an *Iconographia Ecclesiae Fagnanicae*, which describes the Roman Church as reconfigured according to Fagnani's theology.[109]

Caramuel's disappointment at the condemnation of the *Apologema,* and at the lack of support from his former patron, must have been intense.[110] But the scholar was already adjusting to his changed circumstances. By setting up a print shop near his episcopal residence, he could prepare his writings (including the *Apologema*) for distribution, despite the remote location of his diocese. In the year that the *Apologema* was condemned, he published two more volumes of moral theology, the *Theologia Intentionalis* and the *Theologia Praeterintentionalis*, the latter exploring the significance of what we now describe as indirect actions.[111] He also found intellectual stimulation in the *Accademia napoletana degli Investiganti*, a community of scholars devoted to the physical sciences.[112] Caramuel's episcopal duties (which he seems to have taken quite seriously) did not prevent him from revising earlier works and composing new ones, such as his analysis of mental reservations (the *Haplotes*, published in 1672) and of moral logic (the *Pandoxion*, 1668).[113] Most noteworthy perhaps was his publication in 1670 of a huge encyclopedia of mathematics, the *Mathesis Biceps*, which did much to advance his reputation within the scientific community.[114]

In 1673, at the request of the queen-regent of Austria, Caramuel was transferred to the diocese of Vigevano, a more comfortable and more financially secure assignment. Once installed in his new position, the bishop maintained the Cistercian rule and a frugal lifestyle. As he had done in Satriano/Campagna, Caramuel gave alms liberally and set up a print shop to facilitate the publication of his books, including his first treatise on architecture (1678).[115] After the move to Vigevano, he finished the ambitious theological task that he had set for himself by publishing an expanded and revised version of the *Theologia Moralis Fundamentalis* (1675–76). Volume 4 of this last edition (the *Dialexis de Non-Certitudine*) offered a new explanation of probabilism.[116] Despite the progressive loss of his eyesight, Caramuel continued his publications until the end of his life.[117]

Caramuel lived to see the Roman condemnations of errors in morally lax doctrine that took place in 1665/66 and 1679. In each case, the Holy See condemned a group of propositions without identifying their authors. Vereecke asserts that 24 and 25 in the first group, and 48 and 49 in the second, are commonly attributed to Caramuel.[118] Denzinger-Schönmetzer's footnotes, which endeavor to identify the propositions' authors, mention Caramuel more frequently, associating him with propositions 24, 25, 34, and 35 in series one and 35, 41, 44, 48, 49, and 50 in series two.[119] However, even a cursory examination reveals why it is difficult to be sure. In some cases, the *Enchiridion* lists more than one author as the putative source.[120] The various propositions are not direct quotations, and one sometimes searches in vain for a direct parallel in Caramuel's text. In several cases, the propositions reflect issues on which Caramuel had long before changed his views or arguments that he discusses rather than advocates.[121]

The two propositions most commonly associated with Caramuel from the group condemned in 1679 do not, in fact, reflect his mature positions, as evidenced by their treatment in the *Theologia Moralis Fundamentalis*.[122] Number 49, for example, asserts that masturbation is not prohibited by natural law, and hence, if God had not forbidden it, it would "often be good, and sometimes obligatory, under [pain of] mortal [sin]."[123] In both the earliest and latest discussions of this subject in the *Theologia Moralis Fundamentalis*, Caramuel classifies masturbation as a sin contrary to nature and states, "all of us who are doctors hold that it is mortally sinful." He refers to an opinion (attributed to Thomas Sanchez) that excuses this act from sin if it is performed for reasons of health, yet seems unconvinced that Sanchez ever expressed such a conclusion. In addition, he cites another moralist's report that Sanchez expressed this view in the first edition of his work on marriage, but that it was subsequently retracted. Caramuel clearly rejects the argument himself.[124] Thus, his basic position on the morality of masturbation is quite clear.

A discussion that approaches the condemned proposition more closely, however, appears in his comparison of masturbation with foreseeably sterile intercourse, that is, with a pregnant or aged woman. If both acts impede procreation, why is the first condemned and the second permitted? Caramuel notes: "If natural actions, considered *secundum se*, are said to be neither good nor evil, and their entire malice to depend upon [their] prohibition, which pleased Scotus, and today is defended by many very learned men, then the question will cease."[125] In other words, if one adopts John Duns Scotus's argument that acts are wrong because they are forbidden, rather than Thomas's argument that acts are forbidden because they are wrong, then it is easy to explain the difference between masturbation and sterile intercourse: God has forbidden the one and permitted the other. Caramuel believes that the Thomists cannot maintain their position without condemning foreseeably sterile intercourse within marriage: Since everyone is agreed that masturbation is serious sin and marital intercourse without the possibility of procreation is permitted, consistency in moral reasoning supports the Scotist position. Caramuel's discussion, therefore, is really less about practical sexual ethics than it is about moral theory.

The same dynamic appears in reference to proposition 48: "It seems so clear that fornication *secundum se* involves no malice, and is only evil, because it is forbidden, that the contrary appears dissonant from all reason."[126] Again, this proposition is certainly not a literal citation from *Theologia Moralis Fundamentalis*, and it is particularly different from his discussion of "simple fornication" in the last edition. Caramuel begins in this way: "You do not ask *whether simple fornication is a sin*, for you learn this from God and from the Church. Nevertheless, you inquire about that fundamental reason, on account of which it is sinful."[127] As in his discussion of masturbation, Caramuel contrasts the positions of the Scotists and the Thomists, in this case, describing each position as "common and probable [*communem* & *probabilem*]." According to Scotus's principles, Caramuel argues, one ought to say that fornication is evil because God has forbidden it.[128] The Thomists, he acknowledges, take the contrary view, arguing that fornication violates the law of nature because children born out of wedlock are not well educated. Caramuel is unconvinced by this argument. Orphanages or interested parents sometimes provide for the education of the illegitimate. Moreover, if the ability to educate represents a requirement for procreation, then poor people and beggars would be forbidden to marry. Caramuel admits that he finds the Scotist approach more persuasive. Yet, responding to the request of his imaginary interlocutor, he agrees to answer according to the mind of the Angelic Doctor. "I venerate St. Thomas," he remarks.[129] In essence, his solution represents a compromise between the Thomist and Scotist views. Fornication is wrong because God has forbidden it. "But to one asking why it is forbidden, I will say . . . because (among other inconveniences) it makes illegitimate and disagreeable the education of [one's] offspring."[130] Caramuel even supplements Thomas's argument by invoking other negative consequences of fornication for marriage, and for the welfare and security of both sexes. Thus, although he favors the Scotist approach, his answer incorporates elements of the Thomist view, which he also recognizes as probable. Nowhere in this text does Caramuel assert that the Thomist view is contrary to reason.[131] His later analysis, in fact, explores the relationship between two theoretical foundations for a settled practical question.

Without discounting the possibility that Caramuel might have said something that more clearly resembled these two condemned propositions in an earlier work, one must note that they reflect his mature ideas only in a very indirect and distorted fashion.[132] These passages simply tell us that he was inclined to agree with Scotus rather than Thomas concerning the relationship between divine prohibition and moral evil. The practical ethical conclusions are by no means morally lax. One would have to make a determined effort to be scandalized by the full text of these articles.

Finally, proposition 50 of the second series merits special comment because Caramuel refers to this issue directly in the *Apologema*. The condemned proposition states: "Intercourse with a wife, with her husband's consent, is not adultery; for that reason it suffices to say in confession that one has committed fornication."[133] Discussing Fagnani's treatment of resolutions taken from various theologians (sometimes out of context), Caramuel explicitly invokes this example: his text corresponds precisely to the first half of the proposition eventually proscribed in Rome. Caramuel observes:

> He [Fagnani] attributes this to the theologians on the basis of a letter by the Jansenist archbishop of Mechlin. Therefore, let him produce the theologians mad [enough to utter] this absurdity . . . Theologians have said in this case, that the husband . . . cannot kill his wife, or accuse her, or seek satisfaction; but no one has said that they have not committed adultery or violated the Decalogue.[134]

Caramuel's statement would seem to speak for itself. It is particularly interesting, moreover, that he does not explicitly interpret Fagnani's (or Boonen's?) proposition as a misstatement of his own views, but as a spurious argument reflecting no theologian's position.

More than half of the propositions condemned in 1679 were drawn from lists of propositions censured at Louvain in the 1650s and subsequently submitted to the Holy See.[135] In 1677, three members of the university's theology faculty, journeying to Rome to press for the condemnation, made a detour to Vigevano to urge Caramuel to retract his positions. The unexpected confrontation reduced the elderly bishop to a short fit of weeping. But after so long, Caramuel was hardly prepared to yield. Those who did not understand his views had distorted them, he told the unwelcome visitors.[136]

Caramuel's death in 1682 prompted many obsequies and memorials. His diverse accomplishments were reviewed in funeral orations and inscribed in characters of gold upon his monument in Vigevano cathedral.[137] Yet from the perspective of his work in moral theology, perhaps the most touching epitaph was uttered more than twenty years earlier, when the faculty of the College of Discalced Carmelites in the kingdom of Naples held a public disputation in his defense. At the end of the *Apologema*, Caramuel records this group's propositions for debate:

> Whatever Caramuel teaches, he teaches well.
>
> Whatever Caramuel says is probable, is probable.
>
> If others think differently, either they have not read, or have not understood, Caramuel's foundational principles . . .[138]

Caramuel's Approach to Ethical Wisdom and Knowledge

Except perhaps in a negative way, Caramuel was certainly not an example of Henry Davis's famous dictum that, within the discipline of moral theology, "there is no room for originality."[139] The Spanish theologian prided himself on his intellectual independence. In one of his early philosophical works, he offers this explanation of what it means to have Aristotle (and the other ancient philosophers) as one's light, but not as one's leader:

> In the middle of winter, under scant light, you come to a difficult place that you dare not cross, and Peter comes from the other side, furnished with an extremely bright torch. His presence illuminates the spot, and bears away all difficulties. You cross; he crosses; but you do not follow him [simply] because you use his light. Instead you pass through on the opposite path. This often happens to us when we philosophize. We come to an obscure and difficult place. Zeno, Plato, and Aristotle are invoked. Their teaching is a most illuminating torch, which disperses the shadows. We cross in the greatest security. Nevertheless, we do not follow this light, but continue on another [road]. . . .[140]

Caramuel's independence was not limited to his treatment of non-Christian and ancient authors. While he certainly respected the authority of Christian sources, from scripture and the writings of the Fathers to the decrees of Church authorities, Caramuel was careful to emphasize that this heritage often required investigation and interpretation.[141] Relying heavily upon the theologians of his own age (whom he called the "*iuniores*"), he was by no means slavishly dependent upon them, nor was he willing to take their arguments for granted.[142] Moreover, he believed that different branches of inquiry possessed their own proper methods. Much as he esteemed the work of university faculties and the teachings of learned men, Caramuel flatly asserted that when a question's answer depended upon experience, one should trust that experience and the evidence of one's own eyes, even if the doctors said otherwise. "I know learned men," he observed in irritation, "who will not dare to describe the sun as bright, the snow as white, pitch as black, or fire as hot, unless they were aided by the testimony of some ancient philosopher."[143] Such intellectual inertia was hardly to his taste.

Caramuel's treatment of his sources no doubt reflects his awareness of living in a period of rapid change. One of his favorite points of comparison invokes the discoveries of Christopher Columbus. At the time of Augustine and the other Fathers, he points out, there were no clear arguments demonstrating the existence (or non-existence) of lands on the other side of the world. After Columbus, their reality became apparent. Caramuel regards this as a good analogy for the growth of moral knowledge over time. What appears probable today may not have seemed so yesterday; and tomorrow's knowledge may render today's probable opinion either certainly true or certainly false.[144] Caramuel's sense of historical development is thus enormously important for his ethical theory.[145] Yet in addition to history, he also acknowledges the significance of culture in determining appropriate behavior. In contrast to Antonino Diana, for example, he initially questioned whether strict compliance with rules regarding the possession of forbidden books was appropriate in Germany (unlike Italy), because in Germany, "he who does not know what Calvin or Luther says . . . is called ignorant."[146] Such variations in historical and cultural circumstances, as well as in the capacities of individuals, create a necessary space for recourse to probable opinions.

Finally, one should note that Caramuel's characteristic approach to sources—independent, self-consciously innovative, and attentive to historical circumstances and cultural variation—was antithetical to the type of theology favored by many in the late seventeenth century, including (but by no means limited to) the Jansenists. Jansenism, after all, began as a project of recovery, born from its author's reading and re-reading Augustine. Arnauld's *De la fréquente communion*, an influential Jansenist tract concerning sacramental theology and moral practice, bears the sub-title, *ou Les sentiments des peres, des papes, et des councils.* In the preface, the author expresses his basic rule for evaluating the question: conformity to "antiquity, to the traditions of the saints, and to the ancient customs of the church."[147] Fagnani's response to the advocates of probabilism also begins with a catena of proof-texts.[148] That Caramuel recognized the appeal of this method is evident from his attempt in the *Apologema* to give probabilism an ancient Christian (indeed, pre-Christian) pedigree. But it was not his usual *modus operandi.* Even had they agreed with his practical conclusions, Caramuel's opponents would have been profoundly shocked by his approach to moral questions—an approach more likely to begin with citations from his contemporaries than from the Fathers. One must not overstate this point, for Caramuel had great respect for and made significant use of the historic Christian sources, including Augustine and the Scholastics. But he differed from his opponents in what he used their insights to accomplish. At root, the disagreement between Caramuel and his critics concerned the basic nature of moral theology itself: Was it primarily an exercise in recovery or discovery? Between his emphasis on the future, and theirs on the past, lay a gulf too wide for easy empathy or resolution.

Caramuel as a Source Concerning Probabilism

As we have seen, Juan Caramuel was only one of a very large group of moralists who endorsed probabilism during the middle decades of the seventeenth century. Although Caramuel's approach to probabilism certainly came under fire, he was hardly unique in his endorsement of it. At first glance, it is not apparent why he should be any more strongly associated with probabilism than its other proponents. What makes Juan Caramuel a particularly interesting source for the analysis of this moral method?

Caramuel's intellectual background and interests provide one answer to this question. Unlike many commentators on probabilism, Caramuel was not a university or seminary professor. His literary focus is generally exploratory rather than pedagogical. Caramuel is best understood as a theorist who applied his concepts of probability to everything from the astronomy of Copernicus and the functions of dice to the legitimacy of making peace with Protestants. Probabilism was a foundational principle, not merely of his ethical method, but of his general understanding of human knowledge.[149]

In the *Pax Licita*, Caramuel characterizes his writings as concerned with speculative principles as well as practical conclusions.[150] This is what separates his treatments of probabilism from those of many others. It is interesting, for example, to compare Caramuel's analyses of probable opinion with the writings of his friend, the famous casuist Antonino Diana. Diana's literary achievement was a truly monumental collection of case resolutions, published over many years.[151] Although there are references to probable opinion at various points in the text, its central discussion of the subject is eighteen pages long, much of it dealing with specific practical questions.[152] Probabilism is a moral method that Diana used and defended but hardly treated as a subject for intellectual inquiry. Caramuel, on the other hand, was fascinated, not only by its use, but also by its nature. His discussions (which became longer and more complex over the course of his career) also became increasingly philosophical, as he endeavored to analyze the structures and functions of probability. His approach to probabilism thus differed from those of many of his contemporaries.

In part, this reflects, no doubt, the period in which he lived as well as his own intellectual interests. As his earliest writings on the subject reveal, Caramuel was always aware that use of probable opinions could arouse controversy.[153] One could reasonably argue that he defended probabilism throughout his life. Yet Caramuel's most mature works on the subject appeared after the tide had begun to turn against probabilism. The polemical circumstances in which he was writing forced him to confront questions about probability that might have escaped earlier writers. It is interesting to note that he outlived Antonio Escobar, Diana, Thomas Tamburini—indeed, almost all of the so-called "laxist" writers except for Matthieu de Moya.[154] By the time that the Vatican issued its condemnations in 1667 and especially in 1679, Caramuel was one of the very few relevant authors still alive.

In addition, Caramuel's frankness—even effusiveness—renders him a particularly interesting witness to probabilism. As his immense literary corpus suggests, he was anything but a slow and painstaking writer. Nor was he a thinker who hesitated for years before expressing views that might arouse opposition. Discussing one of his controversial theses in the *Theologia Moralis Fundamentalis* (1652), the Cistercian claims to have published his work "in order that, warned by my friends, I may know what I should retain, what I should alter, and what I should prove."[155] Caramuel was not intimidated by fear of making a mistake. In the preface to the same volume, he tells Diana (and his other readers): "I always say what I think; and if today I see yesterday's [position] has lapsed, I will not defend it stubbornly; rather, I will expunge it confidently."[156] Changing one's mind was not a weakness in the opinion of an author who saw his theological writings as a conversation rather than as a monument set in stone.

Precisely because he was not a slow and cautious theologian, however, the development of Caramuel's ideas about probabilism is particularly intriguing. One can trace the evolution of his thought as he considers, and then reconsiders, various positions. His willingness to go out on, and even, on occasion, to fall off of a limb reflects his own understanding of the intellectual enterprise, an enterprise in which probable opinions played a crucial role. Caramuel understands that much of his work is speculative. He is often thinking out loud for the reader, which generally means for the educated elite in a position to weigh his ideas. In general, Caramuel writes for his colleagues, posing theses for their review and criticism. None of his important works on probabilism is a *summa* for confessors, a catechism, or other popular moral work. As a result, his mature treatments of probabilism are on a different plane than those constructed to help seminarians hear confessions.

Caramuel recognized that his outspokenness could create difficulties. An opponent who rejected his defense of the Treaty of Westphalia offered an assessment of Caramuel that has become a favorite of subsequent commentators: our author has the intelligence of eight, the eloquence of five, and the prudence of two. Wryly commenting on this observation, Caramuel noted that his attacker should have added "the sincerity of six: for they call veracity, imprudence."[157] This comment displays not only the value he placed on frankness, but also his sense of humor—an attribute uncommonly displayed in seventeenth-century moral literature, and one of which the reader should remain aware. One should not take everything that Caramuel says literally.

Indeed, one quickly discovers that it is necessary to read Caramuel very, very carefully in order to avoid misinterpretation. He has a fondness for beginning with a claim that is startling or even shocking to the reader, and then explaining its reasonableness through an extended argument.[158] Unfortunately, not all of his critics bothered to cite these clarifications, contenting themselves with the quotation of his provocative theses in order to prove his hubris. Caramuel's style was sometimes his reputation's worst enemy. Yet this does not render his argument absurd. To understand Caramuel, one must always examine his statements in context.

Juan Caramuel is thus a difficult source to consult about probabilism: evolving and loquacious, tendentious and sometimes opaque. Yet his continued fascination with the subject and his philosophical approach to its foundations render him a particularly fascinating witness to the development of this moral theory. Over the years, the increasingly controversial status of probabilism would become evident in Caramuel's works as he labored to analyze, explain, and defend it. For Juan Caramuel, probabilism was both a method and an object of investigation that never relinquished its allure.

CHAPTER TWO

Advocating Probabilism

Caramuel's Early Writings and the Proof-Texts They Provided for His Critics

IN THE *Apologema*, CARAMUEL EXPLAINS HIS EARLY LITERARY INVOLVE-ment in the discussion of probable opinion by referring to his experiences at Louvain, when Libert Froidmont attempted to promote certain theses: "*The use of probabilities is new. He who leaves behind the safe path and relies on probable opinion must be condemned before God. Opinions that are said to be or are probable for us will not be probable for God.*"[1] Noting that upright and learned men opposed Froidmont, Caramuel adds: "I opposed him in the *Theologia Regularis*, which I published in Brussels in 1639 . . . and more copiously and more strongly in the second and the third editions of the same work."[2] With this, Caramuel began his long literary campaign in defense of probable opinion.

In the beginning, Caramuel could treat probabilism as a common moral method, opposed only by a few unnamed adversaries. In the *Benedicti Regulam,* he observes: "There is a common resolution of all the doctors, which asserts that those who act in accordance with probable opinion cannot be judged rash and imprudent."[3] Later in the same text, he claims that Antonino Diana describes this conclusion as the "common opinion of the theologians."[4] Yet even at this stage, Caramuel acknowledges that his position has some opponents: an anonymous prelate, for example, and an unnamed pious critic (Froidmont).[5] It is fair to say that even his earliest discussions of probabilism possess a certain argumentative tinge. The polemical character of the debate, however, grew more serious over time as more and more criticisms of probabilism (and of Caramuel himself) reached the public ear. Paradoxically, in facing Prospero Fagnani and his other critics, Caramuel had to clarify as well as draw upon his own early arguments.

Given Caramuel's ongoing fascination with probabilism, only a theologian who has read his entire corpus could reasonably offer to summarize his early treatments of the subject. This chapter's discussion has a much less ambitious agenda. Two of Caramuel's early works were particularly significant in shaping the debate over probabilism, not only because he drew upon them himself in later works but also because other authors responded to them. These were the tracts on probable opinion from the *In Divi Benedicti Regulam* (1640) and the first edition of the *Theologia Moralis Fundamentalis* (1652).[6] One could reasonably argue that these have been (and continue to be) Caramuel's most influential writings on probabilism. Accordingly, they provide a helpful introduction to his views concerning the nature of probable opinion, his argument that acceptance of its sufficiency is actually "more probable" than the contrary position, his emphasis upon the practical value of "more benign" opinions, and his response to Froidmont's objections against probabilism. However, review of these texts will also reveal how Caramuel's statements were vulnerable to distortion or misunderstanding. As we shall see, these early volumes not only affected the seventeenth-century debates but also exercised a disproportionate influence upon Caramuel's subsequent reputation, including his theological reputation today.

Finally, the conclusion to this chapter will consider the modifications that Caramuel made to *Fundamentum* 11 (i.e., his discussion of probable opinion) in the later editions of the *Theologia Moralis Fundamentalis*. These arguments clarify certain points that receive less attention in the *Apologema* and illustrate the development of Caramuel's basic theory. In addition, since the *Dialexis* explicitly presumes that the reader is already familiar with *Fundamentum* 11, its arguments serve as the background for Caramuel's discussion of noncertitude.[7] Consideration of these preliminary texts and positions thus provides a helpful introduction to Caramuel's mature analyses in the *Apologema* and the *Dialexis*.

The Nature and Types of *Probabilitas*

Given that the *Benedicti Regulam* is a commentary upon religious rules of life, it is not surprising that probabilism appears within these texts as a principle for interpreting law, and that its practical applications receive greater emphasis than its philosophical foundations.[8] Significantly, Caramuel introduces the discussion by referring to the limited character of human knowledge, a circumstance that necessitates our reliance upon probable opinions. "We are not angels, but human beings," he succinctly explains.[9] Thus the treatment of this topic merits inclusion within his explanation of the "most solid and certain foundations" that ground the remainder of the commentary.[10]

The *Benedicti Regulam* follows common practice in distinguishing two types of probability, which Caramuel calls the "authoritatively [*authentice*]" probable and the "rationally [*rationaliter*]" probable. The first becomes apparent from external sources ("*ab extrinseco*"), while the second's probability is intrinsic. One is proven "by the authority and testimony of the doctors," and the other by arguments.[11] Caramuel distinguishes the rationally probable from the rationally improbable on the basis of their foundations. Rationally probable opinions must not militate against faith. They must also "turn away adversaries" on the strength of their arguments and "satisfy objections" on the strength of their foundations. By contrast, intrinsically improbable opinions lack such significant arguments and rely upon sophisms and doubtful or improbable foundations in order to "satisfy the objections of their enemies."[12] This emphasis upon a proposition's power in debate characterizes all of Caramuel's discussions of probabilism. Indeed, one might reasonably translate the word *probabilis* within his works as *solidly defensible*.

The first edition of the *Theologia Moralis Fundamentalis*, Caramuel's systematic effort to analyze the foundations of Christian ethical thinking, also addresses probable opinion within the preliminary phase of its arguments. Caramuel organizes the *Theologia Moralis Fundamentalis* into seven principal divisions (*capita*), each of which considers various "*fundamenta* [foundations], *on which we have built our counsels and resolutions*."[13] *Fundamentum* II, which considers probable opinion, appears at the very end of the first section on speculative foundations, including human liberty, grace, divine omniscience, creation and Providence, the infallibility of the Church, and the authority of various sources of knowledge. Caramuel thus places his consideration of probable opinion within the context of a broader discussion of moral epistemology.

Fundamentum 11 begins with a discussion of the relationship between probability and truth. There is a longstanding philosophical debate, Caramuel explains, as to whether one true proposition can be "truer" than another. Prescinding from that question, Caramuel nonetheless asserts that one thesis can be more or less probable than another. This is because primary truth (which depends upon correspondence between the statement and the thing signified) is distinct from secondary truth (in which a statement *seems* true, whether or not it actually is true, in the primary sense). This secondary truth, Caramuel explains, is usually called *probability*. It rests upon a strong and grave foundation but not an evident foundation, since extrinsic (i.e., secondary) truth "has no place" when intrinsic truth is manifest.[14]

The distinction between primary truth and probability has important consequences for the way in which probable opinions are related to one another. When one is speaking of primary truth, it is correct to assert that contradictory propositions cannot be true at the same time. The claim that "the Turk is sitting [*Turca sedet*]," for example, either corresponds to reality or it does not. Even if the speaker is mistaken, God knows what the Turk is doing. Truth (*veritas*) and falsity are opposites.[15]

Probable opinions, however, are not related in the same way. It is not correct to insist, Caramuel explains, that because I judge one opinion to be probable, I must necessarily judge its opposite to be improbable. A person might have strong arguments in favor of either side, so that he or she could reasonably defend (or challenge) either position. Two contrary theses can indeed be probable at the same time because a judgment of probability presupposes that the speaker has strong but not certain grounds for drawing this conclusion.[16] At the level of primary truth, either the Turk is sitting or the Turk is not sitting. But (to make the conclusions of Caramuel's argument more explicit), one could reasonably say, "it is *probable* that the Turk is sitting; it is *also probable* that the Turk is not sitting," assuming that the available information supports these assertions.[17]

It is impossible to overemphasize the importance of this distinction (which Caramuel will eventually describe as the distinction between truth and veracity)[18] for his understanding of probable opinion. The two types of knowledge operate in very different ways. Truth and falsehood are opposites. What separates the probable claim from the improbable, on the other hand, is the presence or absence of reasonable grounds for supporting it, when clear proof is lacking on either side. If a learned person has sufficient grounds to defend one side of an argument but not the other, Caramuel asserts, then the defensible position is (for that expert) morally certain rather than probable. Probability comes into play when both sides of a debate are reasonably defensible but not demonstrable.[19]

Because the assessment of probability depends upon the information available at any given time, the *Theologia Moralis Fundamentalis* (1652) asserts that such assessments can reasonably change. As an example, Caramuel describes how Columbus's discoveries have transformed our knowledge of the globe. "Similarly it happens in moral theology," he notes, "that today there are many probable opinions that were not seen as such yesterday; and many opinions judged probable yesterday that today—after the matter has been better examined—have passed over into certainties, i.e., as certainly false or certainly true."[20] Moreover, persons living at the same time can reasonably make different assessments of probability depending on the data that they possess. The claim that the emperor is in Prague, for example, can seem probable to Peter (who recently saw the sovereign there), improbable to John (who has heard otherwise from reliable sources), and neither to Frederick (who possesses no information to support either conclusion).[21] An assessment of probability, therefore, says as much about the subject's circumstances and knowledge as it does about the topic under discussion.

Given their shared emphasis upon the capacities of the moral subject, it is not surprising that both the *Benedicti Regulam* and the *Theologia Moralis Fundamentalis* insist upon the necessity of education for the assessment of intrinsic probability. The early text is particularly blunt: "Let them not be judges of intrinsic probability, who are not learned in Theology."[22] The *Theologia Moralis Fundamentalis* refers more generally to ignorance and lack of expertise when it states: "*to the unlearned man, or even to one not sufficiently accomplished in a certain faculty, there is no opinion within that faculty that is either intrinsically probable or improbable.*"[23] (The passage, in fact, compares the uninformed to the blind in terms of their common deficiency in perception.) Because education is so critical to the assessment of moral claims, the *Benedicti Regulam* argues that extrinsic probability is more accessible to all, and for that reason "more secure, morally speaking" than intrinsic probability.[24]

One of the most striking differences between the *Benedicti Regulam* and the first edition of the *Theologia Moralis Fundamentalis* concerns their treatments of authoritative (i.e., extrinsic) probability. In the earlier work, a very brief discussion of intrinsic probability gives way almost immediately to an analysis of the more accessible authoritative probability. Caramuel asks how many authors must support an opinion before it can be considered probable. "At Alcalá," he writes, "I have sometimes seen [the position] defended that the opinion of four doctors is probable."[25] Caramuel nonetheless rejects the necessity of the four-author rule on the grounds that more than four doctors assert that the opinion of a single doctor suffices. Extrinsic probability itself thus tears down the common position that he has inherited concerning extrinsic probability.[26]

One cannot help noticing that the first article in the *Benedicti Regulam*'s treatment of extrinsic probability includes many references to numbers. In addition to the four-doctor rule is the claim that an opinion remains probable as long as no more than eight doctors of equal weight support the contradictory position (an approach that Caramuel attributes to Laurenzo de Portel).[27] But it is very easy to misunderstand Caramuel's analysis if one does not distinguish the positions that he mentions from those that he embraces. Caramuel believes that some of his colleagues rely upon a number count in assessing extrinsic probability. His own view is that "all doctors . . . are morally equal, and for that reason those who do not understand the weight of the reasons are able to rely very securely upon the number of doctors."[28] In other words, counting authorities is an acceptable strategy for those unable to assess the reasons behind an argument. Because (in Caramuel's view) probable opinion requires only a single witness, such attempts to tally the authorities are unnecessary yet unobjectionable. "Truly these are not metaphysical computations, but merely moral [i.e., practical]," he writes, "sufficient nevertheless for security of conscience."[29]

In truth, Caramuel, a gifted mathematician in his own right, believed that his colleagues were applying the wrong branch of the discipline in assessing extrinsic probability. "According to my principles," he asserts, "authors should not be reduced to an arithmetic computation, but to a geometric analogy."[30] In other words, one does not simply count authors because not all authors are of equal weight. Caramuel mentions a number of criteria for assessing a source's significance and then (in most cases) immediately notes that they are not always reliable. Reputation can be a useful guide to trustworthiness, yet fame often depends upon a person's eloquence and sophistication. Personal integrity can be counterfeited; even when it is genuine, the holy person may nonetheless lack the education or the prudence necessary for the direction of others. (A good subject, Caramuel notes, does not always become a good superior.) Caramuel is inclined to give special weight to authors recognized by the most illustrious academies—what we might today call peer review.[31] Finally, he seems to grant greater weight to more recent authors than to their forbears by asserting that the position of a more recent (and exceptionally famous) author is probable, despite his predecessors' contrary views.[32] As soon as he utters this rule of thumb, however, Caramuel asserts that it can prove deceptive since the innovator's colleagues (and those who come after him) may judge the new position improbable. Like reputation and sanctity, chronology provides no infallible guide to assessing the comparative authority of the doctors.

A careful reading of this section from the *Benedicti Regulam* suggests that Caramuel is, in a sense, thinking out loud. In repeating the arguments concerning extrinsic probability that had been part of his Spanish theological education, he reveals his own dissatisfaction with the emphasis upon numbers without yet formulating an alternative. The strongest evidence in support of this interpretation is that the numbers/weight discussion essentially disappears in the first edition of the *Theologia Moralis Fundamentalis*. Although the *Benedicti Regulam* devotes much more space to extrinsic probability than to intrinsic probability, the *Theologia Moralis Fundamentalis* reverses that ratio, disposing of extrinsic probability in a single paragraph in which Caramuel repeats his refutation of the four-author rule. Although he refers the reader to the *Benedicti Regulam,* he does not choose to repeat its various arguments in the later text.[33]

Finally, the *Theologia Moralis Fundamentalis* (1652) provides one interesting clue about Caramuel's presuppositions concerning the relationship between intrinsic and extrinsic probability, a question that he will consider at great length in the *Apologema*. As a young man, Caramuel explains, he learned to appreciate the nature of intrinsic probability from his teacher Angel Manrique,[34] who apparently offered this assessment of a particular philosophical argument:

I have taught for thirty years and have the proof of my abilities confirmed by public testimony; nevertheless, I do not understand this opinion . . . Therefore, whether it belongs to Saint Thomas, or to another, to me, it is intrinsically improbable.[35]

Caramuel acknowledges that these words from a "great man [*magno viro*]" greatly influenced his own conception of intrinsic probability. But the most striking facet of this quotation is what it implies about the connection between authoritative and rational probability. No matter whose name is attached to an opinion, Manrique seems to suggest, it will be intrinsically improbable for qualified scholars who find it unpersuasive. Unfortunately, Caramuel's text does not explicitly examine the implications of his teacher's claim.

The "More Probable" Status of Reliance upon Probable Opinion

Caramuel loved syllogisms and used them repeatedly in his arguments concerning probabilism. A basic example already appears in the *Benedicti Regulam*. According to his opponents, he notes, "we are bound to follow the more probable opinion. Yet the opinion that teaches that the less probable suffices is more probable [than its counterpart]. Therefore, we are bound to assert and think that those who follow the less probable opinion do not sin."[36] To prove the minor premise, Caramuel asserts that, in comparison with his opponents' position, his view has "more solid foundations and nobler reasons" as well as support from "a much greater number of authors." Thus, he concludes that the view that one sins by following a probable opinion is, in fact, improbable.[37]

The appeal to reliance upon probable opinion as the "more probable position" represents a constant in Caramuel's various analyses of probabilism, both early and late.[38] Such an approach reminds us that Caramuel was also a philosopher and amateur scientist, whose belief in logical proof permeated his theological arguments. One has a strong sense that he could never understand his critics' failure to find this argument convincing.

The Defense of "More Benign" Opinions

In Caramuel's view, one of the major advantages of probabilism is that it allows persons to appeal to opinions that are less stringent than their alternatives concerning the requirements of moral law. Thus, he will argue consistently that although every probable opinion is safe (i.e., sufficient to protect the agent from mortal or venial sin), the more benign probable opinions are safer *per accidens*, because they are easier to follow than their counterparts. The first edition of the *Theologia Moralis Fundamentalis* quotes the *Benedicti Regulam* directly in reference to this argument.[39]

As a practical illustration of this point, Caramuel's early works frequently refer to the problem of maintaining "internal attention" during a reading of the Divine Office. One probable opinion asserts that the maintenance of such attention is necessary to fulfill the precept; the more benign position asserts that it is not, assuming that one actually reads what one is required to read.[40] Because both opinions are probable, the agent can (under most circumstances) freely choose between them.[41] There is nothing speculatively or morally wrong with choosing the more demanding position. Yet Caramuel anticipates that this choice will create practical difficulties.

> Who will promise me that I will be able to recite the canonical hours without distraction? Therefore, I foresee a danger, which does not arise from the stricter opinion [itself], but from my own fragility—a danger, nevertheless, which accompanies the stricter opinion, and cannot be present with the more benign position. Therefore, the more benign opinion, even if it presumed to be less probable, is more secure and safer [than the stricter opinion].[42]

In light of human frailty, the gentler opinion thus provides a definite advantage to those who embrace it. This advantage is not reassurance that they have chosen the *only* legitimate answer, for Caramuel believes that those who act on either the strict or the benign opinion are behaving responsibly. Those who choose the latter opinion simply enjoy a freedom from anxiety unavailable to their counterparts, who will never read the Office without fear of vitiating distractions. It is this confidence and release from scruples that Caramuel associates with the access to more benign probable opinions.

The problem of distraction from the Divine Office inspired discordant probable opinions that individuals could apply to their own behavior. Caramuel is even more concerned about access to benign opinions, however, in cases where a superior is imposing a burden or judgment upon someone subject to his control. "It is the ruin of religious life to feign obligations where they do not exist," he warns in the *Benedicti Regulam*.[43] To those superiors who are inclined to reject their subordinates' recourse to probable opinion, Caramuel repeats the admonition of St. Paul that authority's goal is edification rather than destruction.[44] He also poses a test case that pits the less probable opinion of Peter the monk against the more probable (and more severe) opinion of his abbot. If Peter fails to obey (relying upon the probable opinion that he is not bound to do so), can the abbot legitimately punish him for disobedience? In his answer, Caramuel first acknowledges the risk of scandal (i.e., leading others into sin by one's example) that "commonly occurs in such cases."[45] His response assumes that, in this particular case, no such risk is present, because the act occurred either in private or in the presence of those whose education protects them from scandal. Under those conditions, Caramuel believes, Peter did not sin. The abbot is certainly free to regard the stricter opinion as correct, but he must also recognize that the monk acted on probable opinion and (if nothing else) is excused by his invincible ignorance of his obligations.[46]

Caramuel's resolution of this case evidently aroused controversy, as he notes in the 1646 edition of the *Theologia Regularis*. After reading his answer, Caramuel notes, a certain prelate apparently exclaimed, "*From the time that the works of Juan Sanchez, Diana, and Caramuel were published, we prelates have not been prelates!*"[47] Caramuel responds by asking what it means to be a prelate:

> Either it is to be able to issue commands—goods or evils, obligatory or non-obligatory, appropriate or inappropriate, useful or noxious—despotically and arbitrarily; or it is to be able to bring it about that subjects fulfill their obligations. If you think that the authority of a prelate consists in being able to compel subordinates to do even those things that are evil, noxious, or pernicious—in short, those things to which they are not bound—then you are confusing a prelate with a tyrant![48]

In his extremely informative study on the history of confessional practice, Jean Delumeau observes: "From Saint Thomas Aquinas to Saint Alphonsus Liguori, there were numerous counsels of benevolence given to confessors by directors of conscience, who knew, from experience, that of which they spoke."[49] Caramuel was, in fact, only one of a long line of theologians who emphasized the dangers of moral rigorism and the necessity of compassion, especially for those in positions of authority. Divine mercy served as the paradigm for these theologians' ethical approach. Thus, in the face of human frailty, Caramuel and his colleagues clung to the promise of God's benevolence, especially as expressed in Matthew 11:30: "My yoke is easy, and my burden is light." Caramuel invokes this text, for example, at the beginning of his treatment of the Decalogue in the *Theologia Moralis Fundamentalis* (1652):

> *My yoke is sweet, and my burden is light,* says the Lord, where the word *yoke* indicates the Decalogue, and the word *burden*, the rest of precepts. Yet today many interpret this [yoke] and that [burden] so severely, or even cruelly, that either they should be proscribed from the literary world, or we should confess that the yoke of God is extremely bitter, and his burden extremely heavy and insupportable. On account of this, I take up my pen, so that I may show here that true opinions always and everywhere must be preferred to the false, whether they seem benign or severe.[50]

Whether or not he was actually more permissive than other advocates of benevolence, Caramuel was not alone in drawing a connection between probabilism and divine mercy or in emphasizing the dangers of stringency. To some degree, at least, his attitude was more traditional than his opponents'. In an age when moral rigorism (for example, in the delay of absolution) was gaining cachet, Caramuel was, in a sense, a holdover from the "old school" that emphasized benignity.[51]

The Response to Froidmont

In the *Benedicti Regulam*, Caramuel devotes considerable space to answering the complaints of a "certain pious man [*quispiam vir pius*]" concerning probable opinion.[52] From the *Apologema*, we know that this was, in fact, Libert Froidmont and that Caramuel is responding in the *Benedicti Regulam* to arguments that Froidmont proposed at Louvain.[53] Review of this discussion thus illustrates not only Caramuel's early ideas concerning probabilism but also the objections raised against probabilism by one of its early opponents.

Froidmont had argued that a person who relies upon probable opinion and abandons the "safe way" necessarily faces condemnation. Caramuel dismisses this conclusion as a failure to grasp the nature of probable opinion, which itself represents a "safe way" and, in some cases, a safer way than the more probable.[54] A safe opinion "frees you from venial or mortal sin, if you follow it precisely."[55] If one has an obligation to choose the safer course, then logic favors the choice of the option that one is more likely to follow in practice, that is, the more benign opinion. Though he does not say so explicitly, Caramuel seems to treat *safe* and *probable* as synonymous terms. From this perspective, Froidmont's objection is hardly to the point, and his claims about safety fail to recognize probability's moral significance.

"*Oh happy primitive Church, which did not labor under the opinions of so many doctors!*" Froidmont had apparently exclaimed.[56] Caramuel argues that this statement includes two erroneous presuppositions. The first is that probable opinion was unknown in the age of the Fathers. In fact, the learned teachers of Christian antiquity expressed many views that might reasonably be described as probable rather than certain.[57] Caramuel thus interprets recourse to probable opinion as a traditional element of Christian theological method, in contrast to critics such as Froidmont (and later Fagnani), who reject it as a novelty. Yet Froidmont's assertion is also false, in Caramuel's view, because it treats probable opinions as burdens for the Church.

> To say that probable opinions are hardships and even diseases of the Church Militant is manifest error, for they are signs of an easier and more excellent salvation [*salutis*]. The Church is not unhappy because the doctors have opinions in many cases; but from this, it is happier, because it is able to advance its own toward the heavenly crown more benignly and more easily. For many people would be damned, whom probability of opinion saves. Therefore the Catholic Church ought to be described as happier, because it abounds in very holy and learned men, who have introduced benign opinions.[58]

This statement obviously reflects Caramuel's view that access to benign opinions represents one of the benefits of probabilism. Yet the paragraph's precise meaning is (and clearly was in Caramuel's own time) subject to a variety of interpretations. Why does Caramuel describe the Church as "happier" because of the variety of probable opinions? What does it mean to assert that "many would be damned, whom probable opinion saves"?

First, one should note that Caramuel's rhetoric corresponds directly to Froidmont's formulation. The phrase "O happy primitive Church" provokes Caramuel's assertions that "the Church is not unhappy" and "the Church ought to be called happier." Yet it is by no means clear that Caramuel is claiming that the Church of his day is "happier" than the Church of the Fathers, especially since he begins his response by insisting on the antiquity of probable opinion within Christian teaching. Caramuel may simply be saying that the Church is "very happy" because of probable opinions, or even that it is "happier" than it would have been without access to this moral method. Thus, the juxtaposition in this passage may be between the Church as envisioned by Froidmont (i.e., a Church that rejects probable opinions) and the Church that accepts them (both in the past and in the present).

Caramuel certainly believes that a Church open to probabilism is happier than Froidmont's rigorist ideal. In Caramuel's view, probable opinions, especially benign ones, allow persons to avoid sin more easily. Why is this the case? The obvious answer is that benign opinions are easier to follow than stringent ones; more people can meet a lenient moral standard than its rigorous counterpart. Yet this contention also seems to reflect elements of Caramuel's moral theory that are not explicitly articulated in this passage, specifically his understanding of law and its use as a model for interpreting the moral life.

Moral obligation, in Caramuel's view, arises from the imposition of law. "I deny that any moral malice can be understood without [reference to a] precept," he argues earlier in the *Benedicti Regulam*. "As a result, if all laws were to be taken away (whether this is possible or not), there would remain nothing that could be described as morally evil."[59] But Caramuel also believes that law does not oblige unless it is sufficiently promulgated— a Thomist presupposition that Francisco Suarez had emphasized within his theory of probable opinions.[60] Thus, for Caramuel, a person who inculpably fails to recognize a law's obligation—for example, because he or she is following a probable opinion that denies its existence—truly is not bound.[61] For that person, at that time, the law has not been sufficiently promulgated.

In light of this, one can see why Caramuel would describe the Church that recognized probable opinions as happier than its counterpart. No one would argue that it is desirable to impose obligations that do not exist in reality. If a law's requirements are truly doubtful, then it is advantageous that the learned discover this so that Christians can fulfill their moral responsibilities without scrupulous anxiety over imagined "duties." Moreover, without such identifications, there is always the risk that Christians will incur real guilt by choosing to violate apparent "laws" that are (in reality) nonexistent. Probabilism thus offers protection against both anxiety and irresponsibility.

The difficulty with Caramuel's text is that it makes probable opinion sound like a magic talisman, capable of altering the moral character of actions themselves. "Many would be damned, whom probability of opinion saves," he writes. This seems to suggest that probable opinion reconfigures morality itself. Such an idea would, of course, assign enormous power to those who judged opinions to be probable or improbable. In the *Apologema*, Caramuel devotes great effort to explaining the relationship between theological judgments and probability.[62] The early texts are much less clear in this regard. However, the *Benedicti Regulam* does analyze a case that sheds light on the problem.

Suppose that someone has already performed an action. *Ex post facto,* he consults various books to learn whether the deed was acceptable or not. Is such a consultation appropriate? All well and good, Caramuel argues, if the agent anticipates facing the same problem again and seeks guidance regarding this future conduct. But the sinfulness of the past action "does not depend upon the future resolutions of writers or doctors."[63] What matters is the agent's belief at the time of the action itself. If the agent believed that the action was evil and nonetheless chose to perform it, then he sinned, whatever he finds in the books afterwards.[64]

If Caramuel believed that probable opinion altered the moral character of acts, then he would not have resolved the case in this way. The mere existence of a probable opinion would justify any corresponding actions, whether the agent knew about the opinion or not. In that scenario, *"many would be damned, whom probable opinion saves,"* would indeed ascribe an almost magical power to the probabilists. Yet clearly, Caramuel does not believe that probabilism applies *ex opere operato*, so that the simple expression of a probable opinion changes the nature of moral reality. It is not what is in a book, but what is in the mind of the agent that matters. Chapter 5 will pursue this point in greater detail. For now, it is sufficient to note that Caramuel's phrasing was certainly open to misinterpretation.

Finally, Froidmont had rejected recourse to probable opinion on these grounds: *"not all opinions that are probable for us, will be probable for God."*[65] Concerning this claim, Caramuel wishes to make certain distinctions because the accuracy of the statement depends upon the meaning that its author intended. If the statement means that not all opinions that "are thought probable [*putantur probabiles*]" by human beings will receive the same designation from God, then Caramuel has no objections to it. Statements can be "called *probable* [*vocantur probabiles*]" without actually being probable. Caramuel reminds his reader that a probable opinion must possess particular characteristics in order to merit that designation. It is certainly not impossible that someone (especially an unlearned person) might mistakenly describe a thesis as *probable*. Thus one could reasonably posit a distinction between ideas considered probable and ideas that actually are probable. Interpreted in this way, Froidmont's claim is true.[66]

Froidmont's thesis is also accurate, Caramuel believes, if it intends to distinguish human knowledge from divine knowledge. Although human beings can recognize opinions as probable, God, who knows everything, does not perceive these same opinions through the lens of human limitations. God's knowledge, unlike ours, is never probable. Thus, the Spaniard has no objections to the idea that the probable opinion represents a facet of human knowledge but not intuitive divine knowledge, if that is what Froidmont's statement means.[67]

However, Caramuel does reject a third interpretation of Froidmont's statement (one that Caramuel feels corresponds better to his opponent's phrasing). According to this view, opinions that are "truly probable" for us nonetheless "do not suffice, in order that we may be excused by God."[68] Caramuel attacks this position by invoking the limitations in human knowledge. Unlike God, we do not know things intuitively. "I am not an angel, but a man," Caramuel observes; therefore, I must rely upon the type of knowledge available to human beings.[69] Although not developed, this argument seems to reflect the presumption that God does not require us to surpass the capacities of the human intellect.

Caramuel explicitly raises this point in the 1646 edition of the *Theologia Regularis,* where he adds a fourth interpretation of the statement absent from earlier formulations of the argument. "It had not yet come into my mind," Caramuel writes, that a Catholic (or even a Calvinist) who "asserts that God commands the impossible and that invincible ignorance does not excuse from sin" could readily endorse Froidmont's claims.[70] Caramuel objects to this argument's practical consequences: in his view, it renders supernatural merit dependent upon fortune (i.e., predestination?) rather than virtue. These statements in the *Theologia Regularis* represent a very early formulation of an argument that plays a critical role in the *Apologema*: probable opinion suffices because God does not command the impossible.[71] Although Caramuel does not mention Jansenism explicitly within this passage, he does describe Froidmont's position as heretical because of its inconsistency with the Council of Trent's teaching on the availability of grace. Thus, Caramuel seems to identify a connection between Froidmont's theology of grace and his rejection of probabilism—a connection that was not articulated in the *Benedicti Regulam.* With the *Theologia Regularis* (1646), the battle against error becomes a battle against heresy.

Preliminary Concerns, Misconceptions, and Proof-Texts

In a sense, one might describe Caramuel's early treatments of probabilism as experiments in argumentation. Initially probabilism appears a tool for interpreting law and its concomitant obligations, rather than as a subject of investigation in its own right. Like many young scholars, Caramuel repeats arguments that had been part of his own theological education, even though he does not find some of them particularly persuasive. One senses his amusement at the thought that moralists are earnestly weighing and measuring their colleagues' reputations in order to construct assessments of comparative authority. So much unnecessary effort, Caramuel seems to believe. But because he regards the author count as harmless, if philosophically irrelevant, he proffers only mild criticisms at first before his growing independence encourages him to dismiss the subject.

The first edition of the *Theologia Moralis Fundamentalis*, on the other hand, is far more ambitious and sophisticated in its attention to foundational questions regarding probabilism. Here Caramuel attempts to set probability within a framework of human knowledge and to understand its relationship with primary truth. Yet even this text devotes relatively little space to the basic concepts of probability.[72] Caramuel is already thinking about the foundations of probable opinion, yet his attention is focused upon a debate with Juan de Lugo and the resolution of particular (and in some cases, peculiar) test cases. Probabilism itself is not yet the central question.

In part, this reflects the nature of the debate in which Caramuel was engaged. In 1640 and even in 1652, one might describe probabilism as a method in firm "possession" of its place within the world of Catholic moral theory. Caramuel's discussions were always polemical, but these debates have no real sense of urgency. He is not yet facing a concerted assault on probabilism itself or a critic with the influence that Fagnani eventually enjoyed. One suspects that Caramuel may have enjoyed raising the hackles of these early conservative opponents (such as Jacques Boonen?) with his startling statements about probable opinion. The crisis surrounding probabilism was still in the future.

Yet in these early writings, Caramuel inadvertently supplied his future critics with proof-texts for an attack upon his position. The rhetorical tactics that probably served him well as a preacher—his fondness for grabbing the audience's attention with a startling statement that could later be explained—could prove very damaging when others cited these same remarks in isolation from their original context. It is ironic that his most notorious statement concerning probabilism from the first edition of the *Theologia Moralis Fundamentalis* comes not from *Fundamentum* 11 but from a dedicatory epistle that Caramuel addressed to Antonino Diana. Praising his colleague's advocacy of benign opinions, Caramuel writes:

> I venerate the genius of that most learned man, Diana, by whose industry many opinions have become probable, which were not probable before . . . *For if* [these opinions] *now are probable, which were not* [probable] *in the past; then those who follow them do not sin, although they would have sinned before.*[73]

As we shall see, both Pascal and Fagnani explicitly address this statement, the latter remarking: "if this is true, then probable opinions are above the law of God and of nature."[74] In the *Apologema*, Caramuel takes great pains to emphasize that theologians do not "make" a position probable, but one could certainly infer the opposite from statements of this kind.[75] (One suspects that he came to wish that he had been less effusive and more precise in this encomium.)

Similarly, Caramuel's claim that the Church is "happier" because of the prevalence of probable opinions looks quite different when it is divorced from its original context, that is, Froidmont's statement that the primitive Church was happy because it lacked them. Without reading the passage as a whole, one can easily draw the conclusion that Caramuel believes recourse to probable opinion is a blessed novelty (a view he explicitly rejects but which Fagnani seems to assume that he endorses).[76] Caramuel may have relied more heavily upon colleagues and recent theological witnesses than he did upon the Fathers (especially in his early writings), but he did not treat probable opinion as a modern discovery unavailable to Augustine or Aquinas. Without evaluating his adjectives (*happier*) and adverbs (*more easily*) within the context of the entire argument, this famous passage from the *Benedicti Regulam* can prove very misleading.

The Early Texts and Caramuel's Subsequent Reputation

Juan Caramuel analyzed probabilism throughout his life, developing his theories over nearly forty years. Yet his most famous expositions of probabilism were his earliest and least developed treatments of the subject. His contemporaries' emphasis upon these texts is logical because they had greater circulation than the later works and appeared during the period that initiated the great debate over probable opinion. (Moreover, one must acknowledge that some of Caramuel's contemporaries were more interested in using his works as a source of proof-texts against probabilism than they were in engaging him in academic debate.) More striking is the long-term influence of the early texts upon Caramuel's theological reputation. Even today, common theological assumptions regarding his theory of probabilism are more likely to reflect the early writings than the mature works.[77]

In part, this modern reliance upon the early texts may be a matter of accessibility. Because it was placed on the Index of Forbidden Books, printed texts of *Apologema* are relatively rare—although it is apparently now available from a surprising source on compact disk.[78] Copies of the first edition of the *Theologia Moralis Fundamentalis* are more common than the later editions, and this version also appears on microfilm within the Vatican Film Library.[79] But one of the most significant reasons for the heavy modern reliance upon Caramuel's early texts has undoubtedly been the influence of Thomas Deman, whose long encyclopedia article on "Probabilisme" in the *Dictionnaire théologie catholique* continues to be the standard treatment of the subject. In his short paraphrase of Caramuel's position, Deman relies upon and cites the *Theologia Regularis*. Within this summary, he inaccurately claims that Caramuel posits "only opinions, and no certitudes" in moral matters.[80] Moreover, Deman does not mention the development and clarification of Caramuel's ideas in his later treatises. Although the article contains an extended summary of Fagnani's work, Deman discusses the *Apologema* only in reference to its condemnation, without any indication of its contents.[81]

Deman's assessment of Caramuel is quite negative. While acknowledging Caramuel's erudition, Deman calls him the "*enfant terrible* of the new doctrines of probability" and asserts that it would be difficult to excuse him were it not for "the judgment that he was a little deranged."[82] For an author already burdened with the sobriquet *prince of laxists*, this assessment has been, in a sense, the last nail in the coffin of Caramuel's reputation. Small wonder that even investigators anxious to correct misconceptions about moral theology in the seventeenth century have tended to treat Caramuel as the exception that proves the rule. Jean Delumeau warns his readers against imagining "all the laxist casuists on the model of Caramuel, a bustling character, impetuous, . . . sometimes a buffoon."[83] Albert Jonsen and Stephen Toulmin number Caramuel (and Diana) as the "casuists who most merited Pascal's scorn." Concerning the former, they assert: "Once having found any opinion favoring liberty over law, he allowed it to be embraced and so stimulated doubts about the validity of all law."[84] Given the prevalence of such assessments, it is unsurprising that there has been little theological energy for reconsidering Caramuel's ideas concerning probabilism. At present, the best secondary literature on that subject comes from philosophers.[85] References within theological works are likely to represent only reprises of Deman.[86]

Finally, one should note that Caramuel's texts pose many difficulties not only in interpretation but also for comprehension. A particularly interesting example appears in mathematician James Franklin's discussion of Caramuel's ideas within a broader study of probability.[87] Franklin's analysis relies upon the *Theologia Regularis* [88] and the first edition of the *Theologia Moralis Fundamentalis*. Disconcerted by a reference in the *Theologia Regularis*'s sixth disputation to Caramuel's own *Benedicti Regulam*,[89] Franklin remarks: "Not only does Caramuel refer to himself here; the very passage refers to itself. In effecting this postmodern play, Caramuel must be either joking or revealing himself unable to distinguish between joke and non-joke."[90] Although Caramuel does make jokes (and references to himself in the third person) on occasion, the truth in this case is more prosaic. The relevant passage is actually a citation of another author, Eligius Bassaeus, who refers to a specific passage in the *Benedicti Regulam* (published in 1640).[91] Bassaeus, whose work first appeared in 1643, is actually discussing the opinion of Sanchez, and notes that Caramuel subscribes to it in the *Benedicti Regulam*. Caramuel, in turn, quoted Bassaeus's text in later editions of the *Theologia Regularis*.[92] Thus, the reference demonstrates not a peculiarity of Caramuel's but the difficulty in keeping track of the speaker within texts that use neither quotation marks nor block indentation to separate an author's views from those of his sources.

Franklin's mistake is thus completely understandable. Yet it suggests several interesting problems regarding the analysis of Caramuel's views on probabilism. First, Caramuel is difficult to interpret, and the present state of his corpus does not facilitate the task of the modern investigator. There are no critical editions, no theological translations, and no dictionary of Caramuel's terminology (except those that he provides). In addition, the secondary literature can easily lead to an overreliance on the very early texts, such as the *Theologia Regularis*, without consideration of how Caramuel's positions developed over time. In this regard, Franklin only does what others, especially the influential Deman, had done before him. Finally, the passage suggests that modern scholars should always be mindful of the risk that Caramuel's reputation poses for an accurate reading of his text. It is easy to believe that Caramuel is saying something bizarre because so many commentators have regarded him as bizarre. Yet even his harshest contemporaries acknowledged his intellectual gifts. Unfortunately, much of the secondary literature (especially the theological literature) has given too little weight to his intelligence and too much to his reputation as an extreme laxist. For the student of Caramuel, the best rule of thumb is to verify any commentator's assertion by studying the original passage *in its entirety*.

Conclusion: Developments within *Fundamentum* 11 in the Later Editions

In comparison with the 1652 text, later versions of the tract on probabilism in the *Theologia Moralis Fundamentalis* are noteworthy for their emphasis upon the boundaries of legitimate recourse to probable opinion. Especially significant is the role of vows, oaths, and precepts in limiting human freedom. In later editions of *Fundamentum* 11, Caramuel assigns such limiting factors greater prominence. Explaining the precept of charity, for example, he notes: "Therefore, if there is a probable opinion, in accordance with which I am able to refrain from injuring a neighbor (without injury to me or mine), then I am bound to follow it."[93] Similarly, justice requires that "when a debt is certain [*quando debitum est certum*]" one may not appeal to an opinion that "brings in probable circumstances, by force of which the debt is denied."[94]

Caramuel also expands his analysis of limitations by mentioning the significance of "disjunctive" obligations and attendant circumstances in applying probable opinions. Often a precept or contract, he warns, requires us to choose one of several options for compliance. I may choose either white or red wine in celebrating Mass, but the reality that neither is explicitly required does not mean that I am free to use a liquid other than wine. Moreover, one must examine the practical implications of probable opinions very carefully, especially in light of the particular circumstances surrounding their use. Just because it is "probable" that Peter has committed a secret crime, for example, does not mean that others have a "probable" right to reveal the supposed transgression. Translating probable opinion into action can be a complex process because concomitant circumstances may create obligations that limit the agent's freedom.[95]

The later editions of the *Theologia Moralis Fundamentalis* develop Caramuel's earlier arguments about the varied responsibilities of knowledgeable and ignorant persons concerning the assessment of probability, and the distinction between probability and numerical popularity. Repeating his earlier refutation of the four-author rule, Caramuel adds: "In the meantime, whatever [the truth] may be about that subtlety [i.e., whether one author suffices], you follow the opinion that teaches that *the opinion of four authors is sufficiently probable.*"[96] He adds:

> Here the unlearned man is usually happier: because with closed eyes, he can believe in four writers. The learned man ought to have keener vision: for there are authors who do not add to the tally, either because they copy rather than write, and thus pantomime with others (which does not happen infrequently); or, because they are commanded to hold this or that opinion. In such a case, the doctrine and the authority of the one giving the order must be considered, in order that we may judge the probability of the opinion.
>
> Once again, the unlearned man is usually happier: because in doubtful [cases], the learned is under an obligation to examine the reasons and foundations; but the unlearned is not. For the layman, who consults his confessor, or another upright and learned man, and asks whether this or that opinion is secure, is able to believe the [expert] and to be governed according to his direction.[97]

Besides revealing that Caramuel was a child of his time in his assumptions about lay ignorance, this passage sheds important light on the duties of theological experts regarding the assessment of extrinsic probability. First, Caramuel's statements clearly reveal that the author count is a strategy for the nonexpert. Those prepared to evaluate the foundations of an opinion (and the authority of those supporting it) ought to do so. There is nothing here to suggest that theologians have the option of simply shopping for a convenient probable opinion. Moreover, to his longstanding claim that all authors are not equally authoritative, Caramuel adds the problem of constraint: some theologians may be under orders to advocate a particular position. Such lack of freedom poses another complication in the assessment of extrinsic probability, forcing the theologian to evaluate the expertise and authority of the constrainer rather than the constrained. One wishes that Caramuel had explored this problem further, but his laconic remarks raise rather than dissect the issue in detail.

Finally, as he will do in the *Apologema*, Caramuel here emphasizes the connection between intrinsic and extrinsic probability. In fact, the later editions of the *Theologia Moralis Fundamentalis* explicitly raise a question about rational/authoritative probability that the *Apologema* does not: Does intrinsic proof that an argument is improbable destroy its extrinsic probability, since "the approvals of the writers do not prevail against evident reason"?[98] In one sense, yes; in another sense, no, Caramuel answers.

> Extrinsic probability ceases, for the person who perceives the strengths of the demonstration, but not for the person who judges the argument to be strong, but does not judge it to be certain, evident, and undoubted. Accordingly, if Peter, arguing against John, is trying to prove that John's opinion is improbable, he is required to give evident and demonstrative arguments. But what if Peter affirms that they are evident, and John asserts that they are strong and grave, but not evident? Peter ought to have recourse to the authors, and to show that John's opinion is not sustained by the approvals of illustrious men.[99]

In this quotation, one sees the logical conclusion of two of Caramuel's customary arguments. First, certitude and probable opinion are mutually exclusive. When one realizes that an argument has been proved improbable, authoritative advocacy cannot supplant intrinsic certitude. Second, moral obligation arises from the *recognition* of certitude and probability rather than the abstract quality of the propositions themselves. Thesis X can be certainly improbable for Peter yet extrinsically probable for John because only Peter recognizes that intrinsic arguments have *proven* it to be improbable. People can act only upon what they know. This is a theme that Caramuel will push to its logical conclusion in the *Dialexis*.

The later editions of the *Theologia Moralis Fundamentalis*, therefore, provide additional links in Caramuel's long catena of arguments about probabilism. Like an orator adding a few embellishments to a long-polished presentation, Caramuel tweaks and clarifies but does not significantly change his general approach. It is this basic theory of probabilism that Caramuel will explain, develop, and modify in his mature treatises on the subject.

CHAPTER THREE

Using Probabilism

Avoiding Improbable Warfare and
Making Peace with Protestants

MANY OF CARAMUEL'S CRITICS OBJECTED NOT ONLY TO HIS THEO-
RIES about probable opinion but also to his use of those theories
in resolving particular cases. Thus, in order to understand his approach to
probabilism, it is helpful to consider the applications as well as the method
itself. What moral conclusions does Caramuel draw on the basis of probable opinion? What is the practical significance of his ethical method?

A logical place to begin would be with the cases that became notorious—the examples cited by Caramuel's critics to demonstrate the depths
to which probabilism could descend. We have already examined several
of those conclusions in chapter 1. The most infamous example, however,
concerns his resolution of a case regarding homicide in response to the revelation of a guilty secret. Prospero Fagnani (apparently citing the condemnations of the French clergy) invokes this as one of the absurd conclusions
to which probable opinion leads.[1] The censured proposition states the
matter in this way: "By right, one can doubt whether it is by no means licit
for a religious to kill a woman with whom he has disgracefully had sexual
relations, when she reveals the fact. Caramuel, ibid. [*Theologia Moralis Fundamentalis* 1652, *fund.* 55], §7, page 551."[2]

Without question, this represents one of the most outlandish arguments
that Caramuel ever mentioned in the same breath as the word *probable*. Yet
review of the original passage is singularly uninformative. In the first edition of the *Theologia Moralis Fundamentalis*, Caramuel is reporting upon a
consultation that he was asked to give in 1650 regarding Franciscus Amico's

positions on killing in defense of honor.[3] Caramuel's text includes a long citation from Amico, which argues that (under limited circumstances) a cleric or religious may protect his honor (or the honor of his clerical state or religious community) by killing a slanderer.[4]

Caramuel, who had been asked for his evaluation of Amico's arguments, responds at some length. (One should note that a number of theologians examined the question of killing in defense of honor during this period, so it is unsurprising that the Cistercian had developed an opinion on this issue).[5] His basic conclusion is that a priest (like a layman) can reasonably kill a slanderer, provided that the threatened injury is grave, that the victim cannot defend himself with words alone, that the civil law is unwilling to protect him, that violence will be efficacious in protecting his reputation, and that it is the only remedy available to the victim. Although Caramuel regards this conclusion as consistent with natural law, he notes that civil law and canon law may adopt a different position.[6]

After this long excursus, Caramuel mentions the notorious case cited by Fagnani, remarking: "You have read this teaching, and you *inquire whether a religious, who, yielding to frailty, has had relations with a vile woman, may kill her;* [if she], *thinking it an honor to have prostituted herself to so great a man, reveals the matter, and makes him infamous?*"[7] To this question, Caramuel responds: "What do I know? [*Quid scio?*]" Then he quotes an unnamed doctor's assertion: it is probable that the religious may licitly kill the prostitute. (Neither Caramuel nor his anonymous source provides any arguments for this conclusion.) "You weigh the matter accurately," Caramuel instructs his reader, presumably on the basis of his earlier arguments about killing in defense of honor.[8] If one applies the standards that Caramuel applied in the previous case, then the killing seems very dubious. On the other hand, Caramuel offers no direct conclusion, and one could reasonably interpret this passage as evidence that he accepted the anonymous authority's position as extrinsically probable. At any rate, the explicit treatment of the case itself tells the reader almost nothing. The statements are simply too vague.

Caramuel does supply reasons for his resolution of the case in later editions of the *Theologia Moralis Fundamentalis*. However, by that time, his conclusions had clearly changed. Despite the position of his anonymous authority, Caramuel later rejects the justification of the killing as "completely false and improbable." In fact, he argues that the inaccuracy of the conclusion demonstrates the flawed character of the antecedent theory! To prove that the killing is illegitimate, Caramuel invokes a number of different arguments. "It is not permitted to kill for the defense of honor alone," he asserts.[9] Moreover, the religious has ceded his right to honor through his misdeeds, and the woman did not compel him to do wrong. Murder creates greater scandal than fornication. His violence may beget more violence when the woman's relatives attempt to avenge her.[10] Thus, when Caramuel offers concrete warrants concerning the probable solution to this case, they support a conclusion diametrically opposed to the one with which he has traditionally been associated!

Caramuel's treatment of the infamous case in 1652 does teach us that he was sometimes careless in his transmission of the opinions of others (and certainly much less prudent in this case than the anonymous doctor, whose name, unlike Caramuel's, did not become attached to the bizarre opinion). But it tells us little about his theological method because he offers no arguments about the resolution's probability until he has determined that it is, in fact, improbable. Thus, in terms of Caramuel's approach to probabilism, this case is not particularly illuminating. Like many of the examples that made him notorious, this practical conclusion says little about his ethical theory.

One can learn far more about Caramuel's use of probabilism from his analysis of the Peace of Westphalia, which appears in a hastily assembled collection of documents that he published at the behest of the emperor. This is not because this volume (which we will call the *Pax Licita*) provides a highly organized application of Caramuel's favorite theory.[11] Instead, the treatise intrigues the reader through its inconsistency. Caramuel uses probabilism to offer two very different approaches to the problem of accepting Westphalia's provisions. The argument that he mentions (but does not champion) is straightforward and obvious; the position that he ultimately asserts is complex, demanding, and ecclesiastically explosive. The *Pax Licita* thus shows the reader what an ethicist like Caramuel could do with probabilism. It offers a stunning picture not only of his theories but also of his values, his frankness, and his judgment.

Background

According to some estimates, the Peace of Westphalia marked the end of a war that cost Germany one third of its urban and forty percent of its rural populations. Assessing the casualties of this devastation, much of it inflicted by foreign mercenaries, historian Richard Dunn remarks: "Not until the twentieth century could any other European conflict boast such human butchery."[12] In terms of its consequences for religious practice, Westphalia basically reconfirmed and expanded the principle of *cuius regio, eius religio* established a century before in the Peace of Augsburg, which allowed the German princes to maintain territorial churches in accordance with their own religious loyalties.[13]

For the Roman Catholic rulers of the Holy Roman Empire, the Thirty Years War (1618–48) had begun with a Protestant revolt in Bohemia, but the war's initial setbacks were followed by a series of military successes that enhanced imperial power. By 1629, Emperor Ferdinand II was able to issue an Edict of Restitution outlawing Calvinism and demanding the return of ecclesiastical territories and properties that had been seized by the Lutherans since the mid-sixteenth century. These lands included bishoprics, towns, and over 150 monasteries and convents. At this point, Catholic dreams for a complete triumph within the empire seemed quite reasonable. Yet these imperial victories provoked interventions by foreign powers (first the Swedes and then the French) that quickly turned the tide of the war. Emperor Ferdinand III's position in 1644, when peace negotiations began, was far less advantageous than his father's had been in the late 1620s. Peace with the Protestants was going to require concessions, both in terms of religious toleration within the empire and in renunciation of claims to ecclesiastical property and territory.[14]

Given these enormous shifts in military fortune, it is not surprising that Catholic commentators disagreed about the proper response to the situation. Could a Catholic emperor legitimately accept the terms demanded by the Protestants, specifically regarding legal toleration and the concession of ecclesiastical property? Did such compromises constitute moral evil? For some Catholics, the provisions of Westphalia were particularly objectionable because they included permanent concessions, rather than temporary or provisional ones.[15] Permanent concessions precluded the possibility of eventually reversing Catholic losses, even if the volatile political/military situation were to change in the emperor's favor. From this perspective, one might reasonably argue that Westphalia not only compromised with injustice but also perpetuated it.

Jesuit Heinrich Wangnereck (writing under the name Ernestus de Eusebiis) provided the most important expressions of this "militant" position.[16] According to Robert Birely, his goal was not to prolong the war but to encourage a formal protest against the terms of Westphalia that would protect the Church's right to pursue its claims if future circumstances permitted.[17] (The Holy See ultimately followed a similar approach by delaying the release of its formal protest against Westphalia until 1650.[18]) But Juan Caramuel's moral analysis of the situation was very different from Wangnereck's. In response to "Ernestus," the Spaniard argued for the theological legitimacy—indeed, the moral necessity—of the Peace of Westphalia.

Caramuel's *Pax Licita*

The *Pax Licita* has a complex textual history. It poses particular problems for the interpreter because it is a collection of writings, not all of which appear in every edition of the work.[19] In addition to the treatise that responds to the emperor's request, another section of the *Pax Licita* answers questions that had apparently been posed to Caramuel by Anselm Casimir, the late Archbishop of Mainz.[20] The book also outlines Caramuel's evaluation of and response to Wangnereck's arguments. Given these multiple purposes, it is not surprising that the *Pax Licita* poses great challenges for the reader, even in comparison to Caramuel's other volumes. Highly technical in its analysis of counterclaims and historical circumstances, its structure renders it quite repetitive at some points and meandering in others. One could not describe it as a literary masterpiece.

Because it is a defense of certain ethical conclusions rather than an investigation of moral theory, the *Pax Licita* represents (in modern terms) an exercise in applied ethics rather than fundamental moral theology. Here Caramuel uses probabilism without explaining its various nuances. The volume, however, does contain one interesting observation regarding the nature of probabilism itself. It appears within Caramuel's discussion of a historical precedent for Westphalia, that is, the Peace of Augsburg, accepted by the Emperor Charles V in 1555. In evaluating a cardinal's apparent objections to the previous treaty, Caramuel notes: "At that time, moral theology was not as refined as it is now; nor was the force of probable opinions as well examined."[21] This represents an unusual concession on his part, for he generally emphasizes the antiquity of recourse to probable opinion.[22] (One should acknowledge, however, that Caramuel consistently argues that the ancients *used* probable opinions, not that they had developed a theory regarding probabilism.[23]) However, it is noteworthy that, when probabilism itself was not the topic of debate, Caramuel could acknowledge that there had been significant development in the theory during the previous century.

The *Pax Licita,* Caramuel tells us, was not a work that he ever intended to write. The command of his superiors, especially the emperor, drew him away from another extensive and demanding literary project into the reluctant consideration of contemporary politics.[24] In this discussion, he explains, he intends to focus upon general principles rather than upon the concrete features of the situation: indeed, according to its author, "the entire book is hypothetical."[25] In the beginning, Caramuel thus suggests that he intends to provide advice about foundational criteria for assessing Westphalia rather than to defend a particular ethical judgment.

Caramuel also explains his reluctance by pointing out that a concrete assessment depends upon an accurate knowledge of political circumstances. A private person lacks access to the secrets of the commonwealth and to the strategic considerations that the emperor must consider. The entire debate is particularly troubling for a theologian—especially a theologian who is also a foreigner—because its resolution depends upon many questions of fact regarding concrete circumstances. Such questions are not, strictly speaking, matters of theology.[26] Moreover, circumstances can change very quickly, rendering today's conclusions obsolete.[27] Given such limitations, Caramuel warns against the issuance of any absolute opinion about the proposed peace. In his view, some have already spoken rashly, with theologians ignoring political concerns and politicians ignoring theological considerations.[28]

Although Caramuel never raises the point explicitly, one can reasonably assume that part of his reluctance to publish the work came from a desire to avoid ecclesiastical controversy. In letters to Fabio Chigi, he expresses his fear that the book might be condemned, and he later wrote directly to Pope Innocent X to defend the text. Chigi's correspondence with Vatican authorities regarding the work essentially repudiates his former protégé.[29] Both sets of letters demonstrate that Caramuel's argument was ecclesiastically perilous. One finds indirect confirmation of this point in the behavior of other theological commentators. Wangnereck, whose arguments enjoyed Chigi's support, published his book under an assumed name and even listed a spurious place of publication (Ecclesiopolis).[30] The emperor apparently consulted a number of theologians about the Peace of Westphalia, and Caramuel tells us that many preferred to keep their responses private.[31] So did some (though not all) of the experts to whom Caramuel submitted his own arguments for review.[32] It was Caramuel whose argument appeared in a book adorned (eventually) with his own name, in the front lines of a dangerous theological controversy.[33] Even though he was initially unaware of Chigi's connection to the work to which he was responding, Caramuel clearly recognized the dangers of his new project.[34]

One can believe Caramuel when he asserts his hesitation to comply with the imperial command. Yet once the book was published, he defended its argument to the angry Chigi and cited it in later volumes without apparent embarrassment.[35] There is nothing to suggest that Caramuel simply wrote what he thought the emperor wanted to hear. The *Pax Licita* expresses his convictions, albeit his reluctantly expressed convictions.

The *Pax Licita*, of course, was not only an evaluation of the proposed treaty but also a direct response to Wangnereck's attack upon the legitimacy of its terms. Caramuel did not know the author's identity at the time that he wrote his response.[36] Indeed, he speculates about whether Ernestus is a theologian and even toys with the idea that he might not be a Catholic (although Caramuel admits that he does not truly believe this).[37] For the Spaniard, it is not Ernestus's piety that is in question. His opponent clearly loves God and the Church, and honors the pope. The problem is his ignorance about Germany, "which he does not love."[38] Caramuel is amused by Ernestus's objection that toleration will remove the ignominy that heresy deserves. Does he not realize that the Germans feel no shame regarding heresy?[39] (Caramuel apparently did not realize that his anonymous opponent actually was German.[40]) Ernestus's arguments, Caramuel believes, are divorced from the concrete realities of the situation. He has posed his theological questions too broadly, without sufficient consideration of the practical circumstances that shape the emperor's dilemma. Yet for Caramuel, the most objectionable feature of Ernestus's argument seems to be his willingness to preserve the faith by sacrificing Germany. Caramuel quotes Ernestus's assertions that the Church will not be lost, even if it disappears in Germany; and that if the emperor's military resources will not permit an adequate defense, then he must trust in God's promise that the gates of hell will not prevail against the Church. The Spanish theologian has little patience for either argument. The Church in Germany will not be saved, he observes, "by us, without God; or by God, without us."[41] And if Ernestus does not care that the Church is lost in Germany, Caramuel says angrily, "we care [*nos curamus*]."

Indeed, one of the most striking aspects of Caramuel's presentation is his insistence that only those familiar with conditions in Germany are prepared to assess the Treaty of Westphalia. For his theological colleagues, he draws an analogy to medical practice: if one's mother is sick, one calls in the doctor at hand, rather than writing to a famous physician in another city. Similarly, the theologian who lives across the sea or the Alps, "*even if he is the equal of Thomas, Bernard, or even Augustine,*" should defer to those who know the problems of Germany firsthand. "*That controversy is political and practical,*" he writes. "*It depends upon one's eyes, one's ears, one's hands*"—in other words, upon one's personal familiarity with the situation.[42] Someone "chatters of victories, promises triumphs, and . . . [thus] has impeded the concord that all Germany desires."[43] Caramuel's assessment is radically different, in light of his own experiences: "I believe my own eyes . . . I see the losses; I despair of triumphs; I urge the Peace; and I protest that many things must necessarily be conceded to the Protestants."[44] When all is said and done, Caramuel's assessment of the Peace of Westphalia arises not only from his principles but also from his experiences as a Catholic missionary whose work was undone by advancing armies. The memories of the people whom he tried to serve and was forced to leave behind suffuse one of his most passionate applications of probabilism.

The Argument That Caramuel Does Not Emphasize

At first glance, probabilism would seem to provide an easy answer for the emperor's dilemma regarding the Peace of Westphalia. If probable opinion suffices for security of conscience, then Caramuel could reasonably argue that the very uncertainty of the situation renders the treaty legitimate. Faced with contrary probable opinions regarding the acceptance or rejection of the Protestants' terms, the emperor is free to make peace or wage war with a tranquil conscience, since he knows that reliance on probable opinion renders either choice morally responsible. Such an application of probabilism is entirely consistent with Caramuel's moral theory. Moreover, from a tactical vantage point, it would have allowed him to defend the Peace with diminished ecclesiastical risks. In a few paragraphs, Caramuel could have made this argument: My view is probable; Ernestus's view is probable; the emperor is at liberty to adopt either of them.

The beginning of the *Pax Licita* suggests that Caramuel is going to offer a variation of this argument. His initial synopsis of the work proposes four critical questions for resolving the dilemma. Will deferring the settlement and prolonging the war produce better or worse articles of peace, and is such a strategy advantageous or damaging for the Christian world? Second, can peace be obtained by offering fewer concessions than the proposed treaty requires? Third, do the articles of peace involve moral cooperation with evil or simply permission in the face of necessity? Finally, if measures sufficient to obtain religious concord are applied, is the conversion of the heretics mortally certain or beyond reasonable hope? If it is morally certain that delay will produce better articles, fewer concessions, or conversion of the Protestants, then one must continue the war; the treaty must also be rejected if it involves moral cooperation with evil. On the other hand, should all of the opposite consequences be certain, and either morally or evidently true, then one must enter into the treaty under pain of mortal sin. If at least some of these projected outcomes remain merely probable, however, princes have the choice of entering into or rejecting the treaty.[45] That the *Pax Licita* begins in this way leads the reader to expect an extended analysis of political liberty in the face of divergent probable opinions.

Caramuel certainly recognizes the force of this argument and invokes it several times in the volume. Against the claim that one must follow the safer and more secure sentence regarding the concession of ecclesiastical goods, he argues:

> There is no human or divine law that binds the emperor to relinquish a safe and secure path and enter into one that is safer and more secure . . .

> Let us stand firm with the common doctrine of probability: and we will
> find that it suffices for Caesar to have a conscience that is secure and safe;
> . . . [we will find that] probability suffices; nor is *probabilioritas* required.[46]

This represents an obvious application of the view that probable opinion
provides an adequate warrant for moral responsibility, a position that Caramuel defended consistently throughout his career. Yet while he acknowledges its value in guaranteeing the emperor's security of conscience, it is
not (despite the initial synopsis) the major argument of the *Pax Licita*.[47]
This becomes clear from Caramuel's description of the difference between
his approach and other probabilistic arguments concerning the treaty.

> Some defenders of our opinion [i.e., that the treaty is licit], in order that
> they might turn aside ill will, call [this opinion] probable, because they are
> looking toward practice, which is content with mere probability. But we,
> who write not only about practices, but also about speculative matters,
> conclude that Ernestus's opinion is intrinsically improbable, because it
> lacks reasons that are of any importance, and we conclude that it is extrin-
> sically improbable, because it lacks [supporting] authors . . .[48]

Thus, Caramuel does not postulate a choice between two probable opinions in this case. Ernestus's view is improbable, and demonstrating that
point necessarily affects the status of Caramuel's own position. Our author
asserts: "An opinion is manifestly true, if its opposite is improbable . . .
Ernestus's sentence is improbable. Therefore our view, which is opposed
to it, must be considered manifest."[49] Elsewhere, Caramuel expresses this
conclusion even more bluntly by describing his own opinion as "*manifestly
true*" and its opposite as "*manifestly false*."[50] The primary goal of the *Pax
Licita* is to prove this claim. Accordingly, the book illustrates Caramuel's
method for identifying improbable opinions and, as a necessary consequence, for recognizing their opposites as morally certain.

Proving Extrinsic Improbability

Caramuel's theory imposes many demands upon scholars who wish to
argue that an action is improbable, and hence, illicit. First, they must

offer arguments that demonstrate its malice—arguments that cannot be answered with a probable counterclaim. Second, they must show that the arguments in favor of its legitimacy are improbable. Finally, they must show that the rejected conclusion lacks the requisite approval from the experts. In simple terms, the scholars must demonstrate that the position is both intrinsically and extrinsically improbable.[51] This is the case that Caramuel attempts to make against Ernestus de Eusebiis. It is helpful to begin with Caramuel's claims concerning extrinsic improbability, since one can summarize them more briefly than his claims concerning *probabilitas ab intrinseco*.

Ernestus, Caramuel argues, has simply failed to muster sufficient support to render his repudiation of the treaty probable. This is largely because of his misinterpretation of the historical precedents: Ernestus appeals to circumstances that are not analogous to the present case and hence require a different resolution. Ambrose, the fourth-century bishop of Milan, for example, indeed refused to concede churches to the Arians at the Emperor Valentinian's behest, but the bishop was in a different position than the contemporary Catholic emperor, who faced the necessity of conceding some ecclesiastical properties in order to avoid losing more.[52] Caramuel spends a great deal of time examining and refuting such apparent historical precedents, generally arguing that Ernestus has drawn a flawed analogy between historical and contemporary situations. The Spaniard also claims that his opponent has applied his sources' general principles in inappropriate circumstances. Jesuit Martin Becan's argument that a Catholic prince may not "*positively consent to and cooperate*" with the introduction or continued presence of heresy, for example, has no bearing on the present case: The Peace of Westphalia reluctantly acknowledges a *fait accompli* that the emperor is powerless to avoid. Necessary permission is distinct from active cooperation. Becan is correct in principle, but the principle does not suit the present case.[53] In reality, Caramuel argues, Ernestus cannot muster a single authority whose views are immediately relevant to the situation under discussion.[54]

As another challenge to Ernestus's credibility, Caramuel defends the extrinsic probability of his own argument both by citing authors who have accepted his practical conclusions and by pointing to the universal approval of his premises.[55] Historical precedent also plays an important role in Caramuel's claim of extrinsic probability, since he argues that theological approval of the Peace of Augsburg (1555) provides a powerful argument for the similar concessions of Westphalia. Caramuel examines the circumstances and details of the earlier treaty (even including a German text of its provisions), before concluding that the two "peaces" are morally equivalent. (Indeed, Caramuel argues that Westphalia is superior to Augsburg in some respects, especially since it secures Catholics' rights to emigrate from Protestant principalities.[56]) Given the precedent of Augsburg, Caramuel argues that his approach to such treaties has been "in possession [*possessionem*]" for a century.[57] In addition, he argues that acceptance of his opponent's position would force the rejection of other generally accepted agreements between Catholics and non-Catholics. Would one really wish to encourage the emperor to declare war on the Turks or to destroy the peace concluded in Hungary? Should we revoke concordats between the Spaniards and the Muslims, recall the Edict of Nantes, and renew the fighting between Spain and Holland?[58] This long record of precedents is one of Caramuel's chief reasons for concluding that his own assessment is certain, and Ernestus's opposing view, improbable.

Caramuel's theory of extrinsic probability also plays an important role in his response to the question of keeping faith with heretics, another matter on which he believes he differs from Ernestus.[59] Caramuel regards such fidelity as an absolute obligation. Do any reputable Catholic authors, he asks, actually defend the opposite view? Caramuel knows that some Protestants believe that standard Catholic opinion allows bad faith. Some Catholic authors deny that any Catholic has sanctioned such duplicity. On this point, Caramuel is not completely sanguine: perhaps "a few ignorant and stupid men" have indeed professed this scandalous argument, for theology, like other disciplines, enjoys no immunity from "monstrous resolutions."[60] Yet he is concerned that the Protestants might raise the following question:

> Does [the fact that] this is put forward by one person or another suffice that it may be described as probable? For if keeping faith is a merely probable obligation, there will be no security in pacts of this kind. But we [Catholics] . . . hold that [the claim that one need not] keep faith with heretics may have been said by two or three ignorant persons [*idiotas*]—or by none. We deny that the opinion of three or more ignorant persons is probable . . .[61]

(The marginal heading for this section asserts: "It is improbable that the opinion of one ignorant person is probable."[62]) Thus Caramuel, whose discussions of the four-author rule culminate in the conclusion that one author suffices, is at pains here to emphasize that an ignorant person's views do not meet probability's criteria. As he asserts repeatedly in his analyses of probabilism, authoritative credibility is not a simple product of counting signatures (much less coming up with a single signature). In practice, the assessment of extrinsic probability is quite complex. To see how Caramuel distinguishes the extrinsically probable from the extrinsically improbable, therefore, the *Pax Licita* provides a useful case in point.

Proving Intrinsic Improbability

Caramuel's task in refuting Ernestus's intrinsic arguments is even more complex than his discussions of extrinsic probability. At one point, he summarizes his opponent's charges against Westphalia and addresses each in detail.[63] Because the *Pax Licita* is highly repetitive, it is helpful to organize Caramuel's objections into three major categories. First, Caramuel offers an alternate moral interpretation of the treaty by emphasizing the necessity of choosing the lesser evil, and the distinction between cooperation with and unavoidable permission of heresy. Second, Caramuel argues (against Ernestus) that acceptance of Westphalia's provisions is consistent with the duties of a Christian prince. Finally, Caramuel considers the causes of Protestantism's success in Germany, in order to suggest a remedy for the "disease" other than continued warfare. Within all three of these arguments, but especially the last, Caramuel appeals not only to general principles but also to his experiences in Germany and what he has seen with his "own eyes."

The Lesser Evil, Necessary Permission, and Freedom from the Impossible

Early in his text, Caramuel argues that the "entire controversy" can be summarized within a single syllogism.[64] Its major premise is as follows: "between two evils, when both cannot be avoided . . . the lesser must be chosen; and the person will err, who prefers to permit either the greater, or both."[65] No theologian, Caramuel asserts, would deny this principle.[66]

Later he invokes the example of a robbery victim confronted with the threat of death if he does not relinquish his garment, to demonstrate its profound practical and moral significance.

> Natural reason dictates this [concession]. You are able to do it without any human permission, or even if a human being instructs otherwise. For God did not give a pope, an emperor, or a king, the authority validly to order that you lose your life rather than your cloak.[67]

The central strategy of the *Pax Licita* is to demonstrate that the Peace of Westphalia represents the lesser of two evils. Just as the robbery victim must yield his property to save his life, the emperor and the other German Catholic princes must make unavoidable concessions—in this case, to guarantee the survival of the Church within their territories. This argument allows Caramuel to reinterpret Ernestus's descriptions of the treaty's consequences. It is inaccurate, the Spaniard argues, to claim that the emperor is violating his responsibility to defend the Church. Instead, he is defending the most significant element of the Church (its souls) by allowing the loss of some of its property.[68] Nor is the emperor actively cooperating with evil in tolerating heresy. Because he lacks the power to repress it, and the effort to do so would be both ineffective and deleterious, he can reluctantly permit what he cannot avoid.[69] What Ernestus identifies as malfeasance, Caramuel views as a prudent effort to make the best of a bad situation. At both Augsburg and Westphalia, Catholic emperors faced the choice between "casting the luggage into the sea, or allowing the entire ship of Peter to perish in Germany."[70] "I think that Caesar would have sinned mortally, if he had preferred that Germany perish, rather than subscribe to the Peace of Religion," Caramuel says flatly.[71]

To support his argument, Caramuel appeals to many other cases involving the toleration of the lesser evils that are a part of public life. Christian commonwealths, including Rome, tolerate Jews and allow them to practice usury. (Caramuel notes that the pope has far less to fear from the Jews than the emperor does from the Swedish mercenaries.[72]) Moreover, law allows homicide in the case of legitimate self-defense. If loss of life can be sanctioned to save life, then certainly one can justify concessions of ecclesiastical property to save the Church. "Let these things perish, lest we perish," asserts Caramuel.[73] Interestingly, his personal view on the civic toleration of brothels (a traditional test case apparently invoked by Ernestus) is more stringent than his adversary's. Ernestus, if Caramuel has quoted him correctly, apparently argued that brothels might sometimes (though not always) be tolerated as the lesser evil, although cooperation with Protestants could not. Caramuel, who refuses to label the emperor's concessions as *cooperation*, also rejects the claim that brothels are the lesser evil and argues that civic maintenance of such institutions is, in fact, an invitation to sin.[74] Yet Caramuel also cites the case of brothels as an example of civic permission of lesser evils in order to avoid greater ones.[75] Although he does not say so, perhaps he regarded this as an extrinsically probable argument to which he did not personally subscribe.

Even more telling than Caramuel's references to human practice are his appeals to divine tolerance in the face of human evil. Christ's parable of the wheat and the tares illustrates God's governance and provides an example worthy of Caesar's emulation. Rejecting Westphalia's provisions, Caramuel believes, will only lead to greater destruction of the wheat (Catholics) and increased growth of the tares (Protestants).[76] God, in fact, does not always prevent evil, even though God has absolute power, unlike human rulers. "Just as God permits evils on account of a greater good, or lest greater evil follow," Caramuel concludes, Caesar may legitimately practice such toleration.[77] Divine forbearance thus becomes a model for interpreting the Peace of Westphalia.

Choosing the lesser evil—as Birely's discussion of Becan's position illustrates—had played a significant role in arguments justifying concessions to Protestants long before Caramuel's treatise appeared; the Spaniard clearly regards the choice as an ethical dictum.[78] Yet Caramuel associates this principle with another that will play a critical role in his later works on probabilism: the insistence that God does not oblige us to perform the impossible. Since Ernestus faults the emperor for not impeding what he is in no position to impede, Caramuel argues that his opponent has essentially adopted a position that the Council of Trent condemned in reference to Luther and Calvin. In addition, Ernestus's approach resurrects the view of Baianism and Jansenism that human beings sin in what they do out of necessity.[79] Although one might easily be tempted to dismiss such arguments as polemical—an attempt to use guilt by association against an adversary—the insistence upon divine forbearance and the reality of human freedom is a consistent feature of Caramuel's theology. Here one detects a small taste of arguments that will permeate the *Apologema* and the *Dialexis*. For the moment, however, they ground Caramuel's analysis of Westphalia as an inevitable permission of the lesser evil.

The Appropriate Use of Catholic Political Power

Like Ernestus, Caramuel presumes that Catholic princes have a duty to promote the interests of the Church and to protect it from its enemies.[80] Yet for Caramuel, the concrete manner in which rulers fulfill those duties is conditioned first by the limits of their power and second by competing moral obligations that may demand concessions or compromise. The two principles that we have already considered (i.e., the duty to choose the lesser evil and the freedom from performing the impossible) both limit the Catholic prince's response to heresy. Concessions to heretics may be less harmful than the alternative. Eradicating heresy is often impossible. One cannot settle concrete moral questions (such as the assessment of Westphalia) without considering the circumstances that bring these competing principles into play.

The ruler's obligation to protect the common good also shapes what he or she should reasonably do to defend and promote the Church. "I say that the prince is bound to punish heretics, when such punishment is more useful to the commonwealth than tolerance," Caramuel remarks. "But if punishment is pernicious to the commonwealth, and tolerance useful, not only is the prince not bound to punish them, but he is even bound to tolerate them."[81] The ruler must focus his or her priorities on the welfare of the community to make the difficult choices that limited power often requires. Even in reference to the Church's well-being, appropriate concessions are sometimes both necessary and advantageous. Caramuel argues that the prince can promote heretics to high positions in public life, if such honors are useful to the Church. Similarly, if religious liberty benefits the Church, then it is entirely reasonable to grant it to Protestants.[82] Princes do not enjoy unlimited power. In an imperfect world, one must sometimes cede four chapels to protect a hundred others.[83] Though the emperor should try to ensure religious freedom for Catholics living in Protestant regions, he may have to settle for protecting their rights to emigrate.[84] Against Ernestus's objection that such emigration is unjust to the displaced Catholic, Caramuel points out that the common good may

sometimes ask even greater sacrifices of innocent people (such as deten-
tion in quarantine to avoid the spread of plague).[85] The Catholic ruler
always faces the challenge of balancing competing interests, a challenge
compounded by his or her own limited power.

In this particular case, Caramuel points out, the problem under discussion is whether to make peace or continue a war. The emperor must not
forget the limitations of civil power in respect to the lives of others, including his soldiers. Caramuel warns:

> A prince who rashly exposes his soldiers [to death], and loses some with-
> out at least probable hope of public utility, is guilty of shedding innocent
> blood, and is bound to restitution, like others who take human life. He
> rashly exposes his soldiers, if he undertakes an improbable war when he
> ought [to make] peace. A war is called *improbable* either by reason of its
> cause or by reason of its effect: by reason of its cause, when it is unjust,
> and unsupported by any probable argument; by reason of its effect, when
> it is rash, and when there is no probable hope of promoting the authority,
> security, and utility of the Church and the commonwealth.[86]

Despite his claims that the book is hypothetical, Caramuel is obviously
concerned that the specific conflict under debate is becoming (or perhaps
has already become?) an "improbable war."

Caramuel also addresses two specific questions regarding civil responsibility and the Peace of Westphalia: the legitimacy of conceding ecclesiastical property (in perpetuity) to the Protestants and the necessity of
keeping one's word to them. The first question evidently arose from the
claim that secular rulers had no right to alienate property (against the will
of the original donors) that had been given to the Church, and hence, to
God. Caramuel's arguments on this point are varied and ingenious. All
donations, including those given to the Church, are conditioned by the requirements of the common good and are subject to abrogation when they
injure the commonwealth.[87] Moreover, Thomas's argument that goods become common property under conditions of necessity implies that, under the present crisis, the donations have become "common to the whole
empire" and hence, subject to secular concession.[88] Properly speaking, the
emperor is not *giving* the Protestants these properties, but declining to
resist their unjust usurpation. As a result, Protestants will obtain only civil

immunity from being forced to surrender their ill-gotten gains. Caramuel points out that these properties are effectively lost to the Catholics already, and disputing their ownership makes no more sense than arguing over the corpse of a dead horse![89]

Yet despite his attention to these arguments, Caramuel clearly regards the entire debate as a reflection of misplaced priorities. The *Church* that the emperor must defend is primarily its people, and only in a very subsidiary sense, its property. It is not a matter of faith that "God be worshiped in this [particular] place or that one, or that ecclesiastics be rich or poor." Too many people, Caramuel argues, "confuse the Church with its walls."[90] Yet "Christ did not pour out his blood for walls."[91]

> Did the Redeemer of the world die for ecclesiastical goods? Was he crucified, did he die, was he buried, did he descend into Hell, rise from the dead, and ascend into heaven in order to enrich the churches? I deny it; I deny it . . . By dying for souls, he taught us that one single soul must be preferred over many riches.[92]

The priority of a Christian prince, whether secular or ecclesiastical, must be the salvation of his subjects, those who are in danger of losing their lives, their faith, or both, if the war continues. "Let money perish, which brings these miseries," says Caramuel in reference to ecclesiastical property.[93] Elsewhere, he remarks: "I do not regard earthly goods so highly, that I would wish to be at odds with heretics on account of them; nor do I know why one would be unable to concede estates or money to them, lest one be compelled to concede greater things."[94]

If Caramuel allows the prince some latitude regarding the concession of Church property, his prohibition of breaking faith with heretics is absolute. Acceptance of such behavior reminds Caramuel of Machiavelli.[95] "Nothing" is "more pernicious to the commonwealth than perjury and infidelity," he flatly insists.[96] Even if a prince fails in his initial duty by making a pact under inappropriate circumstances (e.g., by making concessions when there is no necessity to do so), he is bound to observe the agreement once it has been made.[97] Catholic rulers owe their Protestant subjects the same fidelity that they give to other Catholics, and the same protection, should the Protestants fall victim to an unjust violation of the Peace.[98]

Against the argument that heretics are unfaithful to God and do not merit faith in return, Caramuel makes a distinction between faith (as a supernatural virtue) and civic fidelity. There is no reason why Protestants cannot maintain the latter.[99] Moreover, Protestant heresy does not justify Catholic perjury. Caramuel also warns against the deviously worded treaties that have caused difficulties in the past, notably between Spain and Holland. Mental reservations, in his view, are simply "true lies decorated with the false name of truth."[100] To protect his own reputation and authority, a prince must be forthright, especially with the Germans, who highly value such candor.[101] In addition, the prince's honesty reflects the ultimate source of his power. God, Caramuel points out, is so faithful that he cannot be unfaithful:

> Since the emperor is [made] in the image of God, and rules in secular matters in the name of God, [the emperor] ought to be supremely faithful; for without fidelity, human affairs are unable to continue; nor will the contracts of commonwealths be able to be made lasting, if princes are not worthy of faith.[102]

Finally, one should note that Caramuel's application of imperial responsibilities to the analysis of Westphalia could hardly be described as morally permissive. The prince must keep faith, even if he errs in entering into an agreement with heretics. The prince must consider the good of souls, even if this requires the sacrifice of property. Most importantly, the prince *must* choose the lesser of two evils. In Caramuel's view, this is a certain obligation, not a probable option. If making concessions to the Protestants is the lesser of two evils, then the emperor has an obligation to do so, under pain of mortal sin.[103] So strongly does Caramuel believe in this conclusion that he is willing to defend it even in the face of hypothetical opposition from Rome. In one of the most ecclesiastically charged passages of the *Pax Licita*, he observes:

> What if a pope should err, through lack of experience, and should say there is no reason why heretics can be tolerated in Germany? Ought we then to allow all to perish [there], and to permit all things to the heretics, rather than permitting some? By no means. We were born in a most learned century; we know that the power of God is innate; and we presuppose that the

power of all human individuals is limited—conceded to them by God for edification. And when we see the commands of superiors turning toward destruction, the purpose of law ceases, and the obligation of obedience ceases. Nor do we wish to cast the whole Catholic religion into peril, on account of their imperfection.[104]

Experience of Germany

As the previous citation illustrates, Caramuel emphasizes the necessity of understanding Germany before one can properly evaluate the Peace of Westphalia. His moral conclusions rely heavily upon his own experiences there, regarding both the miseries of war and the prospects for the future. Caramuel does not believe the Peace necessarily spells the end of progress for German Catholicism. Religious concord with the Protestants is not beyond the realm of possibility. But to address the "disease" of heresy, one must first recognize its causes. Thus, the *Pax Licita* includes (and bases its conclusions on) an analysis of the circumstances behind the German Reformation. In effect, Caramuel offers the emperor an alternative explanation of the present conflict and a method for serving and preserving the faith other than continued war.

For a text that argues that the emperor can yield property to his enemies lest they unjustly seize even more of it, the *Pax Licita* is remarkably free of polemics against German Protestants. For several reasons, the absence of such a diatribe is quite striking, and the explanation for Caramuel's argumentative strategy is not immediately obvious. First, it would be incorrect to presume that Caramuel had scruples about including religious polemics within his work. Although the *Pax Licita* avoids general diatribes against Protestants, one cannot say the same thing regarding its treatment of Jews, to whom the author applies an appalling list of slanders (infidelity, blasphemy, incestuous and invalid marriage, and homicide, including the killing of Christians under the guise of medical treatment).[105] (In fairness to Caramuel, one should point out that the *Pax Licita* also argues that civil relationships do not necessarily require unity in faith: thus, there is no reason why a non-Christian cannot serve as a legitimate superior or play a role in civic life.)[106] The purpose of these references to the Jews is to demonstrate that present civic practice provides a precedent for tolerating Protestants. Yet their inclusion indicates that one cannot explain the absence of a general polemic against the behavior of Protestants from the *Pax Licita* by suggesting that Caramuel had scruples about using such rhetoric.

Nor did Caramuel write as he did because he rejected the use of force in securing religious orthodoxy and wished to defuse the threat of further coercion. Only a few years after publishing the *Pax Licita,* Caramuel would use coercion (as well as persuasion) in the Catholic restoration of Bohemia and Moravia—sometimes against the objections of other Catholics who favored a gentler approach.[107] Whatever explains Caramuel's avoidance of a polemic against the German Protestants, it is not pacifism or even a general commitment to nonviolence in the resolution of conflicts between Christians.

Finally, Caramuel's silence on this subject is not the product of any theological sympathy with Luther, Calvin, and the other reformers. The first edition of the *Theologia Moralis Fundamentalis* very clearly expresses his ecclesiological position: "*the Lutheran religion is not true; nor is the Calvinist religion true; nor any of the others condemned by the Roman* [Church]; *and thus, only the Roman* [Church] *is true.*"[108] Caramuel did not conclude from this that a Catholic theologian could simply ignore or dismiss Protestant theology, and he clearly thought it important to evaluate and respond to the reformers' ideas. But given his own intellectual presuppositions, Caramuel found Lutheran and Calvinist theologies no more congenial than he found Jansenism.[109] The explanation of the *Pax Licita*'s missing diatribe against German Protestantism, in fact, seems to lie in the opposite direction. Caramuel sympathizes with ordinary German Protestants because he believes that their "protest" is not fundamentally a matter of theology at all.

If one begins with the personal, rather than the theoretical, it seems clear that Caramuel left Germany with a favorable impression of many of the Protestants that he encountered there. In the *Pax Licita,* Caramuel repeatedly emphasizes that Protestants frequently exhibit personal and civic virtues. Often, he argues, they even surpass Catholics in their modesty, humility, piety, and other strengths of character.[110] Nor is there any reason that they cannot play a role in public life—even in positions of honor and authority. "If we need a painting, we seek an artist, not a Christian," Caramuel argues.

For health, [we seek] a doctor; nor do we refuse [treatment from] a Jew. Thus it will be possible for a commonwealth to accept heretics into [its] councils, if this is conducive to public peace, or if it judges them to be particularly qualified.[111]

Caramuel does not seem to bear any animus against German Protestants. Indeed, the *Pax Licita* demonstrates far more anger toward the (Catholic) French leaders who have chosen to intervene in Germany to check imperial influence than toward the "heretics" whom Caramuel argues must be granted concessions.[112] Caramuel has great sympathy for ordinary Germans, whom he does not regard (in general) as intellectually committed to Protestant theology. The *Pax Licita* describes an encounter with a Calvinist leader devoted to Francis of Assisi who did not hesitate to speak of the mendicant friar as a "saint" and exhorted his audience to follow Francis's example.[113] In Caramuel's view, some controversies between Catholics and Lutherans are nominal or can "be reduced to some probable position," like the controversies between the Scotists and the Thomists.[114] The root of the problem in Germany is not theology but ecclesiastical practice. Caramuel argues: "the cause of Lutheranism is a certain provocation and scandal . . . But this is not grounded in such strong arguments that it can remain when the provocation and scandal are removed. For they are rational people, as we are. . . ."[115]

The provocation and scandal to which Caramuel is referring are the financial exactions imposed upon German Catholics. The indulgence controversy, to which Caramuel devotes considerable attention, illustrates a more general problem: fiscal malfeasance that has placed excessive burdens on the German Church. Citing the preface to the *95 Theses*, Caramuel argues that Luther was agitated rather than pertinacious in the beginning.[116] The Reformation grew out of a protest over a genuine abuse—an abuse "committed through imprudence and avarice."[117]

"Years and years have passed," Caramuel remarks, regarding the aftermath of the indulgence controversy. "The cancer has gradually spread. We have lived in hope, and we have not known how or have been unwilling to apply the remedy."[118] The tragedy of the German Church is the failure to address the scandals that continue to drive people into the arms of the Protestants. It has been easier to blame the Lutherans, Caramuel complains, than to face our own flaws.[119]

I have said sometimes that flatterers have injured the Catholic Church more than the heresiarchs. I have displeased my [colleague Antonino] Diana; but I maintain [my] position, and with the good leave of my best friend, I must believe my own eyes. The Lutherans do not detest clergy, but clerical pride, avarice, and arrogance.[120]

Caramuel invokes his own experiences in Germany to prove the point. Some of the Germans whom he convinced to abandon Calvinism for Catholicism, he explains, said "*they were able to be Catholic with me, but not with others.*"[121] Certain Catholic clerics misused the property recovered from Protestants in such a way as to scandalize the faithful. Caramuel describes the avarice of many ecclesiastics as intolerable.[122] It is this greed that is driving people away from the Church. People avoid sacramental confession lest they be compelled to pay a stipend. Priests demand money for saying prayers for the dead and offering mass. Small wonder that the Protestants, who deny the utility of such rituals, attract the poor. Caramuel has heard that Catholic paupers are burying their dead in Lutheran cemeteries because they lack the offerings that their own ministers demand.[123] "Oh, we are miserable!" Caramuel exclaims concerning German Catholicism. "We are invaded by an insatiable desire for money, and what we think is heresy, is commonly pure avarice, and a monstrosity born from mere avarice."[124]

One experience moved Caramuel so deeply that he describes it directly for his readers. On April 22, 1647, he was returning to the bridge over the Danube when he encountered a crowd that included "muttering Jews and laughing Lutherans." When he inquired about the cause of the disturbance, the people showed him a poor woman and the corpse of a dead child. The mother had brought the body there so that she could beg for alms to bury her son in the Catholic cemetery. "I was astounded," Caramuel says. "Nor did I judge that one could say—without ignominy for all ecclesiastics—how great the avarice of the parish priest was, that the corpse of a three-year-old had to be cast down at the feet of those who passed by in order to collect money."[125] In reference to this experience, Caramuel says: "I see this, and I am disheartened; and the insolence of the crime suggests many other [abuses] that occur more frequently."[126] "If I seem harsh, it must be imputed to the sadness, which I felt . . . at the misery of this unburied corpse."[127]

Germany's sufferings can be lifted, Caramuel seems to be suggesting in the *Pax Licita,* but not by continued warfare. It is greed that is the prime enemy of the German Church (and concomitantly, of the region's social order). The exactions demanded from the German people may ultimately lead to the types of revolutions that are occurring in other parts of Europe.[128] Caramuel's warning is a plea to Catholic leaders to address the real source of Germany's religious problems. It is also a reminder that concrete moral judgment depends not just upon ethical principles but also upon the evidence of one's own eyes.

Conclusion

Publication of the *Pax Licita* elicited Chigi's comment that Caramuel's judgment did not match his erudition—a critique that has become a staple judgment of the Spanish theologian.[129] One wonders whether Caramuel's disconcerting candor on this occasion effectively ended his prospects for high preferment in the Church.[130] The *Pax Licita* is passionate rather than discreet. Yet our conclusions about value of Caramuel's blunt critique may be quite different than Chigi's. After three centuries, this repetitive, untidy, and forthright book retains its power to move the heart.

The *Pax Licita* is also a striking illustration of Caramuel's ethical theory and of his emphasis upon distinction between probable opinion and ethical certainty—a distinction crucial for his later works on probabilism. One can find no clearer refutation of the canard that the "laxist" Caramuel ignored moral truth and used probabilism to justify any possible behavior than the arguments of the *Pax Licita.* Caramuel sets firm guidelines for the emperor. The probabilism of the *Pax Licita* is anything but a *laissez faire* ethical theory. Like the *Apologema,* this work emphasizes probabilism's role in securing moral responsibility when circumstances limit one's options. The text is also, in another sense, an anticipation of the *Apologema,* for both works swim against the tide of ecclesiastical approval to express what Caramuel views as truth to persons in power.

CHAPTER FOUR

Protecting Probabilism

The Apologema *as an Answer to Probabilism's Critics*

I N THE *Pax Licita,* CARAMUEL TOOK THE RISK OF TELLING CHURCH LEAD-
ers what he felt they needed, but may not have wanted, to hear. Fifteen
years later, he took the same risk in defense of his moral theory. This time,
probabilism itself was under attack, from critics too influential to be ignored. Although Bartolomé de Medina's thesis was becoming increasingly
controversial by the 1660s, the immediate catalyst for Caramuel's apology
was the publication of Prospero Fagnani's tract on probable opinion.

Background

For much of the seventeenth century, Prospero Fagnani was one of the
most influential canonists in the Roman Curia, particularly as secretary
to the Congregation on the Council, a position he occupied between
1613 and 1626. Over the years, Fagnani held a variety of important posts
within the Church's central administration, undeterred by the blindness
that struck him in 1632.[1] Although he was certainly active in Rome during
Caramuel's brief period of residence there, there is nothing in his text or in
the Spaniard's to demonstrate that they knew one another personally.[2]

Fagnani published his famous commentary at the behest of Caramuel's
one-time patron, Pope Alexander VII.[3] His analysis of the legitimacy of
using probable opinion first appeared within this massive canonical treatise, although it was later republished as a separate tract.[4] Although the

first edition of the work was published in 1661, internal evidence suggests that Fagnani composed the treatise on probable opinion at least several years before that date.[5] It would be reasonable to speculate that the canonist supplemented his initial arguments against probabilism with documents that appeared in the late 1650s, including theoretical treatises and letters of complaint about laxism that were submitted to the curia.

Fagnani certainly seems to feel that he is a voice crying in the wilderness against the relentless onslaught of probable opinions. Early in the treatise, he acknowledges "how hard it may be to stop the power of a flood, and to tear away from the ears of princes and private persons this prurient doctrine, fixed in the minds of nearly all."[6] Fagnani clearly regards the use of probable opinion as a pernicious method that has seduced (to varying degrees) "nearly all the theologians of our time [*Theologi nostri temporis fere omnes*]."[7] His tract examines five major questions: "Whether in any matter it is licit to follow any probable opinion whatsoever?" "Whether in moral matters it is licit to follow an opinion probable in itself, prescinding from the probability of any opposite opinion whatsoever?" "Whether from two opposite and equally probable opinions, one is free to follow either one . . . ?" "Whether it is licit to follow an opinion less probable and less safe, having abandoned the more probable and safer [opinion]?" and "Whether the authority of a single doctor renders an opinion probable?"[8]

To the first question, Fagnani responds that it is indeed licit to follow a probable opinion (or even a less probable opinion), provided that the matter concerns neither faith nor morals.[9] Fagnani will allow recourse to probable opinion in what might be called speculative religious matters, provided that no ecclesiastical strictures demand the contrary. He is far more dubious about the appeal to probable opinion in the area of morals. In his eyes, the novelty of this position alone is sufficient to render it suspect.[10] The ancients required certitude for moral action, and one cannot find such certitude in a probable opinion.[11] Fagnani basically regards probabilism as a dangerous innovation that abandons the traditional standards of Christian moral responsibility.

One of the more interesting facets of Fagnani's argument is his effort to trace the history of probabilism. In his view, reliance on probable opinion as a sufficient ground for action was "introduced in this century" (i.e., within the last hundred years).[12] Prior to that point, Fagnani argues, moral certitude served as the prerequisite for licit behavior. This was not because moralists had not yet discovered the efficacy of probable opinion, but because they had already recognized its insufficiency.[13] "Yet after many centuries," he complains, "another teaching crept in, namely that certain judgment is not required for rectitude of action . . . instead probable judgment—with fear that the opposite [might be true])—suffices."[14] Fagnani observes that the famous French theologian Jean Gerson "is said [*dicitur*]" to have held this opinion: however Gerson's dates (1363-1429) would hardly place him within the previous century, so the significance that Fagnani assigns to this claim is unclear. More recent theologians, he notes, have "established three grades of probability" by building upon the basic acceptance of probable opinion as sufficient.[15]

The first grade of probability (or more accurately, the first level of reliance upon probable opinion) occurs when an agent knows that the opinion legitimizing his or her action is probable, but fails to ask whether the opposed position is equally or more probable. Nearly all contemporary theologians, Fagnani believes, accept the legitimacy of following probable opinion under these circumstances. From this position, however, there has been a movement to a second level of reliance upon probable opinion that Fagnani describes as much "laxer, and enveloped in graver difficulties and dangers."[16] This is the view that the agent may legitimately choose either of two equally probable opinions, even if the opinion that the proposed action is illicit is safer than its counterpart. Yet this dangerous development was not the end of the matter. "Because the abyss invokes the abyss," Fagnani explains, "the scholastics of our century have proceeded from this second grade of probability to a third, disseminating a new teaching, unsubmitted in the prior centuries," which accepts the recourse to a probable opinion, even if its opposite is safer and more probable.[17] Fagnani claims that Medina was the first to defend this view.[18] "It is amazing," Fagnani notes in dismay, "how far and wide these grades spread afterwards."[19] He is obviously horrified by the consequences of probabilism's rapid dissemination and acceptance.[20]

Fagnani regards the acceptance of probable opinion as a deviation that threatens the welfare of souls and the social order. Concomitant with any probable opinion supporting an action, he argues, is the fear that its opposite may prove true. Thus, the agent who acts on such opinion always lacks the certitude necessary to render his or her action justifiable.[21] In such a state of doubt, one is bound to follow the more probable or safer opinion.[22]

Fagnani's treatise thus represents a general attack upon the use of probable opinions, especially (although by no means only) in the application of law by jurists.[23] In what sense is it also a direct response to Juan Caramuel? Although the text contains some explicit negative references to Caramuel's work, one would hesitate to identify him as Fagnani's primary target, given the more frequent references to other authors. The range and source of the relevant citations from Caramuel is also quite interesting, for Fagnani had lost his sight more than five years before the publication of the *Theologia Regularis*. How well, one might ask, did Fagnani actually know Caramuel's writings?

To this question, the text of *Ne innitaris* does not provide a clear answer. In general, the passages that Fagnani quotes against Caramuel are his critics' standard proof-texts, such as the suggestion that probable opinion renders licit something that was previously sinful.[24] It is a little odd that at times Fagnani names Caramuel directly and elsewhere refers to him simply as a "modern author."[25] In some passages, the reader cannot discern whether Fagnani used Caramuel's works directly or encountered the Spaniard's views within the responses of others, including his opponents such as Julius Mercorus.[26] Finally, a few explicit references to Caramuel appear within a document that Fagnani reproduces as a warrant for his own arguments: a series of propositions proposed for condemnation by the priests of Paris and Rouen in response to the *Provincial Letters*.[27] Here the references are simply part of a larger document that itself relies upon a work of paraphrase, the *Extrait de quelques-unes des plus dangereuses propositions de la morale des nouveaux casuistes*.[28] Thus, there is little in Fagnani's references to Caramuel that could not have been extracted directly from his critics without reference to the original texts.

Caramuel does not respond to Fagnani's treatise as a personal assault. At one point, he does ask (a little plaintively) why Fagnani has singled him out when the canonist admits that the view in question is widely shared.[29] In general, however, Caramuel does not emphasize the specific references to his own work within Fagnani's treatise. The *Apologema* is not an apology for Caramuel (except indirectly). As the title indicates, it serves instead as an apology for the use of probable opinion.

The Structure of the Text

At less than two hundred pages, the *Apologema* is one of Caramuel's short-
est theological volumes. It is also an epistolary treatise consisting of four
letters with accompanying notes and appendices. The third of these letters addresses an anonymous doctor and friend. Epistles 1, 2, and 4 are directed to Cardinal Pietro Sfortia [Sforza] Pallavicino, S.J., a famous theologian and philosopher, best known today for his history of the Council
of Trent.[30] Sfortia Pallavicino was a scholar for whom Caramuel expressed
his respect in print on several occasions, and the cardinal's service on the
commission to evaluate Jansenism (in addition to his theological expertise) rendered him a logical recipient for the *Apologema*.[31] Sfortia Pallavicino also enjoyed almost daily access to Alexander VII.[32] Thus, Caramuel
chose to direct three of the letters to an intellectual who (unlike himself)
had been elevated to the purple and enjoyed continued influence with
Caramuel's former patron. The last letter, which is much longer than any
of the others, is also the only one to include any indications concerning
its date and place of composition: Rome, in December of 1662.[33] The only
introduction to the text is a summary of the argument. One has the sense
that the *Apologema* was written in haste. It was certainly printed in haste,
or at least released without proper review, since page 181 follows immediately after page 160.[34]

   The *Apologema* does not follow the outline of Fagnani's treatise: Caramuel was apparently unwilling to allow his opponent to frame the pa-
rameters of the debate. Instead, Caramuel's introduction asserts that the
Apologema will focus upon one central question: Does a probable opinion suffice for security of conscience? Caramuel intends to argue that his
own affirmative response represents traditional practice within both civil
society and the Church itself—in fact, he describes it as the "received [*re-
ceptam*]" teaching. By contrast, Fagnani's (novel) negative view necessarily
leads to the conclusion that God commands the impossible, a foundational principle of the Jansenist heresy. In addition, Caramuel wishes to
demonstrate that theologians have become more demanding rather than
more lax during the previous century, and that further stringency would
impede the Church's missionary efforts. Finally, he describes his volume
as apodictic rather than polemical. To others, he announces, he will leave

the task of refuting the many insults and scurrilous claims that Fagnani has made against holy and learned theologians, both living and dead.[35]

In a sense, however, Caramuel's argumentative strategy is more complex (and more interesting) than his own introduction suggests. The *Apologema* actually serves two purposes. On the one hand, it represents a response not merely to Fagnani but also to the different authorities cited by Fagnani and to the Jansenist conclusions that Caramuel believes flow inevitably from Fagnani's position. On the other hand, Caramuel uses the *Apologema* to explain his own theory of probable opinion: what it is, how it works, and why it is important for the welfare of Church and society alike. One might call the first his project of reaction and the second his project of explanation.

When analyzing the *Apologema*, it is helpful to begin with its character as a work of reaction. How does Caramuel regard Fagnani himself? How does Caramuel answer Fagnani's characterization of contemporary moral theologians? How does Caramuel respond in the *Apologema* to other sources invoked by Fagnani? Finally, how and why does Caramuel regard Fagnani's position as an (inadvertent) prop for Jansenism?

The Response to Fagnani Himself

It is reasonable to ask why, from among his many critics, Caramuel responded so directly to Fagnani, who was not a theologian and whose discussion of probabilism represented a relatively minor section in a work devoted to a different subject. As we shall see, it was not because Caramuel regarded Fagnani as particularly knowledgeable regarding moral theory. Fagnani's influence provides a better explanation for Caramuel's choice. With his record of distinguished service to the curia, Fagnani was in an ideal position to influence Roman views regarding the probabilist controversy (indeed, Pietro Palazzini speculates that he might have had some influence upon the later condemnations of laxist propositions[36]). Moreover, Caramuel might reasonably have feared that Fagnani's canonical commentary would enjoy a much wider circulation than tomes specifically devoted to moral theory.

Repeatedly in the *Apologema*, Caramuel distinguishes his view of Fagnani's character and accomplishments from his assessment of the canonist's views on probability. "I venerate . . . the person," he insists, even as he criticizes his opponent's positions.[37] Fagnani, he asserts, has erred "materially" out of "invincible ignorance." Caramuel thus allows Fagnani the excuse that he (Caramuel) had once refused to ascribe to Jansen. Significantly, however, Fagnani is a canonist rather than a theologian, a point to which Caramuel returns several times within his text. "It is not inglorious for a canonist to misunderstand philosophical and theological subtleties."[38] "Matter concerning probability cannot be treated by jurists."[39] Caramuel also distinguishes his view of the tract on probability from his assessment of Fagnani's commentary as a whole, describing the work as highly learned and useful in practice. It would be tragic, he argues, if Fagnani's erroneous writings on probability were to diminish the applause merited by other parts of his text. Caramuel is writing to urge revision rather than condemnation: The fourth letter emphasizes that he is making a personal appeal to Sfortia Pallavicino regarding this matter instead of approaching the cardinal in his capacity as a member of the Inquisition.[40] In general, he seems to regard Fagnani's text as a regrettable (yet dangerous) mistake by a scholar who has wandered too far from his area of expertise.

Although Caramuel delights in pointing to what he regards as Fagnani's theological and philosophical confusions, he also emphasizes the canonist's indiscriminate recourse to unreliable sources, especially the complaints of Archbishop Boonen and other Jansenists.[41] Indeed, it quickly becomes clear that Fagnani is not Caramuel's major subject of concern. Fagnani is dangerous because he has inadvertently lent his authority to a central tenet of Jansenism and to the Jansenist crusade to reintroduce their position under the "mask [*larva*]" of an attack upon lax moral teachings.[42] Fagnani is dangerous because he has denied that probable opinion suffices for security of conscience, a position that Caramuel regards as vital for the welfare of the Church and civil society. But Fagnani is dangerous because of his errors, not because of his intentions. Although one might describe some of Caramuel's references to Fagnani's views as patronizing or even disparaging, the theologian does not classify the canonist as an enemy.

The Response to Fagnani's Treatment of the Theologians

From the beginning of the *Apologema*, Caramuel announces that he is going to ignore the "jeers, injuries, and insults" that Fagnani has inflicted upon learned and holy theologians.[43] He has clearly set himself the task of responding to Fagnani with patience.[44] At times, however, that self-imposed patience seems to be wearing thin. Particularly striking are his letters' references to Antonino Diana, who would in fact die in the year that the *Apologema* was published, as "sick and blind," having lost his sight "through too much reading and writing" on behalf of the Church.[45] Caramuel leaves no doubt that he regards Fagnani's statements about his colleagues (and himself) as unjust. Fagnani has even dared to describe such dedicated scholars as *novatores* (innovators), a term commonly used in reference to Protestants (as Caramuel demonstrates in pedantic detail). The Spaniard's sense of outrage at this injustice is patent, despite his resolve to maintain an argumentative equilibrium.[46]

Caramuel certainly does not address all the objections that Fagnani raises against the views of particular theologians, but he does offer some general arguments against Fagnani's treatment of his contemporaries. One of the most interesting is his response to Fagnani's fortieth argument against the legitimacy of recourse to a less probable opinion. To demonstrate the negative consequences of this practice, Fagnani cites twenty-two "false, rash, and scandalous" examples of casuistry from "the writers of our time."[47] Commenting on this collection, Caramuel asserts that his opponent has expended great effort in mining the authors without proving anything. "From these [resolutions], many are evidently true, others [are] probable, and [there are] also some that do not please me," he remarks.[48]

> Furthermore, I wish to warn my reader that theologians very prudently propose all the circumstances that can come under consideration, and thus define cases [within] due limits. Yet Fagnani, in order that he might stir up the hatred of the readers, proposes the resolutions of these same cases universally, abstracted from the limitations.[49]

In other words, Caramuel argues that his opponent has cited his sources out of context. Yet eventually, for the sake of argument, Caramuel grants the possibility that a theologian might have abused the teaching concerning probable opinions. Should recourse to such opinions be condemned as a result? Would one condemn canon or civil law, sacred scripture, or divine mercy because persons misinterpret or misuse them? "I laugh [*rideo*]," Caramuel remarks, instructing the reader to laugh as well.[50]

Caramuel devotes particular attention to the charge that recent authors have strayed from the rigor of their theological predecessors. In Letter 4, the theologian discusses a number of cases in which he and his contemporaries are more demanding than earlier theologians such as Cajetan or Melchior Cano: omission of the Divine Office, fasting and other observances, papal inerrancy in the approval of religious orders, Mass attendance, and conformity with the precepts of the Church.[51] Most of these cases concern obedience to ecclesiastical law, and Caramuel himself notes that historical circumstances (specifically, Luther's objections to papal power) led to a change in the attitude of Catholic authors toward the moral necessity of such submission.[52] Fagnani's contention that theologians have become more lax in the last century, Caramuel concludes, only demonstrates the canonist's unfamiliarity with the prior authors.[53] Indeed, his call to relinquish the innovations of the *iuniores* in favor of the now antiquated views of their elders would endanger the entire jurisdiction of the Church.[54] Caramuel hopes that he and his colleagues will be allowed to maintain their "strict" teaching, instead of being forced to return to the "very lax" opinions of their predecessors.[55]

That Caramuel devotes so much space to this argument reminds one of the historical circumstances under which he was writing. In an age when *innovator* had become a synonym for Protestant and when attacks against "laxists" were flying on every side, Caramuel could not allow Fagnani to apply these labels with impunity. Yet paradoxically, the need to portray the probabilists as theological traditionalists could not have reflected all of the deepest instincts of his heart. Caramuel sincerely regarded recourse to probable opinion as an ancient method and defended it on those grounds, yet he had never maintained that new ideas were necessarily bad or inferior to the old.[56] Caramuel was outraged at the claim that he and his colleagues were too lax in their opinions, yet he had never endorsed the conclusion that the stringent is necessarily better than the gentle. When Caramuel reminds his readers that Thomas Aquinas's opinions were new in their day, and repeats his long-held view that a more benign opinion is (*per accidens*) "safer" than its stricter counterpart, his arguments seem far closer to those used in his earlier works than to the *Apologema*'s effort to seize the conservative high ground.[57] A blend of the two appears in his decision to cite Jean Gerson rather than rely only on more recent authors to demonstrate the dangers of moral rigorism and the risk of plunging persons into despair rather than freeing them from sin.[58] Fagnani, Caramuel warns, should reflect on Gerson's assertion: God *"does not wish us to be tested and burdened beyond that which we are able* [to bear]."[59] Such an argument reminds one that the author of the *Apologema* was also the author of the *Theologia Moralis Fundamentalis.*

The Response to Other Critics

In a sense, Fagnani's commentary provided an opportunity for Caramuel to respond to other critics of his position, sometimes because the canonist cites or draws upon them explicitly, on other occasions because his criticism coincides with theirs.[60] Caramuel nonetheless devotes little direct attention in the *Apologema* to critics other than Fagnani, with the exception of the Jansenists (who will be discussed in the next section) and the Dominicans.

The most intriguing response to (non-Jansenist) criticisms in the *Apologema* is its apparent answer to the Dominican community's Admonition of 1656. (One must call this "apparent" because Caramuel never refers to the event or to the document explicitly.[61]) Yet the number of the *Apologema*'s references to Thomas and other Dominican sources is very striking, especially since Caramuel's theology tends to rely more heavily upon Scotus than upon the Angelic Doctor.[62] In the *Apologema*, however, Thomas not only serves as an important theological source but also provides a precedent for the legitimacy of theological innovation and for the way in which such innovations can be misunderstood. Letter 3, for example, begins with this quotation (which Caramuel attributes to Martin Bucer): *"Take away Thomas . . . and I will vanquish the Roman Church."*[63] Caramuel agrees, describing Thomas as the Atlas who holds up the Church's sky. Then he uses Thomas as an analogy: "I say, take away this proposition (*probable opinion suffices for security of conscience in matters of faith and morals*) and you will destroy not only the Church, but also the entire Christian commonwealth (ecclesiastical and secular)."[64]

Within the *Apologema*, however, Thomas is far more than a symbol for the significance of probable opinion. Thomas's example legitimizes theological innovation. "When Thomas was alive, [his ideas] were new," Caramuel reminds his readers. "Should he be rejected for that reason?"[65]

Thomas, the Cistercian points out, was justly praised for his theological discoveries in ethics and in other facets of the discipline.[66] Unfortunately, Thomas's successors are abandoning the precedent of their own master. What they celebrate in respect to Thomas, Caramuel reports regretfully, "*modern Thomists condemn in other doctors. Novelties in Thomas are praised and extolled, as you see, when in other doctors, they are blamed and detested.*"[67] Thomas also developed many theological positions that might be described as probable. "But God did not give a dispensation in the case of Saint Thomas, so that he alone could do what was forbidden to others," Caramuel asserts.[68]

> Therefore, *what after Jerome, Augustine, Gregory, and Ambrose was permitted to Thomas, and after Thomas, to Scotus, Ockham, Durand, Cajetan, and others; today, after all these, will be permitted to Juan and Thomas Sanchez, Suarez, Vasquez, Diana, Mascurenhas, and even Caramuel.*[69]

Not only does Caramuel invoke Thomas as a precedent for theological development, he also uses Thomas to demonstrate that divergent theological opinions are not necessarily an indication of theological error. In his discussion of Thomas's theological authority, Caramuel raises this problem: Do the traditional praises of Thomas uttered by various popes and even (according to hagiographical tradition) by Christ himself, indicate that anyone who disagrees with Thomas is automatically wrong?[70] No, remarks Caramuel, because Thomas did not always claim that his own position was certain (either as a matter of faith or logical proof).[71] One must recognize that Thomas treated "some things as certain, others, as probable."[72] The difficulty is that some "emulators" of Thomas forget this point, confusing absolute claims with what one might call relative claims.[73] Thus, Caramuel (again without making the point explicitly) provides a means for Dominicans to disagree with Thomas without concluding that the Angelic Doctor erred.

As a demonstration of this principle, Caramuel invokes an interesting case: the Thomist/Scotist debate over Mary's conception with or without original sin.[74] By the late seventeenth century, the Scotist position favoring Mary's freedom from such sin had become the dominant theological view. In 1661, in fact, Alexander VII's *Sollicitudo omnium ecclesiarum* had once again proscribed the public defense of the position traditionally ascribed

to Thomas.[75] Caramuel's distinction between certain and probable assertions thus offered help for the Thomist caught between official church
regulations and fidelity to the Angelic Doctor. According to Caramuel,
one can acknowledge the disagreement between Scotus and Thomas without accusing either theologian of error, for each asserted his view as probable (rather than as certainly true).[76] Reliance on probable opinion is not
antithetical to Thomism, Caramuel seems to suggest. Instead, recognizing
the distinction between probable claims and certain claims can allow one
to be (in modern terms) a faithful Thomist rather than a fundamentalist
Thomist.

Finally, the *Apologema* presents a long discussion of the controversy
that surrounded Thomas's teachings between his death and his canonization a half-century later. In 1277, Caramuel reminds his audience, the
bishop of Paris, with the support of at least some of the university faculty, condemned a number of propositions taken (in the literal sense of
the words, at least) from the *Summa*. Although the decree did not name
Thomas, these literal quotations led to the perception that he had been
condemned.[77] Caramuel cites a writer of the time to indicate that the
scandal was created not by Thomas's ideas, but by the action taken against
them.[78] Caramuel makes himself Thomas's defender, arguing that envy
drove the campaign against the Angelic Doctor and that the bishop's decree condemned Thomas's words (which were taken out of context), but
not his original meaning.[79] Concerning the argument that Thomas's ideas
(while blameless in themselves) might have inadvertently led those who
misinterpreted them into error, Caramuel proclaims his skepticism. Today, he asserts, Thomas's theology "is read by the expert and the inexpert,
and introduces no error. Therefore it did not introduce [error] then."[80]
Such a charge, if true, moreover, might merit the prohibition of a good
book (such as vernacular scriptures) but not its condemnation.[81] Caramuel makes it very clear that he agrees with a later bishop's decision to
revoke the sentence.

Why does Caramuel devote such extensive attention to this episode,
citing contemporary sources at length and, in some cases, even identifying the library in which the relevant texts can be found?[82] His expressed
goal is to demonstrate that theologians and church leaders were relying
upon probable opinions in the late thirteenth and early fourteenth centuries. Between Thomas's death and his canonization, Paris theologians

differed in their assessments of his theology, with some supporting and some opposing the condemnation. No unanimous conclusion supported either view. Caramuel points out that, when annulling his predecessor's sentence, the later bishop did not assert that Thomas's positions were certainly true; instead, without approbation or blame, he left them for academic debate.[83] In Caramuel's formulation, the bishop treated the positions as probable. Because Thomas's teaching concerned faith and morals, this was essentially an acknowledgment that probable opinion sufficed for security of conscience.[84] Caramuel also cites an anonymous author who, while the condemnation was still in place, raised this question: "*Whether the doctrine of Father Thomas is able to be taught licitly at Paris as far as all of his conclusions?*" Against the argument that many of these conclusions were condemned under pain of excommunication, the unnamed canon observes: "*This teaching is received everywhere as probably true, containing faith and good morals, because truth is not lost on account of any sort of penalty.*"[85] Caramuel again uses this argument to prove that churchmen were relying upon probable opinion in the late Scholastic period, while noting that the claim that probable opinions cannot be prohibited is broader and more lax than the contemporary theories of probability. Perhaps with his tongue in his cheek, he asserts again that the *iuniores* are sometimes more stringent than their predecessors.[86]

The obvious sense of this discussion is to demonstrate that probable opinion has a long history in Christian practice. But the ironic subtext of the analysis is perhaps more striking than its convoluted arguments. There was a time, Caramuel seems to be reminding the Dominicans, when Thomas's views were not only novel but also controversial—even worse, subjected to an unjust condemnation. What would the modern Thomists have thought, if they had been writing in 1300 like Caramuel's anonymous canon? Would they have insisted on certitude and safety, like Fagnani, or would have they relied upon probable opinion to defend the Angelic Doctor?

Moreover, although he does not make the point explicitly, Caramuel could hardly have failed to compare Thomas's situation with the tribulations of the *iuniores*, including himself. Like Thomas, they were becoming the objects (in Caramuel's view) of malicious persecution. Like Thomas's, their words were quoted out of context and then condemned for scandalizing those who misunderstood them. When Caramuel wrote about an ancient bishop of Paris, was he remembering a recent archbishop of Mechlin? Perhaps Caramuel is urging the Dominicans to remember that their history made them natural allies of the *iuniores*. It would have been unnecessary to appeal to Bartolomé de Medina, even if Caramuel attributed probabilism to Medina as he clearly did not. The example of Thomas provided sufficient parallels with contemporary events. Just as Caramuel had long opposed slavish reliance upon Augustine, the *Apologema*—much more gently—rebukes a slavish and literal Thomism that ignores the innovative and controversial aspects of Thomas's theology. The response to Thomism is thus the subtlest element in the *Apologema*'s project of reaction.

The Response to Jansenism

Although Caramuel's approach to the Dominicans is gentle and indirect, he responds to Jansenism with all the restraint of a cavalry charge. In the *Apologema*, it is the Jansenists, rather than Fagnani, whom Caramuel has cast as the villains. Fagnani, in Caramuel's view, has relied heavily and uncritically upon Jansenist sources. By failing or not wishing to recognize the consequences of his positions, he has become caught up in a campaign against probable opinion that the Jansenists initiated long ago and in the scurrilous attacks against laxity that they are now using to win public approval. But most seriously, Fagnani has not understood the logical connection between his "false postulate [*pseudolemma*]" (i.e., that probable opinion does not suffice for security of conscience) and the foundations of Jansenist theology.[87] Caramuel develops all three of these complaints in some detail.

In the long notes to Epistle 1, Caramuel documents Fagnani's heavy reliance upon sources influenced by Jansenism. Usually, he notes, Fagnani does not quote his sources at length, remaining "content with one line or another." Yet "from page 95, number 336 to page 103, inclusive, through seventeen columns . . . we are compelled to read Jansenists."[88] Caramuel is referring to four sources that Fagnani refers to or includes within his commentary: the propositions condemned by the parish priests of Paris and Rouen (in response to the controversy raised by the *Provincial Letters*) in 1656; Archbishop Boonen's letter to the Roman Inquisition (1654), containing seventeen assertions that he regards as intolerable in practice; a letter from Antony Triest (the bishop of Ghent) to the faculty of Louvain; and finally, the response of that faculty concerning the propositions submitted by the bishop (May 1657).[89] As Caramuel observes, Fagnani reproduces each of these documents as a warrant for his rejection of the freedom to follow a less probable or less safe opinion. The theologian is obviously horrified that the canonist has given these sources such authority. Moreover, Fagnani has given them a publicity that they would not otherwise have enjoyed. The "censures of the Jansenist doctors," Caramuel argues, would have quickly faded away had not Fagnani included them within his commentary.[90]

Caramuel, one should note, makes no concerted effort to prove that the authors of these various texts are Jansenists; he simply assumes that his reader will agree with his identification. He tells us nothing, for example, of the circumstances surrounding the Paris/Rouen condemnations.[91] Regarding the bishop of Ghent, Caramuel argues that Triest's adherence to Jansenism was motivated by a hatred of the Jesuits rather than intellectual conviction, and that he had followed in the footsteps of Archbishop Boonen by defying the Holy See in print.[92] The *Apologema* does provide more extensive information concerning Boonen's adherence to Jansenism, including several references to his *apologia* for refusing to publish the bull against the *Augustinus*.[93] Caramuel seems particularly incensed by Fagnani's reliance upon Boonen, especially regarding the interpretation of scripture.[94] Finally, in reference to the faculty at Louvain, Caramuel remarks that it was "plainly dominated by Jansenists" at the time of the condemnations.[95] Caramuel concludes, "Clearly all those chosen by Fagnani (priests, bishops, and doctors) are Jansenists."[96]

Caramuel was not mistaken in his claim that some of Fagnani's sources were associated with Jansenism: indeed, in certain cases the connections may have run far deeper than he himself recognized. After the publication in 1643 of the papal bull *In eminenti* regarding the *Augustinus,* the faculty at Louvain sent a delegation to Rome to request an authoritative text of the document.[97] One of the faculty representatives was the Jansenist theologian John Sinnigh, commonly believed to have compiled the index for the *Augustinus*.[98] The deputation carried letters of introduction from Archbishop Boonen.[99] When Sinnigh returned from Rome in 1645, he encouraged the continued resistance of Boonen and of others, including Bishop

Triest of Ghent, to publishing the bull.[100] Eventually, Boonen and Triest became the last Belgian prelates to refuse to disseminate *In eminenti*.[101] In 1651, the Holy Office proscribed both bishops' writings on the subject. After extended wrangling, the two were suspended from exercising their offices and, after submitting to the Church, received absolution in the fall of 1653.[102] The complaint from Boonen that Fagnani includes among his sources was written less than a year later; Triest's address is dated 1657.[103] Thus, these bishops' complaints against laxism appeared very shortly after they had been disciplined for recalcitrance regarding Jansen's theology.

As for the continued influence of Jansenism at Louvain, it is worth noting that, in the decade after the *Apologema*'s publication, the Vatican had come to view Louvain's theology faculty with such suspicion that the professors had to request help from the Spanish king to gain permission to send their representatives to Rome. The delegation of 1677, which succeeded in obtaining the condemnation of 65 laxist propositions, had in fact set out with a broader agenda, including an appeal for the approval of Louvain's articles concerning grace and free will. Such a concern harkened back to the theological quarrels of the sixteenth century that had preceded and, in a sense, given rise to Jansenism. (In the matter of grace, Louvain's representatives enjoyed less overt success at the Vatican than in their triumph over laxism).[104] Claeys Bouuaert suggests that one of the major sources for the faculty's list of laxist propositions was, in fact, an early Jansenist polemical tract, the *Théologie morale des Jésuites* (1643), an anonymous compilation commonly attributed to the Parisian Jansenist leader Antoine Arnauld. One of Louvain's emissaries to Rome, Martin Steyaert, actually stayed with Arnauld during his trip back to the university.[105]

All this lay well in the future when Caramuel was writing the *Apologema*. Yet it certainly suggests that Jansenist influence at Louvain did not evaporate with the publication of *Cum occasione*. In fact, the struggle between various factions at the university over questions of Jansenism and laxism would extend well beyond Caramuel's lifetime.[106] Although he may have exaggerated the influence of Jansenism at Louvain, Caramuel was certainly not making a bizarre claim in associating the faculty's campaign against laxism with its quarrels over Jansenism. Jansenist influences did shape the attacks upon laxist morality in Belgium and also in France. (In addition to his *Provincial Letters*, for example, Blaise Pascal composed several of the pamphlets that were published in the name of the Paris clergy in response to the Jesuit Georges Pirot's *Apologie pour les casuistes*).[107] Thus, it seems decidedly odd that Fagnani, whose status in the curia should have given him better information than Caramuel's regarding current ecclesiastical politics, chose to cite these sources without acknowledging the significance of Jansenism for the quarrel over permissive morality. One is hardly surprised by Caramuel's alarm at his opponent's argumentative strategy.

Caramuel by no means limited the *Apologema*'s attack upon Jansenism to comments concerning Fagnani's choice of sources. Without hesitation, he characterizes the campaign against probable opinion (and the concomitant accusation of "laxism" raised against its proponents) as products of a longstanding Jansenist agenda. He explains:

> I was at Louvain while the executors of the dead Jansen's will were deliberating secretly about the clandestine edition of his *Augustinus*. And Libert Froidmont, the chorus leader among the followers of this new doctrine, in order that he might open a path for the coming error; or more accurately, so that he might disseminate it, while the doctors of the academy foresaw nothing of the kind, tried to put forth into the school . . . propositions, . . . which, in light of the author's intentions, are equivalent to this: *probable opinion does not suffice for surety of conscience.*[108]
>
> The Jansenist heresy, again and again suppressed, condemned, and proscribed, is brought back to the literary world in an altered disguise . . . Yesterday, it lied in respect to religion, and said that all orthodox doctors were Pelagians . . . Today, it lies in respect to piety . . . and accuses all theologians of rash and lax teaching.
>
> But what, I ask, do the Jansenists allege when they pretend to be the reformers of relaxed morals . . . ? [They wish] to obtain that, in the court of vulgar opinion, the last sentence may be annulled, which the Holy Spirit pronounced through Innocent X in the supreme tribunal of the Roman Church, against the pernicious delusion of Jansen.[109]

Repeatedly the *Apologema* returns to this theme: Jansenism is trying to worm its way back into the Church under the guise of an attack upon lax moral teaching.[110] Central to this guerilla war is the assault upon probable opinion. Caramuel states his conclusion quite baldly:

These words, *All sin, who in matter of conscience follow probable opinion,* are of the Jansenist dialect, and they encompass all the heresies that the Holy See condemned . . . in the year 1653. For anyone who rejects this proposition, condemns the entire Jansenist heresy. But anyone who is a Jansenist is unable to deny it.[111]

The war against "resurrected" Jansenism, in Caramuel's view, depends on repudiation of Fagnani's claim that probable opinion does not suffice for security of conscience. Fagnani's "false postulate" represents what we might today call a condensed version of Jansenism's central convictions about grace and human freedom.

One need not embrace Caramuel's theory of a calculated Jansenist conspiracy to acknowledge the significance of his historical observations. First, it is clear that an important Jansenist (Froidmont) opposed probabilism long before Pascal developed the theme, and that he put forward some of the same arguments later repeated by Fagnani and others, that is, that reliance upon probable opinion is a new theory and that its acceptance leads to damaging consequences. Second, it is clear that the Jansenists regarded their opponents (especially the Jesuits) as advocates of moral laxity and that they did not hesitate to proffer such accusations. This was, in fact, their most successful counterargument, as the response to the *Provincial Letters* makes clear. Fagnani was clearly influenced by Boonen's complaints or he would not have included the archbishop's letter within his treatise. Nor is there any doubt that Pascal (whom Caramuel never mentions directly)[112] wrote his satires precisely to stir up popular opinion. No wonder that Caramuel saw Jansenism as invading Belgium, France, and even Italy "under the form of a stricter life."[113] Though his view of the origins of the attack upon laxism is too simplistic, it is certainly not without foundation.[114]

Furthermore, Caramuel's narrative suggests that there existed at least a recurrent pattern (and perhaps even an ongoing pattern) of Jansenist hostility toward reliance on probable opinion. Froidmont attacked it early. Pascal must have learned about it from Pierre Nicole and Arnauld, the Jansenist leaders who supplied his theological references, in order to focus upon it so effectively in his sixth letter. It is certainly reasonable to ask whether opposition to probabilism represented an early element of Jansenist moral theory. Caramuel believed that no Jansenist could embrace probabilism. It would hardly be surprising if the Jansenists reached the same conclusion.

Probable opinion must suffice for surety of conscience, Caramuel asserts over and over again, because God does not command the impossible. This argument represents the core of his case against Jansenism, for he identifies the claim that God commands the impossible as "the foundation and basis of the Jansenist heresy."[115] Caramuel dwells upon this point in the *Apologema,* even though he acknowledges that it is not one of Fagnani's arguments. Fagnani, in fact, develops Caramuel's basic presupposition in a different way. The canonist agrees that God does not command the impossible but denies that it surpasses human capacity to have certainty about moral choices—an assurance that he describes as "not only . . . possible, but even easy."[116] Caramuel's reaction is predictably ironic: "A most witty response! Therefore, let Fagnani write *The Book of Moral Certitudes* and all contention will cease!"[117] One can only imagine the list of moral controversies that Caramuel might have assembled to refute Fagnani's claims. With regret, perhaps, he remarks instead that many topics lie beyond the range of his letter's notes. Instead of skewering Fagnani's "hallucinations" concerning moral certainty,[118] Caramuel returns over and over again to the presupposition his opponent accepts: God does not command the impossible.

Caramuel was certainly not the only theorist to argue that probable opinion suffices because God does not command the impossible. The *Apologema* provides a short catalogue of authors who make similar arguments and then directs the reader to Diana's more extensive compilation.[119] Yet because of his encounters with competing theologies of grace, Caramuel may have felt a greater need than his predecessors did to defend the premise as well as the conclusion. In the face of questions about predestination and grace, the assertion that God does not command the impossible raises problems of its own. For Caramuel, therefore, what seems at first glance to be a straightforward problem of ethical method (does probable opinion suffice, etc.?) becomes a conundrum of theological anthropology regarding the relationship between grace and human freedom.

These, of course, were precisely the same issues that had concerned Cornelius Jansen. More than twenty years ago, Caramuel tells us in the *Apologema,* he (Caramuel) had written a book concerning Jansenism's foundations. The controversy with Fagnani provided an opportunity to recycle certain arguments from that never-published manuscript.[120] Some of these arguments appear near the end of the *Apologema* in a brief section titled the "catena of the Jansenist heresies."[121] Here Caramuel describes Jansenism as a "continuous chain [*Catena continua*]." Its links, though few, he argues, are so intertwined that a person cannot retain one of them without accepting the others.[122]

The first link, which Jansenism shares with other heresies, concerns the limited capacity of human volition after the Fall. Post–lapsarian free will "consists in freedom from compulsion rather than freedom from necessity."[123] God does not compel us to do evil. However, our evildoing becomes inevitable if God denies us the grace to avoid it. This anthropological assertion has crucial consequences for moral responsibility: human beings sin in committing acts they cannot avoid (and in omitting acts they cannot perform), because they lack the assistance of grace that is necessary for appropriate moral action. As a result, one must draw the following theological inference: God does command the impossible on occasion, for persons who desire and attempt to obey the divine precepts are sometimes denied the grace requisite for their fulfillment. (By contrast, the bestowal of grace renders disobedience impossible.) Thus grace (or its absence) inevitably produces meritorious action or sin. According to this understanding, human beings truly sin out of necessity.

If human beings can be obliged to do the impossible, the fourth link in the chain asserts, then they can be obliged to know what they could not possibly know. Invincible ignorance does not excuse an agent from sin.[124] The obligation to know what one cannot know simply represents another facet of the obligation to fulfill God's impossible commands.

As a result of these postulates about grace and moral responsibility, we reach the fifth link in the chain of Jansenism. Caramuel summarizes it in this way:

> Therefore, the way that leads to life is so narrow that it admits no probable opinions.
>
> Therefore, he who in practice acts according to the benignity of probable opinion is not excused before God.[125]

Caramuel's précis of Jansenism (as he understood it) thus moves from the assertion that invincible ignorance is not exculpatory to the conclusion that probable opinion is not exculpatory. The connection between the two is explained a bit more directly in an analytical discourse that he might reasonably have called the catena of probable opinion.

Why does reliance upon probable opinion excuse a person from sin? Caramuel asks. The answer is that every legitimate appeal to probable opinion involves invincible ignorance. By definition, if the agent has certain knowledge of the truth, or can attain it with reasonable effort, then he or she cannot appeal to probable opinion. Legitimate recourse to its "benignity" presupposes that the agent truly suffers (here and now) from invincible ignorance. But why is invincible ignorance exculpatory? Because if it were not, Caramuel answers, *"God would command the impossible, for he would prescribe that one know what one is unable to know."*[126]

With this conclusion, the argument has moved from human agency to divine action. What is wrong with conceding that God commands the impossible? Granting this, Caramuel asserts, would force one to conclude that persons violate divine precepts out of necessity. If God commands the impossible, persons will inevitably sin when they fail to fulfill those impossible commands. Caramuel pursues this logic a bit further and ultimately reaches the conclusion that he had previously identified as the initial postulate of Jansenism: free will entails liberty from compulsion but not from necessity. At this point, his response to the Jansenist chain has come full circle.[127]

As Caramuel recognized, his defense of probable opinion relied upon a view of moral responsibility profoundly different from that of the Jansenists. In respect to personal (as opposed to original) sin, Caramuel believes that one is responsible only for acts that one could have avoided at the time of their commission, and that human limitations, especially invincible ignorance, diminish culpability. The Jansenists (in Caramuel's view) hold human beings responsible for acts they could have avoided before the Fall yet cannot now avoid without the irresistible assistance of grace, even if they wish to avoid the acts and attempt to do so.[128] Behind these different assessments of blameworthiness stand starkly opposed conceptions of how God deals with limited and sinful creatures. It is noteworthy that Caramuel refers in this section not merely to probable opinions but also to the "benignity of probable opinions."[129] At root, this is a dispute about the extent of divine mercy. For Caramuel, that is what is really at stake in the argument over whether probable opinion suffices for security of conscience. It also explains why he devotes such space, in a treatise intended to refute Fagnani, to an argument that Fagnani never made.

Conclusion

The *Apologema,* then, is an answer not only to the arguments of its proximate opponent Prospero Fagnani but also to the other critics of probable opinion and the casuistry it inspired. One doubts that any of them would have been satisfied with his response. (Indeed, his quickly condemned volume inspired some to formulate responses of their own.[130]) Yet Caramuel's energies in the *Apologema* were not devoted exclusively to answering the critics of probable opinion. As the next chapter will make clear, the *Apologema* was also a work of education and explanation, in which Caramuel attempted to dispel common misunderstandings of his theory and to highlight its practical value for civil society and for the Church.

CHAPTER FIVE

Explaining Probabilism
The Apologema's *Project of Education*

THE READER OF THE *Apologema* WILL QUICKLY RECOGNIZE THAT PROSpero Fagnani's arguments have left Caramuel worried, angry, and amused, yet also clearly puzzled by his critic's inability to accept what he regards as obvious conclusions. Why (one can imagine Caramuel asking himself) were Fagnani, Julius Mercorus, and others so blind to the truth? What if Church authorities shared their conclusions? What other arguments might be necessary to demonstrate probabilism's virtues and values?

By the time Caramuel published the *Apologema,* he had clearly become aware that some criticisms of his method arose from what he regarded as misconceptions about its origins, its consequences, and even its nature. The most interesting element of the *Apologema* is Caramuel's effort to explain probabilism for Church authorities as well as for moral theologians. Is this method new, as Fagnani and others had asserted? What are the consequences of accepting or rejecting the reliance upon probable opinion? How should we understand its nature, and what makes an opinion probable or improbable? Finally, how is extrinsic probability related to intrinsic probability?

The Antiquity of Reliance upon Probable Opinion

From the very beginning of his literary efforts in defense of probabilism, Caramuel had faced the objection that reliance upon probable opinion was new. For critics such as Libert Froidmont and Fagnani, this charge alone was sufficient to render the method suspect. Caramuel, of course, rejected the assumption that innovation necessarily represents deviation.[1] But he also believed that the historical claim itself was false. Against Froidmont, he had asserted in the *Benedicti Regulam* that not all teachings in the Early Church came directly from the Apostles and the Holy Spirit, with the result that the teachers of Christian antiquity had a need for probable opinions.[2] At this stage, however, Caramuel's argument might better be described as an assertion rather than as a proof. In response to Fagnani, the *Apologema* devotes more extensive consideration to the historical question. Here Caramuel attempts to document the antiquity, both Christian and pre-Christian, of recourse to probable opinion.

To understand Caramuel's historical claims, however, it is important to note how Fagnani's statement of the question has shaped the Spaniard's arguments. First, Fagnani's initial claim is that one may indeed rely upon probable opinion, provided that the matter in question does not "belong to faith or to morals."[3] By *faith*, Fagnani seems to mean *defined by the Church,* since he asserts that the significance of original sin for the Incarnation is not a matter of faith.[4] However, he does not analyze this aspect of the argument extensively, and it is clear that the focus of his presentation concerns the recourse to probable opinion in matters of morals.[5] The reference to probable opinions regarding faith is essentially an unexplored assertion within Fagnani's argument.

Caramuel, however, frequently argues against Fagnani's conclusion as the canonist originally stated it, that is, that probable opinion does not suffice in *either* faith or morals.[6] Although Caramuel agrees that such opinions do not remain probable in the face of a contrary ecclesiastical definition, his concept of faith is far more expansive than Fagnani's.[7] Regarding the significance of original sin for the Incarnation, for example, the bishop explains that this *is* a matter of faith; it is simply not a question currently defined by the Church.[8] The consequence of this tactic for the present discussion, however, is that Caramuel poses the historical question (i.e., Is reliance upon probable opinion new?) in terms of opinions regarding faith and opinions regarding morals. Thus, much of his evidence is not particularly relevant to an investigation of the origins of probabilism per se.

In addition, one should note that neither Fagnani nor Caramuel focuses on the first appearance of the argument that probable opinion suffices, in the face of a more probable opinion to the contrary—that is, on the innovation associated with Bartolomé de Medina. As we have seen, Fagnani begins the story of probability's acceptance with Jean Gerson, and identifies Medina only as the proponent of the third and most radical grade of probability.[9] For Caramuel, the issue is not when theorists began to refer to probable opinion as sufficient, but when human beings began to rely upon it as sufficient *in practice*. Although it is true that one will not find the explicit claim that "probable opinion suffices for security of conscience" among the older writers, he argues, neither will one find Fagnani's thesis. In Caramuel's view, the ancients presumed the legitimacy of reliance upon probable opinion, and as a result, simply did not pose the question in these terms.[10]

In an appendix to his fourth letter, Caramuel argues that even the angels use probable opinion on occasion.[11] However, his discussion of probable opinion's history begins not with heaven, but with earth and the actions of Adam and Eve before the Fall. "I pronounce that the state of human nature and the laudable use of probable opinions are simultaneous," argues Caramuel.[12] In other words, probable opinion has been part of human experience from the very beginning.

Caramuel's analysis of the behavior of Adam and Eve brings him into dialogue with Augustine. Like the bishop of Hippo, he argues that the first mortal sin of our first parents was pride.[13] But how is one to understand the acts that led up to this behavior (i.e., Eve's misinterpretation of God's warning regarding the consequences of eating from the tree, and Adam's failure to recognize the danger in his excessive love for his wife)? For Caramuel, the factor that renders these failures venial rather than mortal was the agents' probable grounds for holding a materially false opinion.[14] Adam, for example, recognized that his affection for Eve was excessive but did not comprehend the full extent of the danger. He had reasonable grounds for thinking it to be venial sin, and as a result, it was venial sin. Caramuel applies this precedent to contemporary human experience.

> Therefore, even today, he who does what materially is mortal sin, commits a sin that is only venial, formally and as far as God [is concerned]; if, having been led by probable reasons, he thinks it to be venial. Therefore, even today, he who does what materially involves lethal guilt, commits no sin, if nevertheless he judges it to be no sin, [on the basis of] probable [opinion].[15]

Just as our first parents were excused from mortal sin on the basis of probable opinion, Caramuel asserts, we too can rely upon such opinion as a basis for our actions. In fact, we have, in a sense, better grounds for doing so than the prelapsarian Adam and Eve. One of the consequences of the Fall is our invincible ignorance of many things, a characteristic that we inherited from the primal couple. "Therefore under a just God," Caramuel asserts, "human beings do not have an obligation of understanding beyond the powers of the mind, or of acting beyond the powers of the body, and they satisfy the precepts of God if they understand them in a human mode, and follow them in a human mode."[16]

As historical analysis, of course, this argument leaves much to be desired. It is better understood as an anthropological argument—invincible ignorance has been part of human experience from the very beginning—and as a theological conviction regarding divine mercy. Interestingly enough, although Caramuel argues that invincible ignorance was exacerbated by the Fall, he associates its basic existence with finitude rather than sin. Like the prelapsarian Adam and Eve, innocent angels required probable opinion, for even angels cannot know what God has not yet revealed.[17] Invincible ignorance is thus a concomitant feature of the limited knowledge that characterizes all creatures.

From Adam and Eve, Caramuel moves on to other biblical examples: Abimelech attempted to take Sarah as his wife, but God excused him because he had sufficient cause to identify her as Abraham's sister rather than as his spouse.[18] Judas Maccabeus repulsed the army that attacked him on the Sabbath and, in Caramuel's words, "proposed a singular and new opinion to his troops in a matter of faith and morals."[19] The Spaniard also finds precedents in the New Testament. Caramuel notes the contradictory "probable opinions" that were initially available in the early Church regarding continued submission to the Jewish law—opinions that (in his view) explain the different behaviors of Peter and Paul.[20] Moreover, according to Christian tradition, Peter followed what the seventeenth century would regard as the "less probable" position by naming his own successor.[21] Thus Caramuel believes that one can identify many precedents for the use of probable opinion within the scriptures themselves.

Caramuel also ascribes reliance on probable opinion to the Fathers and to the giants of the Christian theological tradition. He discusses, for example, Augustine's acknowledgment that the second chapter of Paul's letter to the Romans could be interpreted in two different ways, and Bernard's unwillingness to act upon a charge of irregularity unless it could be proven.[22] For the modern reader, all these examples are likely to prove tedious rather than convincing. Caramuel's argument is, on the one hand, insufficiently developed, and on the other, too wide ranging to provide an effective defense of ecclesiastical precedents for reliance on probable opinion.

Ironically, Caramuel's strongest case for historical precedents appears at a different point in his text, when the discussion focuses on evolving church practices, especially those concerning expansions in papal power.[23] As the *Apologema* indicates, developing ecclesiastical praxis in granting dispensations (e.g., from solemn vows or from ratified but unconsummated marriages) did not always conform to the "more probable" theological position. (In Caramuel's day, pontiffs were certainly exercising powers to issue dispensations that Scholastic theologians would not have recognized.[24]) These decisions (e.g., releasing a prince from religious vows in order to stabilize a dynastic succession) certainly involved matters of faith and morals. Caramuel by no means questions the legitimacy of these developments: in fact, he appeals to them as proof that other persons can reasonably utilize the same principle of moral action. Popes and ordinary people are equally subject to the Decalogue. If it is licit for the supreme pontiffs to act on probable opinion, Caramuel asks, "why will it not be licit for others as well?"[25]

The implicit point of the historical precedents' discussion concerns the role of probable opinion in the development of Christian doctrine and practice. As Caramuel points out, virtually every ancient practice was new at one time. The claim that Mary was conceived without sin was a novelty in Bernard's day (and without roots in Thomas's), yet now, Caramuel asserts, it is "piously defended in papal bulls."[26] "Were not those things, which today are read with applause, and even veneration," he asks, ". . . rejected by the prudent, when they were new?"[27] That the Church has changed demonstrates the legitimacy of recourse to probable opinion, for the movement from ignorance to certitude is often gradual. The transition from midnight's darkness to the noontime's blazing sun, the bishop reminds us, is not the illumination of an instant.[28] Slowly and painstakingly, probable opinion leads us toward the truth. Yet there are always moments when a Columbus teaches us that lands exist on the other side of the world—even if Augustine and the Fathers believed the opposite.[29]

The reliance on probable opinion—with the possibility that the truth could ultimately prove to be otherwise—thus represents a constant in the evolving search for human knowledge.

The Consequences of Accepting or Rejecting Probabilism

Fagnani may not have described probabilism as an invention of the devil, but he certainly believed that it could lead persons to hell.[30] Behind his attack upon probabilism lies the conviction that the spread of this method has led to the "destruction of souls," and that it provides apparent justification for a wide variety of sins and crimes.[31] In his view, the Church must repudiate this theory not only because of its inconsistency with Christian tradition but also because of its practical consequences.

The *Apologema* rejects both Fagnani's historical and his teleological arguments against probabilism. Caramuel goes to great pains to demonstrate that human beings have relied and continue to rely upon probable opinion. This is necessary, he seems to presume, because the gaps in human knowledge leave us no reasonable alternative. Caramuel regards Fagnani's rejection of this approach as a recipe for practical disaster. It is enormously instructive to compare the two authors' claims concerning the consequences of accepting or rejecting probabilism.

To demonstrate the absurdity of permitting reliance upon a less probable opinion, Fagnani mentions a number of cases that were, as his own text indicates, also the subject of intense discussion among probabilism's proponents. These were precisely the situations that raised questions about the limits of probabilism and inspired theologians (including Antonino Diana and Caramuel) to consider the circumstances under which it could not reasonably be applied.[32] Fagnani poses these cases in terms of probable opinion as license. A judge rules in favor of the litigant with the weaker case, who happens to be his friend, on the grounds that the friend's position is probable. A doctor withholds the treatment that is more likely to benefit his patient and administers a less probable (and riskier) remedy. Princes use probable opinion as an excuse to wage war on the flimsiest of pretexts, rejecting the more probable warnings of their confessors. Priests risk invalid administration of the sacraments and, in their role as confessors, find their judgments subverted by clever penitents who appeal to probable opinions. "In the forum of the soul, the judge is compelled to follow the judgment of the criminal!" remarks Fagnani in disgust.[33] Such malfeasance, he seems to suggest, is the inevitable result of sanctioning reliance on probable opinion.

The *Apologema* examines cases set in many of the same professional venues (the judge in the courtroom, the doctor at the bedside, etc.) to emphasize the consequences of accepting or rejecting probable opinion. Yet where Fagnani invokes the miscreant looking for an excuse, Caramuel describes the agent seeking rectitude in the midst of uncertainty. Tribunals can err because judges often must proceed on the basis of what is probable, rather than what is certain.[34] Medical practice raises the same problems. The disciples of Galen often disagree with the disciples of Paracelsus, to the distress of the ordinary doctor faced with contradictory advice about a patient's treatment. Yet there is no alternative to acting upon probable opinion, which could conceivably be wrong and might even kill the patient. Should we close down courts and condemn doctors because they cannot exceed the limitations of human knowledge?[35]

Caramuel raises similar arguments concerning probable opinion and war. A commander, he notes, violates the fifth commandment if he risks his soldiers' lives "without utility [*sine utilitate*]," that is, without reasonable hope that the results will merit the sacrifice. Yet in warfare, the outcome is inevitably uncertain and the anticipated victory merely probable. No prince will be able to wage war, no matter how just the cause, if we demand more than probable opinion concerning its outcome.[36]

Caramuel's priest faces the same dilemma as his doctor and his prince. The *Apologema* invokes not the reckless sacramental minister but the responsible cleric who must act in the face of contradictory theological opinions. Imagine, Caramuel asserts, that this priest is called to the bedside of an unconscious dying person who has lived as a Christian but did not seek through any external sign to make a last confession. Should the priest absolve the person or not? One opinion refuses the absolution, the other says that the priest not only may absolve but also must absolve; both positions are probable.[37] Between absolution and forgoing absolution, Caramuel notes, stands no middle ground. Whatever he decides, the priest is going to act upon a probable opinion.[38] Again, Caramuel focuses upon the perplexed and well-intentioned agent rather than the villain searching for a loophole.

In reference to the requirement that the priest should follow the penitent's opinion rather than his own, Caramuel, who devotes significant attention to this claim,[39] emphasizes the burden that the opposite approach would impose upon the person making confession. Mentioning an act that a Scotist might classify differently than a Thomist, the bishop considers the implications of focusing upon the confessor rather than the penitent regarding its assessment. Has Titius committed two types of sin if he approaches a Franciscan, but only one greater sin if he approaches a Dominican? Surely that is absurd. The decisive question is what Titius believes that he has done, not which ethical theory the confessor holds. Of course, Caramuel acknowledges that penitents sometimes embrace improbable rather than probable opinions. In that case, the confessor's role is to educate them, after assessing whether their mistakes were the result of invincible ignorance. The confessor must not use his superior knowledge to demand a "sacrilegious confession" of apparent *sin* that was, in truth, unavoidable error. It is one thing to commit sin, Caramuel explains, and another to "require instruction."[40]

In each of these cases, it is striking that Caramuel highlights the positive and Fagnani, the negative. Fagnani is concerned that probable opinion makes it easier for persons to do what is wrong. Caramuel, by contrast, emphasizes its role in assisting those who are trying to do what is right, especially in situations of uncertainty. Probable opinion protects the judge, the doctor, the prince, the priest, and even the penitent. Any of their concrete decisions may be mistaken, yet all can feel confident that they have acted responsibly. Where Fagnani sees an incentive for misbehavior, Caramuel sees a safety device.

Just as Fagnani fears the negative practical consequences of embracing probabilism, Caramuel fears the consequences of rejecting probabilism. Indeed, he regards this approach as a prescription for social chaos. Because the hierarchy relies upon probable opinion in its decisions (e.g., regarding dispensations), repudiating probabilism will cast Church leaders into disrepute.[41] Secular leaders will fare no better. Indeed, if Fagnani is correct in his view that probable opinion is an insufficient warrant for action, most of the commands offered by superiors will necessarily be unjust, and subordinates will rarely have an obligation to obey. Caramuel also warns: "what Superior will be able to persuade deviant subjects that the things he orders are certainly or more probably necessary or useful?"[42]

Caramuel pursues the same theme by introducing an ad hominem consequentialist argument against Fagnani himself. Christians have a certain duty to help the poor, especially those in extreme necessity; and probable opinion holds that one must even sacrifice property necessary for one's status and authority in order to do so. This is certainly the stricter and materially safer view of Christian duty and, as such, presumably represents the standard that Fagnani would accept as a moral obligation, since he rejects recourse to probable opinion. In light of this, what is his responsibility toward the poor, especially those captured by bandits, pirates, or the Turks, who stand in special peril unless they are redeemed? Because Fagnani insists on the safer position, Caramuel muses, presumably he does not have a home, furnishings, or even two tunics, because he has sold everything to raise money for the poor. "If he has not done this, he scandalizes us," Caramuel remarks, "because he lives differently than he teaches." Noting that he could make many more claims along this line if he were willing to vex "an excellent old man," the Spaniard argues instead that Fagnani lives a most holy life—according to the less strict opinion![43]

On the question of almsgiving, Caramuel pushes the argument one step further by invoking the problem of civil obligations. It is certainly probable that princes have a duty to require the rich to give alms. But if this safer duty were "always [*semper*]" imposed in practice, how greatly would the commonwealth be disturbed! Must a theologian really demand that a Catholic prince require his wealthy subjects to sell their possessions, in order to assist the poor?[44] This, for Caramuel, is one of the many proofs that imposing the safer opinion would lead to social upheaval.

The argument about probable opinions and possessions (which must have outraged Fagnani) is a reminder that the *Apologema* represented an appeal to Church leaders and, as such, an appeal to social conservatism, in order to make its point. But one wonders whether it was also, perhaps unconsciously, a reminder to those leaders that persons who live in glass houses should stay away from stones. As the *Pax Licita* makes clear, Caramuel was very sensitive to the problem of clerical avarice and its impact upon the faithful. Whatever Fagnani's financial situation may have been, there were certainly many ecclesiastics in late seventeenth-century Rome who were not living according to the stricter opinion regarding property and almsgiving. Was Caramuel, from his very poor diocese, reminding them that they did not live by the standard that *Ne innitaris* wished to impose?

The discussion regarding property and almsgiving also reminds the reader that Fagnani's arguments have made Caramuel very angry, even though he tries (not always successfully) to avoid ad hominem attacks in his response. Caramuel seems most outraged by Fagnani's general conclusion that probabilism opens the door to moral laxity and the endangerment of souls. If probable opinion does suffice for security of conscience, the theologian argues, then it is beneficial rather than harmful to the Church, for it reassures people that they have acted responsibly.[45] Excessive rigor is more likely to drive people to despair or even overt rebellion than to lead them away from sin.[46] Earlier in the *Apologema*, Caramuel illustrates the same point by describing the practical dangers of imposing more stringent opinions. As an example, he mentions a difference of theological views concerning the limits of appropriate physical contact, including kisses. If one insists upon the stricter and safer proscription of such contact, he notes, "all France will be disturbed" and the young will enter marriage prematurely.[47] Why attack a custom that Jesus accepted in Palestine, and Bernard accepted in Italy, centuries ago? Similarly, he suggests that Fagnani go to "Germany, Bohemia, Hungary, and Belgium," to gauge the audience reaction when he advocates the more stringent opinions about fasting and mortal sin.[48] Caramuel believes that the benignity of probable opinion better serves the public good, and the good of individuals, than Fagnani's stricter approach.

Yet Caramuel also suggests that accepting probabilism reflects divine mercy. Although the *Apologema*'s primary appeal to Christ's easy yoke relies upon quotations from Gerson and Brother Jerome (since Fagnani had disparaged Caramuel's own reference to this passage in the *Theologia Regularis),* the underlying argument remains the same.[49] Probable opinion suffices for security of conscience because God shows mercy toward human creatures, who are both sinful and finite. God does not ask us to know more than we can know. The worst consequence of Fagnani's approach, in Caramuel's view, is that it rejects a lifeline provided for us by a merciful God.

The Nature and Types of Probable Opinion

Caramuel certainly believed that his opponents had fundamentally misconstrued the nature and function of probable opinion in providing security of conscience. He may well have wondered whether some of the Church leaders to whom he was appealing understood it either. In any case, the *Apologema* attempts to clear up such misunderstandings by explaining what a probable opinion is, when its use is (or is not) appropriate, why it suffices for security of conscience, and how authoritative probability is related to rational probability. Although elements of this analysis appear throughout the volume, *Epistola* 2 specifically concentrates upon the examination of probabilism's "*prototheoremata*."[50] References to Fagnani are infrequent within this section, as Caramuel carefully and painstakingly explains his moral theory.

Caramuel begins by situating probability within the broader framework of human knowledge. Some truths are self-evident. Others (which Caramuel describes as "*undoubted and certain*") are established by logical demonstration.[51] (Elsewhere in the *Apologema*, he identifies three sources of certitude: revelation, definition by the church, and logical proof.[52]) Propositions that are neither self-evident nor certain are classified according to the strength of the reasons supporting them, and such support can be entirely absent, light, or grave. It is this last level of support that characterizes probability. Caramuel thus defines a probable opinion as one "*that has strong reasons on its behalf, but no logical demonstration; and has strong reasons against it, but no logical demonstration.*"[53] In *Epistola* 4, he explains probability's nature more poetically by invoking the biblical image of the seven seals:

> Between night and day, between manifest falsehood and manifest truth, [there is] a middle [way] that we call *probability*. Saint John seems to show this light of truth in his Apocalypse, under the form of the book closed with seven seals. As long as no seal is opened, we walk in darkness and we are entirely ignorant of the truth. When natural demonstration or divine faith in this life, or beatific vision in the next, opens the seventh, we follow truth infallibly, and we depart from every fear of error. But when some are opened, and some are not, shadows and lights conflict in our intellect, and we are led to truth by probable footpaths.[54]

Probability thus lies between certitude and complete ignorance. In practical terms, however, it represents the minimum standard for action. Although Caramuel asserts that there is a logical distinction between having no reasons and having light reasons in support of one's position, that distinction has no consequences for behavior. A person who has only light warrants for his or her action might as well have none, because neither suffices for security of conscience. One must have grave reasons (i.e., probable opinion) backing one's position in order to behave responsibly.[55]

Caramuel also describes a probable opinion as a position that a learned person could defend publicly without fear of embarrassment. Yet probability is never the same as absolute certainty. Moreover, it always involves invincible ignorance.[56] (If agents can discover the truth by using the capacities available to them here and now, then Caramuel regards their ignorance as virtual knowledge, and their appeal to probable opinion as illegitimate.[57]) Because invincible ignorance is inevitably present, recourse to probable opinion always involves a certain type of fear, that is, the fear that one's judgment could ultimately prove to be mistaken. But Caramuel insists that this fear (which he calls fear of the object) must always be distinguished from fear of the act, that is, the fear that one has acted irresponsibly in relying upon probable opinion. This, he argues, is where Fagnani has become confused. Fagnani has conflated uncertainty about the *accuracy* of one's decision with uncertainty about the *legitimacy* of one's decision. Caramuel argues that the two are quite distinct. The Dominican who knows that Scotus and Thomas disagreed about a particular philosophical point may not be absolutely certain that Thomas's view is superior to Scotus's, but he (the Dominican) can be sure that he is behaving responsibly in defending the probable opinion of the Angelic Doctor.[58] Similarly, agents who cannot know whether their choices will ultimately prove to be correct can nonetheless have confidence that they have behaved responsibly in adopting a probable opinion. Because grave foundations render an opinion probable, persons can trust probable opinion to identify the actions that are safe in practice.

Caramuel recognizes that there are special circumstances that render recourse to probable opinion inappropriate. Although it considers none of them in detail, the *Apologema* specifically mentions three of these: situations in which the agent is bound by a vow; an oath; or a precept, including the precept of charity.[59] In the first two cases, the agent has voluntarily limited his or her own freedom to adopt a probable opinion by taking a vow or swearing an oath. In the third, the agent is constrained by a precept, either human or divine. Concerning the human precept, Caramuel observes:

When a superior prescribes what is probable within the limits of his jurisdiction, the subject is bound to obey; for he has promised obedience, and
all things, which are necessary in order that he might be governed, he has
promised at the same time. Unless the subject cedes his right of following
opinion as he wishes, what superior will be able to govern? Scarcely any
law will be universal and common; for always or nearly always the subject
will be able to say that the opposite seems probable, or even, if he wishes,
more probable; and so the entire Church, the entire commonwealth, and
all communities will be disturbed.[60]

Caramuel's argument here is certainly more conservative than his assessment of the disagreement between Peter and his superior in the *Benedicti
Regulam*.[61] What is particularly interesting in its formulation, however,
is his emphasis upon the subject as *yielding* his right to follow probable
opinion. In other words, the superior can constrain the subject because the
subject has promised obedience and, in doing so, has made a concomitant
promise ceding his freedom. Thus Caramuel apparently treats this human
precept as another example of constraint through prior concession, just
like obedience to an oath and a vow.

The idea that the precept of charity limited legitimate recourse to probable opinion played an important role in the theories of those who defended its use under other circumstances. Investigating the question of
whether one may use probable opinion in the administration of the sacraments, for example, Diana argues that this would be a sin against charity because of the risk that such a choice would pose for the sacrament's
recipient.[62] Diana acknowledges that there are exceptions to this rule, as
for example, when the minister cannot follow the more probable opinion
because the required elements are lacking.[63] Caramuel, on the other hand,
does not discuss the general rule regarding charity extensively in the *Apologema*. His most significant reference to the subject focuses upon a case in
which charity requires rather than forbids reliance upon the less probable
approach—in other words, upon one of the cases that Diana treats as an
exception:

Since I ought to assist my neighbor situated in extreme peril as far as I am
able, and since it is better for an infant to have a less probable baptism
than no baptism at all; in a case where I have neither certain nor more

probable material [for administering the sacrament], I ought to use the less probable material.[64]

Thus Caramuel admits that charity limits the appeal to probable opinion and immediately invokes a case in which charity demands reliance upon probable opinion! In general, it is fair to say that the *Apologema* devotes little attention to what Caramuel describes as the extrinsic limits on the use of his favorite method. Here Caramuel is less interested in discussing the effect of vows, oaths, and precepts than in investigating how knowledge limits one's recourse to probable opinion.

Within the *Apologema*, Caramuel repeats his customary arguments about the safety of all probable opinions and the greater safety of probable opinions that are also more benign. Such greater reliability, he notes, occurs *per accidens* from "adjacent and external circumstances" rather than from the nature of probable opinion itself.[65] Gentler opinions are safer, he argues (speaking from the perspective of the confessor), because weak human beings are more likely to comply with them. But any probable opinion by definition suffices for security of conscience. Here Caramuel uses Francisco Suarez's theology of law to argue that probable opinion allows the agent to escape both formal and material sin. Invincible ignorance obviously explains the absence of the first. As to the second, Caramuel argues:

> Law does not oblige those upon whom it has not been imposed; and where there is no law, there is no transgression (either formal or material). Law (whether it be human or divine) is not imposed on those to whom it has not been sufficiently communicated and proposed . . . But a law, the existence of which is disputed by the learned with probable opinions on either side, is invincibly and unconquerably unknown.[66]

Thus, Caramuel maintains that the person who unwittingly violates such a "law" is in fact guilty of only "hypothetical malice [*malitia hypothetica*]" in contravening not what the law presently is, but what it would be, should it be promulgated sufficiently.[67]

Caramuel's approach here is not without its problems. It would certainly be helpful if he explained the corresponding roles of invincible ignorance and insufficient promulgation of law within probabilism. If law that is insufficiently promulgated imposes no obligation, why speak of invincible ignorance as *excusing* a person from guilt, as he does in his discussion of Jansenism?[68] Perhaps this represents an unresolved tension between the theory of probabilism that he had inherited and his own developing rejection of the concept of material sins. In this regard, the *Apologema* is a transitional text.

Intrinsic and Extrinsic Probability

In *Epistola* 2 of the *Apologema,* Caramuel also addresses a topic to which he had previously devoted relatively little explicit attention: the relationship between the probability grounded in reason and the probability grounded in authority. Perhaps this represents his response to critics who had interpreted his arguments (especially the encomium to Diana) as a claim that theologians had the power to justify a previously sinful action by describing it as *probable.* Fagnani certainly attacked him on those grounds, disparaging a certain "modern author, who was not embarrassed to disseminate this proposition in his letter, namely: All probable opinions bring it about that what was once sin, no longer will be [sin]."[69] One of the few explicit references to Caramuel in the *Provincial Letters* cites the same dedicatory epistle in the *Theologia Moralis Fundamentalis.*

> And so it happens that the learned Caramuel, in the letter in which he addresses to Diana his *Fundamental Theology,* says that this great *Diana has rendered many opinions probable that were not [probable] before (quae ante non errant) and hence, one no longer sins in following them, although one would have sinned before (jam non peccant, licet ante peccaverint).*[70]

Whether or not he had read Pascal, Caramuel had certainly read Fagnani! He could not have been unaware of how his statements were being interpreted. Although he never refers to such criticisms directly in the *Apologema,* the text answers them nonetheless. Here Caramuel takes great care to explain the origins and nature of probability, especially extrinsic probability. "For all do not understand what authoritative probability is, considered according to its own Metaphysical concept," he remarks.[71]

As in his earlier works, Caramuel emphasizes that assessing authoritative probability (and distinguishing the authoritatively more probable from the less probable) is not a simple matter of poll results. The "bare names of authors" do not make an opinion probable. In some cases, this is true because their opinion diverges from something that has been established as true, and "against certitude, probability does not exist."[72] (As an illustration of this point, Caramuel mentions the large cadre of Lutheran theologians, whose views contradict the truths established as certain through the definitions of the Church.) Attestation cannot render an opinion probable when the opposite view is certain. And Caramuel seems to believe that this is true even when the *certainty* in question is not necessarily available to humanity (or even to the Church) as a whole. In a particularly interesting passage, he contrasts the probable opinions held by the Scotists and the Thomists with the knowledge that Saints Brigitta and Teresa have received through revelation. Whereas the Dominicans and Franciscans can assert their positions as probable, Brigitta and Teresa cannot, because they know the truth, no matter how many mendicants assert their positions on either side. The authority of the theologians cannot make something probable for those who possess certain knowledge.[73]

The distinction between probability and certitude is not Caramuel's only reason for arguing that establishing the former is not a matter of counting positive references. Sometimes, a list of authors does not guarantee probability because various writers are not independent witnesses. Theologians can and do quote one another unreflectively, just as "sheep [follow] sheep."[74] Thus, assembling a bare catalogue of proponents does not make an opinion probable.

The problem is only exacerbated, of course, when one is attempting to distinguish the extrinsically more probable from the extrinsically less probable, a task that Caramuel describes as "very difficult" and "often impossible."[75] His argument here echoes the observations in his earlier works: all authorities are not equally authoritative. Imagine a case in which "four authors are as learned as eight; and Peter is as learned as a hundred."[76] If there is a disagreement between Peter and his colleagues, who can claim to hold the *more probable* opinion? Is it Peter (because of his greater acumen) or his four opponents (because of their numerical superiority)? Though Caramuel presents a short list of his favorite authorities (a list, on this occasion, more heavily weighted in favor of his predecessors than his contemporaries), he admits that precise identification of the extrinsically more probable often exceeds the power of the human mind. Assessing the intrinsically more probable is no easier. Indeed, Caramuel equates the demand that persons follow only the more probable opinion with the command that they exceed the capacities of human knowledge.[77]

Caramuel, one must emphasize, believes that some arguments are genuinely more probable than others and that some sources are genuinely more authoritative than others. The difficulty is not the reality of the more probable, but the perception of that reality. How do limited human beings tell whether one argument is more probable than another, or one authority more weighty than another? In reference to the assessment of arguments, Caramuel uses an analogy to make the point. Suppose that one considers a handful of similar coins, each stamped with the same image. Are they all equally valuable? A natural philosopher armed with a scale would say no, for measurement of every coin's precise weight would reveal disparities in the level of precious metals that each contains. To the person who plans to spend them in the marketplace, however, no coin has greater value than the others. The logically distinct is, at the same time, the practically identical.[78]

This analogy reflects Caramuel's basic concept of the significance of probable opinion and explains why he chose what we now call probabilism rather than probabiliorism. It is not simply that the assessment of the more probable often "hangs on disposition and prejudice," although Caramuel does make this argument.[79] More significantly, the distinction between the more and less probable is *"not always perceptible and discernible."*[80] Moreover, it is unnecessary for moral practice, because every probable opinion suffices for security of conscience. Returning to the marketplace metaphor, Caramuel proclaims that all probable opinions are "stamped with the sign of prudence, and are equally good, so that we may buy eternal glory."[81] For him, the basic and most significant distinction separates the probable from the improbable, not the more probable from the less probable. Finding the probable is complex enough, in Caramuel's view.

What then identifies an opinion as probable, and what role do theologians play in this assessment? While maintaining the traditional distinctions between the intrinsically and extrinsically probable, Caramuel investigates their intersection. Subtly, he shifts the debate by beginning with our *knowledge* of probability rather than with the *origins* of probability. How does one decide whether an opinion is probable? The answer,

Caramuel argues, depends upon the arguments offered in support of the opinion and upon the agent's own capacity to assess them.

> But how do I know whether this [opinion] has a grave reason [supporting it]? If this reason is proposed, and I am a good theologian, and I have sufficient [resources] in respect to intelligence and learning in order to weigh and examine it, and if, on the scale of sincerity, I perceive it to be grave, that opinion will be intrinsically probable for me.[82]

With this long list of clauses, Caramuel identifies the conditions necessary for the assessment of intrinsic probability. The first concerns the opinion itself. Its author must identify the reasons underlying the conclusions. Second, the reader (a good theologian) must be intellectually prepared to assess those reasons. Third, the theologian must use his or her intellectual prowess to weigh the arguments and decide whether they represent a grave foundation. If they do, then the opinion is (for the evaluating theologian) intrinsically probable.

One should note, however, that Caramuel asserts that the opinion is intrinsically probable "for me [*mihi*]" rather than for a general audience, the theological community at large, the Church as a whole, and so forth. In the first edition of the *Theologia Moralis Fundamentalis*, Caramuel had pointed out that the same proposition could seem probable to one person, improbable to another, and neither to a third, depending upon the relevant information that any of them possesses at the time.[83] Intrinsic probability is only accessible to a person in a position to evaluate it. Thus, it is always a judgment that says as much about the judge as it says about the object.

Even more interesting is what this argument suggests about the responsibility of the theologian for the assessment of intrinsic probability. Caramuel does not phrase his argument in this way: If the reason is proposed, and if I am a good theologian with sufficient intellectual attributes, then I can *decide* whether I wish to assess it or whether I prefer to depend upon the assessments of others. Caramuel's formulation instead suggests that a theologian capable of investigating an argument's foundations has a responsibility to do so. Admittedly, the *Apologema* never considers that point explicitly. But as we have seen, the later editions of the *Theologia Moralis Fundamentalis* assert: "in doubtful cases, the learned person will be under obligation to examine the reasons and foundations, but the un-learned will not."[84] Recall also that, in this text, Caramuel describes the unlearned person as "happier" than his educated counterpart because the first can rely upon authority in a way that the second cannot.[85] It is not unreasonable to assume that this presupposition is implicitly operative in the *Apologema* as well, and that Caramuel presumes that the assessment of intrinsic probability is not optional for those in an intellectual position to do so.

Caramuel's procedure for the identification of intrinsic probability, however, involves a number of stipulations: *if* the reason is proposed; *if* I am a good theologian, and so forth. What if these conditions are not present? "What if the argument, on which the opinion depends, is not proposed?"[86] What if it is proposed, but I lack the intellectual resources to evaluate it? What is one to do, in short, when some or all of the criteria for assessing intrinsic probability are lacking? Regarding this situation, Caramuel describes four different scenarios for resolution. Perhaps the agent has read the arguments posed for this position by a number of learned authorities. Perhaps he has heard about this authoritative support through the writings of or even through a personal consultation with another expert. Perhaps he knows that the doctor who has formulated a unique solution to the case has nonetheless studied it thoroughly and has a proven record of success in moral assessment. Or perhaps he knows that the opinion of the only doctor who has discussed the case as yet remains unchallenged. In each scenario, the agent can responsibly rely upon the word of the experts who tell him that it rests upon a grave foundation.[87]

What precisely do these authorities provide for Caramuel's agent, who is in no position to evaluate the intrinsic probability of the argument? In each case, what the inquirer learns from the expert(s) is the same: This opinion possesses the grave foundation requisite for probability. This leads Caramuel to a crucial conclusion about the relationship between the in-trinsically probable and the extrinsically probable.

> From this it is evident that the authors who are cited in favor of some opinion do not give it probability, but testify either expressly or implicitly that it is probable. As a result, so that I may expose the difference between the two types of probability in another way (which comes back to the same point), I will say [this]: *an intrinsically probable opinion is one that I*

see is supported by a grave reason. An authoritatively and extrinsically probable opinion is one that (although I do not see its support from a grave reason)
I *hear* is supported by a grave reason from [the testimony of] a very learned
man or men.[88]

One could hardly imagine a stronger rejection of the idea that theologians create probability. Lest his readers miss the point, however, Caramuel returns to it in his discussion of the extrinsically more probable. Here
the theologian uses two analogies, comparing probable opinions to food
and music. We speak commonly of sweeter foods and sweeter music, and
it is clear that many people find them more pleasing to the palate and the
ear than less sweet foods and music. But is it this popularity that renders
them sweeter? No, Caramuel answers. In reality, they please more people
because they *are* sweeter. "As a result, to give pleasure is neither the formal
nor the efficient cause of sweetness, but its effect."[89] In other words, the
popularity that such foods and music enjoy is the consequence of their
inherent qualities. It testifies to their virtues, but it does not create them.

Caramuel makes a similar claim about the origins of greater probability.
"It is the better reason that pleases many learned men," he writes. "But
speaking a priori, the learned do not give goodness to the reason; instead
the reason [itself] supplies this."[90] This argument about *probabilioritas*
leads him in turn to a critical conclusion concerning the relationship between greater intrinsic and extrinsic probability:

Therefore the plurality of authors does not give *probabilioritas* to an opinion, but their consensus testifies that it is intrinsically more probable.
Therefore authoritative *probabilioritas* ought to be reduced to intrinsic
probabilioritas.[91]

Caramuel's immediate statement concerns the more probable, but it
logically applies to the probable opinion as well. There is really only one
source of probability: the grave foundation upon which an opinion rests.
Reason and authority are the two ways in which we discover the existence
of such a foundation. In and of itself, the testimony of the learned renders
an opinion neither probable nor more probable. Instead it offers evidence.
One should thus describe theologians as the witnesses of probability rather
than its creators.

Within the *Apologema*, therefore, Juan Caramuel makes it very clear that he does not regard probable opinion as a magic wand that theologians can wave at their pleasure to transform the moral nature of actions. Grave reason, not theological judgment per se, is what makes an opinion probable. Yet his critics did have some grounds for assuming the opposite (as they evidently did). How else is one to understand his dedicatory epistle's reference to Diana in the first edition of the *Theologia Moralis Fundamentalis*, or his claim in the *Benedicti Regulam* that "many would be damned, whom probable opinion saves"?[92] Did he change his mind, or can one interpret those statements in a way that is consistent with the *Apologema*?

On the one hand, it is reasonable to assume that the criticisms of Fagnani and others forced Caramuel to raise questions about the nature of probability that he had previously never considered. One should remember that reliance on probable opinion was a feature of Caramuel's early theological education and hence, something that he probably took for granted, to a certain extent. He certainly revised his theory of probable opinion over the course of many years, both before and even after the publication of the *Apologema*. Thus it is remotely possible that Caramuel changed his mind about the type of power that theologians wielded when they asserted that an opinion sufficed for security of conscience.

Nonetheless, other evidence suggests that the other possibility is "more probable." According to this interpretation, Caramuel never changed his mind about the relationship between theological opinion and probability: the criticisms of Fagnani and others simply forced him to choose his words and explain his presuppositions more carefully than he had done in the past. In this regard, one should note the important consistencies between the *Apologema* and his earlier arguments. As we have seen, the *Benedicti Regulam* considers the case of an individual who has doubts about the legitimacy of action that he has already performed and consults various books to obtain an opinion. Caramuel asserts that probable opinions unknown to the agent are irrelevant in the assessment of the past action. It is hard to believe that Caramuel would have resolved the case in this way if he thought that theological opinion alone was sufficient to change the nature of a moral act. Moreover, even in the first edition of the *Theologia Moralis Fundamentalis*, Caramuel says (in reference to an opinion of Diana's with which he disagrees) that Diana has not offered any probable arguments for his position. "For that reason," he argues, "the opinion of

Diana is not rendered probable [by these words], if it was not probable before."[93] Unlike the introductory encomium, this statement seems to recognize clear limits to Diana's influence upon an argument's probability. Perhaps what the *Apologema* asserts about theologians as discoverers of probability was assumed but not explained in the earlier texts.

One must remember that Caramuel's theory of probable opinion represents an answer to the quest for moral responsibility in the face of speculative uncertainty. It is not that he believes that Diana (or any other theologian) has the power to transform sin into morally legitimate action. Instead, the agent's *reliance* upon probable opinion changes the nature of the *choice* to perform the act. Imagine two agents who are uncertain that something that they are proposing to do is legitimate. The first simply takes action without resolving the uncertainties. In traditional terms, that person has acted out of doubtful conscience and has committed sin. The second searches (either directly or through the mediation of an expert) for a probable opinion about the proposed act. The concrete actions that the two perform are exactly the same. Nonetheless, their choices reflect very different exercises of moral responsibility. Unlike the first agent, the second can be sure that he or she has acted prudently, by relying (in a situation of invincible ignorance) upon an answer supported by a grave foundation.[94] What would have been sinful (without the agent's reliance upon probable opinion) becomes morally responsible, not because theological opinion changed the nature of the act, but because reliance upon that opinion changed the nature of the choice.[95] To demand more of finite human minds, as Caramuel was so fond of saying, is to demand the impossible.

The *Apologema*, therefore, explains Caramuel's theory of probabilism and attempts to explain common misconceptions surrounding the method. Here Caramuel identifies probability's place in the continuum of human knowledge and its role as the minimum standard for responsible action. Reliance upon probable opinion, he asserts, has played a constant role in human history, although not necessarily under the aegis of an articulated theory. Human limitation renders its use necessary and unavoidable. The welfare of the Church and civil society depend upon the acceptance of probable opinion, and any attempt to impose Fagnani's more rigorous standard is a prescription for disaster. Finally, probable opinion is not a license to embrace any conceivable behavior or to sacrifice truth on the altar of expertise. Whether one recognizes it through intrinsic or extrinsic means, probability always arises from a grave foundation. In a world of finite creatures, it often represents the best available means of attaining moral responsibility.

Conclusion

One cannot read the *Apologema* without entertaining this question: Would Caramuel's debate with his critics have proceeded differently if its clarifications concerning probable opinion had appeared in the earlier works, or if the treatise itself had not been condemned? It is impossible to say, although one at least hopes that later commentators would have relied less heavily upon statements taken out of context from his early writings in summarizing his position. The polemical atmosphere surrounding discussions of laxism in the late seventeenth century was so harsh that one wonders how much genuine dialogue would have taken place, even if Caramuel's views had been clear from the beginning. Moreover, it is reasonable to assume that many of Caramuel's critics would have been no happier with the *Apologema* than with the earlier texts. Yet had the red herrings been swept away (e.g., the claim that theologians could change the moral character of actions), perhaps the parties could have devoted more energy to the question that, for Caramuel, represented the true core of the debate: What is the response of a merciful God to sinful and finite human beings? As we shall see, when he formulated a strikingly distinct approach to probabilism in the *Dialexis*, this emphasis upon divine mercy remained constant.

CHAPTER SIX

Redefining Probabilism
The Dialexis de Non-Certitudine

L OGIC SUGGESTS THAT THE *Apologema* SHOULD HAVE BEEN BISHOP Caramuel's last major analysis of probable opinion. He had explained probabilism to the authorities of his Church with passion and an enormous sense of urgency. Yet the rebuff from those Church leaders, especially the pope who had once been his patron, could not have been more evident. For Caramuel, who took ecclesiastical censures seriously, the consignment of the *Apologema* to the Index of Forbidden Books must have been incredibly distressing. Given his broad range of interests, it would not have been surprising if the bishop had abandoned theological probability and devoted himself to science, linguistics, and the other subjects that captured his imagination. Yet less than a decade after the condemnation of his *Apology*, Caramuel essentially redefined his treatment of probable opinion in a work entitled the *Dialexis de Non-Certitudine*.[1]

The *Apologema* and the *Dialexis* illustrate Caramuel's mature thought concerning probable opinion. If the *Apologema* is pastoral and polemical in its approach, the *Dialexis* is philosophical and academic, with a display of erudition that includes Hebrew and Greek quotations as well as Caramuel's usual mining of the Latin sources. It is definitely a work directed to his colleagues, rather than one composed for the edification of ordinary Christians. The *Dialexis's* theoretical sophistication renders it an appropriate addition to the *Theologia Moralis Fundamentalis* (1675–76), for which it serves as the fourth volume. As we shall see, Caramuel regarded his approaches to probability in *Fundamentum* 11 and the *Dialexis* as distinct but complementary. Together, they represent a remarkable explanation of probable opinion from an author who had devoted much of his career to its analysis.

To evaluate the significance of the *Dialexis*, it is helpful to note certain circumstances surrounding its publication. The discussion will then consider the novelty of its central thesis and the significance of its emphasis upon certitude and "noncertitude." To understand the latter, it is helpful to examine the *Dialexis*'s presuppositions regarding law, human freedom, and the mediating role exercised between the two by the so-called principle of possession. All of these developments, of course, have important implications for Caramuel's understanding of probable opinion, as the discussion shall make clear. After addressing these foundational issues, I will consider Caramuel's response to two possible objections to his theory. From there, discussion moves to the theology of the *Dialexis* and to the *Dialexis* as the culmination of Caramuel's approach to probable opinion.

The Publication of the *Dialexis*

The title page of the *Dialexis de Non-Certitudine* gives its publication date as 1675. The text itself, however, reveals that it must have had, in comparison to Caramuel's other works, an unusually long hiatus between composition and actual circulation. The first edition of the *Theologia Moralis Fundamentalis,* for example, received the *censura* (i.e., the required examination and permission for publication) in 1651 and was published during the following year. All of the *Apologema*'s permissions were issued in 1663—the same year as its publication. But the *Dialexis*'s censures are dated 1671 and 1672—three and four years, respectively, before the date on the title page. Thus the book that Caramuel wrote as bishop of Satriano/Campagna was published only after his transfer to Vigevano.

Many practical factors—not least of which was the bishop's move to a new assignment—may explain the delay. Yet it is also clear that Caramuel demonstrated uncharacteristic caution in bringing this text to the public view. The *Dialexis* ends with a long section of letters regarding both the matters treated in the volume and the history of its production. To his correspondent Marcus Bravo, a consulter to the Congregation of the Index, Caramuel explains the steps that he took to protect his volume from "those who tried to suffocate it before it was sent into the light."[2] As a precautionary measure, the bishop sent his treatise to two professors at the University of Salamanca, Michael de Fuentes and Antonio de San Pedro, for their evaluation. The date of their replies indicates that Caramuel must have developed a rough draft of the *Dialexis* before the end of 1670.

The *Dialexis* does not include Caramuel's original letter to these two professors, but it does publish their responses, both written in December of that year.[3] It is probably significant that these evaluators were not only professors of theology but also leaders of the Cistercian Order in Spain.[4] Thus, Caramuel could have pointed out to any detractors that he had submitted his text for the approval of leaders in his religious community—leaders who were also noted theologians. San Pedro's response was particularly helpful to Caramuel. Not only did the professor endorse the bishop's central thesis, describing it as true rather than probable, but he also offered some important objections and amendments that Caramuel incorporated into the final version of his text.[5] The "Epistles" section of the *Dialexis*, in fact, provides a valuable glimpse of Caramuel as a theologian in correspondence with his colleagues and other interested persons regarding the contents of his work.

In this case, however, Caramuel's efforts at collaboration were clearly spurred by anxiety as well as a desire for conversation with the learned.[6] It would certainly be helpful if he had said more about those who allegedly tried to "suffocate" his forthcoming work.[7] Whatever the precise nature of his ecclesiastical concerns, however, Caramuel must have also experienced the anxiety of a theorist who proposes to take a longstanding debate in a new and surprising direction. After many years of study, the longtime defender of probable opinion was about to break new ground.

The Novelty of the *Dialexis*

The opening statement of the treatise's "Index of Chapters and Articles" lulls Caramuel's audience into a false sense of security. "Here, Splendid and Erudite Reader," he remarks, "I do not set out any new teachings for ingenious curiosity, but common and ancient [teachings] more clearly explained, which the whole body of elder and junior writers presupposes; which all admit and exercise in practice, even if they have handed on these same [ideas] in very obscure words."[8] Caramuel repeatedly insists that the central argument of the *Dialexis* is nothing novel, either in his own works or the works of others. "I have always held [this position], and have passed it on to readers, when the occasion demanded it," he remarks.[9] In fact, the theologian sees continuity between the *Dialexis* and his earlier discussions of probable opinion. "I do not repeat what I have explained in our *Fundamental Theology* at number 435, for I presume that you have already read it," he writes, referring to *Fundamentum* 11.[10] "There I explain the common teaching *de* [about] *Probabilitate*; now, with some [issues] having been overcome, I advance to the concomitant difficulties."[11] This statement suggests that Caramuel regards the relationship between the earlier analyses and the *Dialexis* as a logical progression from a central argument to related (and presumably more complex) questions.

Nonetheless, Caramuel seems to acknowledge that his new text involves not only development but also a radical shift in thinking, especially regarding the topic of "noncertitude." Even Caramuel must admit that, in the past, he and other theologians expressed the significance of this concept only "in very obscure words." "Before today, I think the formal reason that renders consciences secure was undiscovered,"[12] he explains. "For we thought [it] to be probability; yet it was not probability, but something distinct, which accompanies probability and certitude equally."[13]

Dissemination of the argument concerning noncertitude, in Caramuel's view, will greatly advance the "teaching about human acts, . . . about which I thus far spoke foolishly, along with others."[14] Though he tries to emphasize his argument's continuity with tradition, Caramuel is obviously excited by this new approach to a question that had occupied him for many years. Perhaps his simplest concession about the text's novelty is this statement, which echoes some of the *Apologema*'s responses to Fagnani's criticisms of probabilism: "And what if I am transmitting something new? A new [opinion] is not bad, if it is true."[15]

The Significance of Certitude and Noncertitude

In the *Dialexis*, the article devoted specifically to probable opinion is the very last to appear in the main body of the treatise, instead of appearing near the beginning as it does in Caramuel's other works.[16] Here the theologian has decided to approach the problem from a new direction. "The formal reason, which renders consciences secure in practice," he asserts, "is neither the certitude of the opinion that we sustain, nor its greater, equal, or lesser probability, but the mere noncertitude of the contrary [position]."[17] From this central thesis, he formulates a new explanation for the moral implications of probable opinion.

To understand the *Dialexis*'s central argument, it is helpful to decipher its title. Caramuel explains this for the reader within his preliminary section of definitions: The Greek term *dialexis* translates the Latin *disputatio* (i.e., debate). But why hold a debate about "noncertitude" rather than uncertainty? Caramuel insists that there is an important difference between the two: "there are many things that are not certainly true, which nevertheless are not uncertain. For things that are certainly false ought not to be called *uncertain*."[18] As we shall see, this distinction reflects his belief that moral law is either certainly imposed or nonexistent (at least for those operating under conditions of invincible ignorance). As a result, Caramuel speaks throughout this work of *noncertitude* rather than *uncertainty*.

The central argument of the *Dialexis* provides a response to this question: What precisely is it that renders consciences secure? As he had done throughout his career, Caramuel asserts that probable opinion is sufficient for tranquility of conscience. Yet probable opinion is not the only warrant for morally responsible action, since certitude provides another mode of assurance. In that case, Caramuel observes, it is not probability that provides security. "Therefore, the cause by which security of conscience is established," he concludes, "will be something common to certitude and probability."[19] In other words, security of conscience must be the result of some factor that probability and certitude share.

Before proceeding further, it may be helpful to review Caramuel's position on the complex relationship between certitude and probability. On the one hand, every responsible moral action, even one grounded in probable opinion, involves a type of certitude, namely certitude about the "honesty" (acceptability) of one's action. Caramuel illustrates this point in the *Dialexis* by invoking the practices of the criminal courts. Suppose that a judge must acquit a defendant because the accusers have provided insufficient evidence to support their charges. Considered in reference to reality itself, the verdict (X is not guilty) is only probable. However, the appropriateness of issuing that verdict is certain, in light of the failure to prove the defendant's guilt. Thus, one act (issuing a judgment) can encompass both probability (in reference to the facts) and certitude (in reference to the legitimacy—indeed, in this case, to the obligatory character—of issuing the acquittal).[20] However, if one is discussing an agent's assessment of a proposition's truth at a particular time, then probability and certitude are mutually exclusive categories. Recall the argument from the *Apologema* about the difference between St. Teresa's certain knowledge (through revelation) and the probable opinions of the Scotists and Thomists regarding the same mysteries of faith. For Caramuel, a person who regards a thesis as certain cannot regard it as probable at the same time. Yet because either certain or probable opinions suffice for responsible action, the factor rendering each secure must be something common to these two distinct categories of knowledge.[21] This, as we shall see, Caramuel identifies as the noncertitude of the contrary opinion.

Perhaps in response to the opponents who had attacked him for "skepticism," Caramuel is careful to insist that certitude in moral matters is possible.[22] "Even if there are disputes about very many particular notions," he asserts, " general and universal [principles] are infallible."[23] He also insists that, without certitude, there would be no probability.[24] Thus, in the *Dialexis* (as, in fact, in the *Apologema*), Caramuel's notion of probability is closely connected to his notion of certitude.

In comparison with the *Apologema*, however, the *Dialexis* devotes far greater attention to the definition of certitude, explaining its relationship to probability more concretely. Caramuel identifies three basic types of certitude: metaphysical, physical, and moral. Metaphysical certitude encompasses that *"which necessarily is true, because from the absolute power of God it is not able to be otherwise."*[25] Caramuel mentions the principle of noncontradiction as an example. By contrast, *physical certitude* applies to those things that could conceivably be otherwise (in light of God's absolute power) but remain constant where such miraculous intervention is lacking. God can override the normal laws of the physical world or dispense persons from obedience to the Second Table of the Decalogue, but in the absence of such divine dispensation, these laws remain physically certain.[26] Thus the terms *physically* and *metaphysically certain* refer to basic realities of existence that God either can or cannot change.

Things described as *morally certain*, on the other hand, can conceivably be "otherwise [*aliter*]" as the result of human action as well as divine intervention.[27] One must have evidence, however, to assert that such a variation from the norm has occurred. As illustrations, Caramuel mentions the presumptions that immemorial possession is legitimate, that a stranger is a decent person, and that a particular father loves his child. In concrete cases, any of these assertions can prove false. Perhaps someone has documents to prove that a family originally stole the land they have possessed quietly for hundreds of years. Perhaps the stranger is a cad. Perhaps the father is only feigning affection for his offspring. But in the absence of evidence to support these conclusions, the opposite presumptions remain morally certain.[28] "I am not able to say, *perhaps it is otherwise*," Caramuel notes, "because I have no argument upon which to ground this suspicion."[29]

How then does moral certitude differ from probability? Caramuel notes that they have two features in common. Each is *"supported by some grave reason (particular or general)."*[30] In addition, each could conceivably be "other" than it appears. What separates the two is the agent's possession (or lack of possession) of prudent grounds for questioning the initial presumption. If the agent has no such grounds, then the assertion (or law) is morally certain; if the agent has grounds, such as the existence of a defensible position to the contrary, then the hypothesis is probable.[31] Moreover, moral certitude excludes fear.[32] By contrast, fear (concerning the assessment of the action rather than the legitimacy of its performance) necessarily accompanies every probable opinion.[33] Finally, the practical consequences of probable opinion and moral certitude are overlapping but not identical. Both, under given conditions, suffice for security of conscience. But only certitude (indeed, certitude of any type) creates moral obligation. Caramuel flatly asserts:

> It is certain that the person who violates a precept [that is] metaphysically, physically, or morally certain, commits sin . . . It is certain, that the person who acts contrary to a precept that is neither metaphysically, nor physically, nor morally certain, sins in no way.[34]

In fact, it is the lack of certitude (in this case, concerning the accuracy of the opposing view) that makes it safe for one to rely on probable opinion. This conclusion depends, however, not only upon Caramuel's analysis of certitude but also upon his theories of human liberty, law, and the ethical significance of possession.

Liberty, Law, and the Mediating Principle of Possession

"Human beings are clearly in the most certain possession of their own liberty," argues Caramuel, "and so essential is their free will, that the person who dares to deny it, should be considered insane."[35] Without liberty, Caramuel believes, the concept of moral responsibility makes no sense. Although law constrains freedom, it renders actions legitimate or illegitimate rather than physically or psychologically impossible.[36] Even in the presence of law, the human capacity to obey or to disregard its precepts remains intact. Moreover, only a law that is certain (as opposed to one that is simply probable) can limit persons' free exercise of their liberty. Liberty is "in possession," for Caramuel, prior to the clear imposition of law.[37]

As a proponent of the position that actions are evil because they are forbidden rather than vice versa, Caramuel, of course, assigns enormous importance to law as a principle of the moral life. Moral obligation, in fact, arises from law. Caramuel derives the word *law* [*lex*] from *ligare* (to bind), and argues that a precept that imposes no obligation is not law at all.[38] Conversely, "*what is prohibited by no law is said to be licit.*"[39] Theological sin is a violation of divine law, and without such law, there can be no theological sin.[40]

However, as previously mentioned, law does not oblige unless its existence is certain.[41] This is true (in part) because of another principle that plays a mediating role between law and liberty: the principle of possession. Caramuel typically states it in this way: "the one who possesses, must be maintained."[42] To illustrate this principle, Caramuel invokes two examples, one from civil and the other from criminal law. Suppose that John is suing Peter over the possession of a house. Peter was born in the house, grew up there, and has lived in it throughout his life. In order to prevail, John is going to need more than probable reasons to prove that he, rather than Peter, is the rightful owner. Peter is in peaceful possession of the property, and according to civil law, the burden of proof falls upon the adversary of the peaceful possessor. Similarly, in the second example, when Frederick has been charged with but not convicted of, a crime, his accusers will need full proof rather than probable arguments to establish his guilt juridically. Frederick is in peaceful possession of his life and reputation. If the truth is uncertain, those in possession are entitled to the benefit of the doubt.[43]

Riches and even physical liberty, Caramuel argues, are nothing in comparison to one's soul and security of conscience. Noting that, in human courts, more serious punishments require greater justification than lesser ones, he warns his colleagues to be wary when handing down a "sentence of mortal sin, i.e., of eternal death."[44] To substantiate such a claim, theologians should be able to offer proofs as certain as those that are necessary for a criminal conviction. In reference to another case, Caramuel applies this general principle: "For everything is considered free, unless servitude and obligation are proven."[45] Without proof, liberty remains in possession.

Caramuel was certainly not the first or the only theologian to apply the principle of possession to the debate over probabilism. (Fagnani's counterarguments, in fact, bear witness to its popularity.[46]) Nor is the *Dialexis* the first treatise on probabilism in which Caramuel invokes this principle. However, it is fair to say that its role is much less central in his other treatments of the question. Here, Caramuel even explains eighty-eight fundamental rules of practice as logical conclusions from the principle of possession. "*In penalties, the more benign interpretation should be made*" (rule 49).[47] Why is this true? It is because those to be punished are in possession of their liberty, reputation, and so forth. "*Once something has been declared* [to belong] *to God, it must not be transferred further to human uses*" (rule 51). In this case, God has become the possessor.[48] As these examples reveal, the principle of possession plays a central role in the *Dialexis*'s moral approach. Caramuel even applies it to one of his favorite arguments from the *Apologema*, the assertion that God does not command the impossible. When I am unable to do something, he argues, my disability is in possession and must be maintained until God gives me the capacity to do otherwise.[49]

The principle of possession thus plays a mediating role in the imposition of law upon liberty. Yet Caramuel also insists that moral obligation arises not from law as it is in itself, but from law as it is recognized by the subject.[50] Like Thomas, Caramuel identifies promulgation as part of the essence of law.[51] "A law that is not yet established, or not yet intimated, is not true and actual law. As a result, that law, of which I am invincibly ignorant, is not sufficiently intimated to me, nor (in respect to me), is it true and actual law."[52] Here, we find the emphasis upon invincible ignorance that is so characteristic of the *Apologema*. Caramuel does offer certain clarifications of his arguments in this regard. Unlearned persons, the

Dialexis insists, for example, have a responsibility to recognize that they lack adequate education and to seek help from experts in resolving moral dilemmas (assuming that circumstances permit this).[53] Invincible ignorance does not excuse an agent from sin, if he or she can reasonably delay the action and seek further enlightenment. (Caramuel gives the example of a judge who realizes that he has insufficient information to resolve a case and chooses to issue a ruling immediately rather than requiring further witnesses.[54]) But as in the *Apologema*, invincible ignorance plays a critical role in explaining why law does not impose identical moral obligations upon everyone. Caramuel's basic explanation for this point is the same: God does not demand the impossible.[55]

Finally, his new understanding of the significance of noncertitude for moral action leads Caramuel to move beyond the *Apologema* in an explicit rejection of so-called material sins. Although recognizing that others use the concept, he argues that it makes no sense. "Law, if it does not bind, does not exist; and unless it is known, it does not bind," he argues. "Therefore, a law that is unknown can be violated neither formally nor materially."[56] The designation *material sin*, in other words, is illogical because there can be no sin without the deliberate violation of (perceived) law. Caramuel prefers to speak of these acts as *hypothetical sins*, that is, actions that would indeed become sinful if law were sufficiently intimated to the agent.[57] One cannot break the law when one's ignorance means that there is no law to break. This represents one of the most significant theoretical implications of Caramuel's emphasis upon noncertitude.

Implications for the Analysis of Probable Opinion

In the *Dialexis*'s treatment of probable opinion, therefore, Caramuel intertwines his traditional arguments with his new emphasis upon possession and noncertitude. The claims that a law is not law for those invincibly ignorant of it and that law only obliges if its existence is certain have obvious consequences for the theory of probabilism. Caramuel argues, for example, that even laws that certainly exist do not oblige when the experts interpret them in opposite ways.[58] The principle of possession also helps to explain why noncertitude plays the critical role in making the conscience that relies upon probable opinion secure. I cannot be deprived of my liberty unless the existence of a precept is certain, Caramuel asserts. Thus, my liberty remains in possession not because I have proved that there is no precept but because my opponent has not succeeded in proving the opposite.[59] Noncertitude of obligation thus maintains agents' freedom and justifies their reliance upon probable opinion.

In light of his focus upon certitude, Caramuel reexamines certain aspects of the concept of probability itself. A leader of the contemporary Thomists, he observes, argues that all certain propositions are equally certain, and all probable propositions are equally probable. Caramuel (very respectfully) rejects the latter position. In reality, some opinions are more probable, and some less probable, than others. The practical difficulty lies in distinguishing one from the other. Thus, from a practical perspective, all probable opinions are equally probable, that is, equally sufficient for security of conscience.[60] Moreover, Caramuel supplements that conclusion by arguing that the distinction between "more" and "less" probable opinions is really philosophical rather than theological in nature. For theological probability, the critical factor is the noncertitude of the opposed position and hence, the maintenance "in possession" of human freedom. This factor is present in all probable opinions, whatever the extent of their philosophical probability.[61] Caramuel makes the point that if a certain number of witnesses are required for a will's validity, supplying extra witnesses does not make it "more" valid than a will that has only the requisite number. Similarly, if two persons each owe a third ten gold pieces, the borrower who returns twenty has not repaid the debt "more" than has her counterpart who supplies only the required ten. In practical terms, theological probability represents a basic (and indivisible) designation.[62] Attempts to distinguish the more from the less probable are thus unnecessary.[63]

For these reasons, Caramuel concludes in the *Dialexis* that the traditional distinction between rationally and authentically probable opinions really reflects the "accidents" rather than the essence of probability. Thus, he compares the categorization of probable opinions as rational or authoritative to the description of human beings as white or black. Probability formally arises from the noncertitude of the contrary position. Special warrants and expert testimony can be present or absent without affecting the basic nature of a thesis's probability.[64]

But what of the claim that probability must be grounded in "grave reason," which Caramuel had so emphasized in the *Apologema* and which he still includes within the basic definition of probable opinion in the *Dialexis*? Caramuel anticipates this objection, and asserts that the grave reason in question can be general as well as special. The general reason that grounds every probable opinion—indeed, all licit human actions—is *"liberty's possession"* in the absence of certain obligation. [65] Some probable opinions may be supported by other special grave reasons (i.e., particular arguments), but all share this common foundation. A rational warrant is still necessary; however, Caramuel now argues that it can be the general priority of possession rather than a particular argument.

Anticipating Possible Objections

In addition to explaining Caramuel's revised concept of probability, the *Dialexis* also attempts to forestall some possible objections to the new focus upon noncertitude. In this case, Caramuel had the comments of his consultants from Salamanca to draw upon, and he tells us that he inserted a new section into the text precisely to respond to their various concerns. [66] In answer to his correspondent San Pedro (and perhaps also remembering the approach of Fagnani), Caramuel attempts to demonstrate that accepting his idea will not have negative ethical consequences. And, as he had done in the *Apologema*, he tries to provide a historical pedigree for the idea that noncertitude of the contrary view can ground security of conscience.

In his letter of evaluation to Caramuel regarding the *Dialexis*, Antonio de San Pedro makes this observation:

> I do not know whether what happened to me will happen to others. When first I read through the teaching of the most illustrious lord, most difficult appeared to be the statement of the third conclusion: *it is licit to choose any action whatsoever that is not certainly forbidden* . . . From this opinion follow very many absurd [consequences.][67]

As an illustration, San Pedro mentions three cases regarding the sacraments. Suppose that I am not absolutely certain that I have been validly baptized or ordained. May I legitimately seek another baptism or another ordination, since I am not certain regarding the original rites? What if

I question whether a host, which is displayed for the veneration of the faithful, was validly consecrated? May I take it down and even trample it underfoot, because I am unsure? San Pedro assumes, of course, that one has an obligation not to do any of these things, and he has no doubt that Caramuel holds the same position. In essence, he is suggesting that Caramuel clarify his terms to prevent others from drawing the wrong conclusions from his arguments.[68]

Caramuel pays great attention to his consultant's observations, even describing these particular objections as "most grave [*gravissimae*]" in the marginal notes.[69] (One suspects that the 1665–66 condemnations of laxist propositions made the bishop particularly anxious to demonstrate that his theory would not justify outrageous behavior.) In addition to the three cases regarding profanation of the sacraments, Caramuel also considers the significance of his theory for the prohibition of rash judgment. According to his position, are people entitled to suspect their neighbors of theft, adultery, and other sins, since they cannot be sure that these persons are not malefactors?[70]

In respect to all these cases, Caramuel argues that his position does not justify such obviously illicit behaviors, and that any assumptions to the contrary rest upon a confusion between probability and moral certitude.[71] In a sense, all the cases hinge on the nature of the knowledge available to the agent. God does not prohibit human beings from making any judgments, but from making rash judgments, that is, judgments in which one's evidence and arguments are insufficient to justify one's conclusions.[72] Such unsubstantiated judgments are sins—sins against oneself (as a misuse of reason) and against the neighbor whom one holds in insufficient esteem.[73] Moreover, it is certain that I have an obligation to avoid this sin and to give my neighbors the benefit of the doubt, unless I have sufficient grounds to override the presumption in their favor.[74] The duty to avoid rash judgment is undeniable, whatever the hidden state of my neighbors' souls.

This conclusion about rash judgment, in effect, solves the other cases regarding sacramental profanation. How can I know that the priest who baptized me, and the bishop who ordained me, performed these rites appropriately? Caramuel asks. "Because I do not know the opposite. Because God orders me *to presume innocence, where guilt is not proven*."[75] To seek a second baptism or ordination, without grave reasons for questioning the validity of the first, is, in essence, to commit rash judgment against the sacramental minister. Similarly, one ought not presume that the priest who consecrated the host exposed for veneration has committed sacrilege.[76] The priest is in "possession of his innocence."[77] In effect, Caramuel solves these objections by redefining the issue. The question is not whether the agents are entitled to doubt their neighbors (including their sacramental ministers) because they cannot be absolutely assured of their sanctity and appropriate behavior. The real question is whether they have an obligation to presume the opposite in the absence of compelling evidence to the contrary. Speculative doubt does not create a license for action in the face of certain duty.

San Pedro had also mentioned (in order to refute it) the claim that Caramuel's position violates traditional teaching—a charge with which the bishop had by this time become quite familiar.[78] Like the *Apologema*, the *Dialexis* attempts to counter the attack that its author's teaching is new and, therefore, automatically suspect.[79] Although there was no doubt that probabilism had many other defenders, Caramuel here faces the charge that "no [other] doctor has asserted" the sufficiency of noncertitude.[80] In response, the Cistercian argues that his teaching is "extremely ancient and common," with a pedigree that extends from the classical past to the present. From Plato to Caramuel's contemporaries such as Verde, the learned "expressly conspire in this one truth."[81]

In comparison to the *Apologema*'s historical pedigree for probabilism, the *Dialexis*'s parallel section devotes relatively little attention to the Bible. Caramuel, however, does draw one interesting example from Paul's instructions to the Church at Corinth regarding meat that might have been sacrificed to idols. Citing the Apostle's instructions that the Corinthians need not have scruples about eating meat sold in the market, Caramuel observes that this advice has practical applications for the present.[82] Amidst the religious diversity of seventeenth-century Europe, Catholic travelers might well need to consume food cooked by someone who does not share their faith. Must a Catholic who eats in a public inn on a fast day be absolutely sure that the non-Catholic owners have not used meat to flavor the fish or the beans? No, says Caramuel, advising the reader that inquiry is unlikely to provide reliable information, since cooks tend to say anything necessary to make a sale. As Paul's instructions indicate, it suffices that the Catholic remains uncertain that meat has been used.[83]

Caramuel's most striking illustrations of reliance upon noncertitude, however, are taken not from the Bible but from Augustine. Indeed, the

Cistercian's "genealogy" of noncertitude lists Augustine as its "mother."[84] In what can only be described as a rhetorical tour de force, Caramuel draws upon a statement of Augustine's that had been a favorite proof-text of his adversaries: "*hold the certain, and dismiss the uncertain.*"[85] Noting that some theologians have misinterpreted this passage and now "disturb theology" as a consequence, Caramuel considers the original context of the statement.[86] Augustine was urging his audience not to delay in undertaking penance, and warning them of the dangers inherent in reserving it for the time of one's last illness. Within this exhortation, the bishop of Hippo describes his own procedure when a person seeks penance on his or her deathbed. Though he cooperates with the request, Augustine reports, he has no way to be sure that such delayed penitence is efficacious: "*We are able to give penance; we are not able to give security.*"[87] As a result, he gives penance under these circumstances not because he is certain that it will benefit the dying sinner, but because he is uncertain about its effects: "*for if I knew* [absolution] *would not benefit you, I would not give* [it] *to you.*"[88]

Caramuel pounces upon this admission. "It seems that the Holy Father has expressed my entire *Dialexis* with these words," he remarks.[89] It is the uncertainty of the opposite position—that is, that delayed penance will not benefit the dying person—that the bishop of Hippo requires as a necessary condition for action. Augustine's choice to use it in such a case is telling, because all theologians are inclined to be particularly strict in matters regarding the sacraments, whether they typically resolve cases "rigorously or benignly."[90]

In support of this point, Caramuel notes that Augustine seems to apply the same principle to other sacraments. Regarding the case of a woman who unwittingly marries an already-married man, for example, Augustine argues that she does not commit adultery as long as she remains ignorant of her partner's deceit.[91] From this, Caramuel concludes that one need not be absolutely certain that one's proposed spouse is free before entering into marriage—a type of certainty that might have been difficult to obtain in some places, both in Augustine's day and in Caramuel's. It is sufficient that one does not *know* that the partner has another spouse. Similarly, Augustine allows the baptism of a catechumen who has fallen into a mortal sickness and is no longer able to express his or her wishes about the rite's administration. If the desire for sacrament is uncertain, the bishop of Hippo observes, it is better "*to give* [baptism] *to the unwilling, than to deny*

[it] *to the willing.*"[92] Once again, the lack of certainty that the catechumen has changed his or her mind provides adequate grounds for action.

Caramuel himself considers the application of Augustine's principle to other situations surrounding sacramental administration. In hearing confessions, for example, the priest often lacks the means to be absolutely sure that the conditions necessary for absolution are present. What if the person was never baptized? What if he or she did not really commit the act just mentioned in confession? What if the penitent is not truly sorry or has no intention to avoid such acts in the future? Often, the confessor cannot provide a certain answers to these questions. Must he be able to do so in order to absolve the penitent? "By no means [*minime*]," Caramuel answers. It suffices that he is not certain that the person is unbaptized, or acting in bad faith.[93] A similar principle holds in reference to confirmation, where the bishop has no absolute proof that those approaching the chrism are not acting sacrilegiously, and in the administration of the Eucharist to persons who might conceivably be, but are not actually known to be, public sinners.[94] Even in reference to Holy Orders, where the bishop has a duty to exercise oversight regarding the worthiness of the candidates, Caramuel notes that information about external worthiness (e.g., has the candidate been excommunicated?) differs from knowledge of his internal worthiness (i.e., is he presently in a state of grace?).[95] In all these cases, the minister is justified in giving the sacrament's recipient what we might call the benefit of the doubt, on the basis of what Caramuel calls noncertitude of the opposite conclusion.

Augustine's sacramental practice, therefore, functions in Caramuel's argument as a major warrant for the sufficiency of noncertitude and for its recognition by theological authorities. (One can only imagine how pleased Caramuel must have been to draw such conclusions from a passage that his opponents had invoked against probabilism!) Interestingly enough, the influence of Augustine is evident not only when Caramuel cites the bishop himself but also when he refers to the work of other authors who provide a precedent for his views, such as Bartolomé de Medina. Caramuel, who never mentions Medina in the *Apologema*'s pedigree for probabilism, invokes him here as an implicit believer in the sufficiency of noncertitude. To prove the point, Caramuel discusses Medina's defense of the position that it is not sinful to act in the face of speculative (as opposed to practical) doubt. The relevant arguments that Caramuel draws from Medina rely primarily upon precedents from Augustine, some already invoked by Caramuel himself (e.g., the unwitting bigamist) and others that point in the same direction (e.g., the claim that one may fight in a war that one does not know to be unjust).[96] The parallel between these arguments is quite striking and suggests the utility of investigating the significance of Augustine's casuistry for probabilism—a topic that, unfortunately, lies well beyond the scope of the current analysis. Here, one should note only that Medina and Caramuel draw similar lessons from Augustine—lessons one of them describes as the legitimacy of acting on speculative doubt, and the other, as the sufficiency of noncertitude.

Caramuel's identification of other (implicit) adherents to his theory is sixty pages long and devotes far more space to his contemporaries and recent authors than to traditional authorities such as Cyprian, Aquinas, and Bernard. This list includes (among others) Matthieu de Moya, Eligius Bassaeus, Domingo de Soto, Navarrus, Franciscus Amico, Heinrich Busenbaum, and even Caramuel's earlier works ("if perhaps . . . I may be numbered among the theologians").[97] Yet the bishop does assign one author particular importance in reference to the theory of noncertitude. According to Caramuel, Bishop Stephen Spinula "many years before us" taught this position: *"an opinion that removes the obligation of doing or omitting something . . . is probable, even if it is supported by no positive reason, as long as it dissolves all arguments of the contrary* [positions]."[98] This very learned author, asserts Caramuel, "says more . . . than we did in our *Apology.*"[99] Indeed, Caramuel describes Spinula's opinion as a virtual compendium of the *Dialexis*.[100]

Caramuel, however, does not clearly explain the relationship between Spinula's volume (which was published in 1648) and his own.[101] Did Caramuel draw the idea of noncertitude from Spinula, or is he simply identifying Spinula as an earlier writer who proposed a position similar to his central thesis? One can hardly interpret Spinula's statement as a literal anticipation of the *Dialexis*. Caramuel also acknowledges that Spinula speaks "more broadly [*latius*]" than he does.[102] Thus, despite Caramuel's eagerness to invoke the example of another author, Spinula's precise influence upon the *Dialexis* remains a bit murky.

From Plato and Paul to Spinula, the *Dialexis* devotes extended attention to alleged antecedents and fellow adherents of its central argument. Caramuel is unprepared to allow the claim of novelty to pass unchallenged.

Yet, as in the *Apologema*, he also attacks that charge from the opposite direction, again rejecting the presupposition that a new idea is necessarily a bad idea.[103] By drawing distinctions, Caramuel attempts to shift the tenor of the debate.

As we have seen, Caramuel lived in an age in which *heresy* and *innovation* had become interchangeable terms. Yet while acknowledging this usage, the Spanish theologian asserts: "This objection does not touch us. For we do not disagree about orthodox faith, but about another matter . . . which, even if [it is] extremely serious, is disputed on one side or another, without danger of heresies."[104] The claim that novelty equals heresy is true, but only in respect to teachings that contradict the truths of faith revealed to the primitive Church or subsequently defined. This debate over noncertitude involves a different type of question, on which experts can disagree without violating the requirements of faith.

In addition to distinguishing different levels of theological consensus (or lack of consensus), Caramuel also invokes the type of historical argument that he had raised in the *Apologema* by pointing to Thomas's innovations. Augustine's exegesis of Genesis 1, the Cistercian argues, differed from those of his predecessors. The assumption that no development is possible in matters of faith, even when a theologian can offer "plausible . . . and probable" grounds for the innovation, contradicts the lessons of Christian theological history.[105] The great teachers of the past, therefore, provide a precedent for change.

Finally, although it shifts the argument away from theology to secular culture, Caramuel cannot resist invoking marvelous recent inventions and discoveries such as the printing press, the telescope, and logarithms. When one considers such advances in the arts and sciences, one must regard the attack upon new ideas as a slander rather than a valid objection. To the person who never bothers to read, Caramuel points out, everything is new. But to the person who constantly consults the works of others, "nothing is new, nothing is astounding, under the sun."[106]

The Theology of the *Dialexis*

In the chapters "on definitions [*de definitionibus*]" that begin the "Prodromus," *Deus* is the first term that Caramuel chooses to consider. If the

Dialexis is an analysis of the relationship between knowledge and moral responsibility, it rests upon a conception of God and how God deals with weak and finite human beings. As in the *Apologema*, Caramuel emphasizes divine mercy. Once again, his insistence (against Jansen and others) that God does not command the impossible spurs him to explain how God's commands to humanity should be understood.

Caramuel has no sympathy with the vision of a Creator who imposes obligations upon human beings that they cannot possibly fulfill. "The rule of one who commands the impossible is unjust and tyrannical." he asserts. "Therefore God does not order human beings to understand beyond the abilities of the human mind, or to act beyond the abilities of the other [human] powers."[107] Caramuel thus describes the view that only certain truth suffices for security of conscience as heretical, because of what it effectively implies about God. Only a tyrant commands persons to do what they cannot do and (in particular) to know what they could not possibly know.[108] Caramuel's conclusions about invincible ignorance and probable opinion reflect his faith that God is not a tyrant.

If the *Dialexis* tells us how God *does not behave* in reference to humanity, it also provides a picture of how divine mercy shapes the character of moral law. Law, of course, represents Caramuel's basic model for understanding the moral life. But he believes that it is important to understand precisely what divine law does and does not require. The Eighth Commandment, for example, does not demand that we never utter a false statement, but it does enjoin us to avoid lies. It is as if God says to us:

> *When I forbid lies and false testimonies, I certainly command nothing that exceeds human powers. I command that your speech proceed from your mouth, in such a way that it agrees with your heart and your mind . . . It will be quite easy for you to obey this precept, for I ordain nothing above the powers of the human mind.*[109]

The scope of divine commands, in other words, reflects God's knowledge of human limitations.

Caramuel's emphasis upon this point is even more striking in his interpretation of the First Commandment. In this life, he acknowledges, no one can love God perfectly. Does this mean that God commands the impossible? No, Caramuel insists. There is a distinction between performing an act perfectly and obeying a precept perfectly. A monk whose musical deficiencies make him a poor chorister does not thereby disobey the command to chant the canonical hours. A youngster commanded to copy a psalm is not disobedient because inexperience distorts his handwriting. Caramuel notes that he was disturbed to read of a bishop who had ordered the rebaptism of persons whose priest, through his ignorance of Latin, had baptized them "*in nomine Patria, & Filia, & Spiritua sancta.*" The defect in pronunciation, in Caramuel's view, did not render the baptisms invalid because the priest had obeyed the precepts regarding baptismal form insofar as his insufficient knowledge of Latin would permit. Performing an action imperfectly—even badly—does not mean that one necessarily failed to obey the law enjoining that same act.[110]

These examples provide an arresting illustration of how Caramuel regards the commandments and how he envisions God. He explicitly rejects the argument (which he attributes to Philipp Melanchthon) that the command to love God is as impossible as the command to fly across the Caucasus.[111] For Caramuel, the commandments are not impossible moral standards that inevitably convict us of sin. Instead, they are the precepts of a merciful God whose expectations reflect the limits of human nature. We can obey them, even though we do not perfectly perform the actions that they enjoin. Caramuel's God is the lawgiver and judge who sees the heart and looks for obedience rather than perfection—a God of incalculable mercy.[112]

Caramuel illustrates these points in his resolution of another case that seems, at first glance, to turn his argument on its head. Claudius (who is in a state of mortal sin) knows that he is about to die and has no opportunity for sacramental confession. Caramuel asserts that Claudius must make an act of contrition, yet acknowledges a possible objection from his reader. An act of contrition requires charity in the soul, which Claudius lacks. Would the charge that he should make an act of contrition require him to do the impossible? By no means, Caramuel answers:

> [God] either orders us to do what we are able to do; or, by giving the order, warns us that we should seek what is lacking. And if we seek [what we do not have], he gives us all things necessary for us to be able [to do what is commanded]—indeed, frequently [God gives] us these things, even if we do not seek [them].[113]

God provides such great mercy to all human beings, Caramuel remarks, "that [God can] be called *God* [*Deum*] from [the word] *giving* [*dando*]."[114] The Imposer of laws shapes them in light of human weakness, supplies the grace necessary to render their fulfillment possible, and judges their execution in light of human capacities and intentions (including invincible ignorance). This theological presupposition stands behind the various analytical conclusions of the *Dialexis*. Its claims about the sufficiency of noncertitude (and hence, of probable opinion) for security of conscience arise from faith in the boundless mercy of God.

The *Dialexis* as Culmination

Despite the *Dialexis*'s novelty, the reader of Caramuel's earlier works would have no difficulty in identifying this last treatise's author if the title page should happen to be missing. Many claims that shaped the earlier treatises reappear here and even gain further development. At one point, for example, Caramuel returns to his favorite argument that the opinion of one author, not four, suffices for extrinsic probability, to demonstrate that it does not properly fall under a papal condemnation (presumably a reference to the condemnations of 1665).[115] Explicitly citing the *Theologia Regularis*, he offers an amendment to his syllogism to render it "certain": "*the opinion of one doctor is probable, provided that it falls within the limits to which theologians adhere.*"[116] With this clarification, he confirms his reliance, even in the *Dialexis*, upon this familiar argument. He also invokes the *Theologia Regularis* in reference to another favorite syllogism, his demonstration that probable opinion suffices for security of conscience. This argument, notes Caramuel, has remained unconquered "in the arena" for "forty or more years."[117] The *Dialexis* thus bears witness to the longstanding continuities in his arguments over probabilism, as well as his innovations.

Caramuel turned seventy in 1676, the year that publication of the *Theologia Moralis Fundamentalis* (including the *Dialexis*) was completed. He had been defending probabilism, in public disputations and in his writings, for his entire public career. Yet after so many years, he still found new clarifications to offer, new examples to illustrate his arguments, and even (in the *Dialexis*) a new philosophical approach to the relationship between probability and security of conscience. The creativity of his intellect is as striking as his continued fascination with the problem.

Caramuel's mature works regarding probabilism, the *Apologema*, the *Dialexis*, and the later editions of the *Theologia Moralis Fundamentalis*, clearly build upon his early writings such as the *Theologia Regularis* and the *Benedicti Regulam*. Yet in the sophistication of their arguments and the clarity of their definitions, the later volumes are light years beyond Caramuel's initial musings. Caramuel's developed theory of probable opinion appears in his last works, not in the treatments that are better known and habitually quoted. Ironically, the theologian who spent his life investigating probabilism has been remembered almost exclusively for his least developed (and least clear) observations on the subject. The result has been unfortunate not only for Caramuel's reputation but also for our appreciation of the history of moral theology.

Despite setbacks such as the condemnation of the *Apologema*, the furor surrounding the *Provincial Letters*, and the general reaction against "laxism," Juan Caramuel never lost his fascination with probabilism. After decades of studying the question, a new insight—the significance of noncertitude—encouraged him to believe that he had finally grasped the basic reason that probable opinion sufficed for security of conscience. Yet even at that, one wonders whether Caramuel was truly satisfied with his understanding of probable opinion. If he had lived for another decade, with his eyesight intact, might he have revised the *Theologia Moralis Fundamentalis* yet again, perhaps analyzing and defending probabilism from another new perspective? In light of his past history, that speculation does not seem improbable.

Afterword

Remembering Probabilism: The Contemporary Significance of Caramuel's Legacy

In the twenty-first century, it is good for moral theologians to read Caramuel, if for no other reason than to recognize how much the presuppositions of ethical theory have changed since he labored over the *Theologia Moralia Fundamentalis*. The triumph of the Thomist assumption that actions are commanded because they are good and forbidden because they are evil becomes evident when one confronts an advocate of the opposite view, which today is almost exotic in its unfamiliarity. For the students of those who have struggled to redefine the Christian life in terms of a metaphor other than law, Caramuel's complete reliance upon that model is disconcerting, intriguing, and ultimately, thought provoking. One can marvel at the ingenuity with which Caramuel and his fellows exploited the legal image in order to understand Christian discipleship, without wishing that moral theology would again embrace law as its dominant metaphor. The world of Caramuel's ethical foundations is a good place to visit, although the "*iuniores*" of our age would not want to live there.

This book is not the product of a hope, much less a desire, for the advent of a great Caramuelian revival, or of a dream that probabilism might emerge as a popular topic for ethical reflection. Yet if Caramuel's probabilism is not a method for our age, this does not imply that it provides no significant lessons for our age. The legacy of the Spanish Cistercian illustrates several important problems for modern moral theology. We need a better understanding of our own history. We need a better appreciation of the value of provisional knowledge. And finally, we need to consider the implications of recognizing moral theology as theology, that is, as speech about God.

The Historical Problem

The debate surrounding probabilism was moral theology's most significant methodological question during the seventeenth and eighteenth centuries. Given probabilism's importance for the history of the discipline, one would expect to find a plethora of recent studies devoted to the question. Yet this is hardly the case, although there are, of course, important exceptions, such as Jonsen and Toulmin's *Abuse of Casuistry*. Is this because all of the important questions regarding probabilism have been answered? Would further research into the topic be meaningless labor, the repetition of investigations effectively completed long ago?

As far as Caramuel's theory of probabilism is concerned, the answer is clearly no. Many of the common conceptions of his approach are simply inaccurate and draw upon extracts from his early works (sometimes taken out of context) without consideration of his later clarifications. The mature Caramuel, for example, did not emphasize extrinsic probability at the expense of intrinsic probability; indeed, the *Apologema* treats the former as an extension of the latter. He never regarded the number-count as anything more than a practical rule of thumb for the uneducated, and insisted that those in a position to do so had a responsibility to consider the reasons behind any opinion. A bare list of names did not create probability for Caramuel; he was sometimes reluctant to ascribe probability to positions that others accepted and did not hesitate to label opinions improbable. Nor did Caramuel believe that moral truth was unattainable, only that its acquisition was often difficult and slow. As the *Dialexis* makes clear, he certainly did not ignore the relationship between probability and certitude. For Caramuel, probable opinion is not moral license. It is a tool for ensuring responsibility in the absence of ethical certainty. In short, Caramuel's approach to probabilism simply does not conform to the common portrait of his "laxist" ethical theory.

If the present discussion proves nothing else, it demonstrates the need for a fresh consideration of Caramuel's moral theology. One cannot assess Caramuel's place within the discipline by focusing only on his theory of probabilism; the present analysis is simply too narrow to ground any firm conclusions. Nor does it answer the question of whether Caramuel deserved to be known as the "prince of laxists." But the results of his long, theoretical investigations concerning probabilism do suggest that he merits more careful attention than he has received from moral theologians to this point. Caramuel may not have been a great saint or an ethical genius of Aquinas's caliber. Yet neither was he a crank, a fool, or an expert available to justify any conceivable behavior. The theologian who reminded his superiors that "Christ did not die for walls" and used a volume demanded by his secular patron to rail against the exploitation of German Catholics deserves to be heard by his successors.

If the standard portrait of Caramuel is so skewed, one reasonably wonders whether conventional views of other probabilists, and of seventeenth-century moral theology in general, also require reconsideration. There is a strong temptation to write the history of Early Modern moral theology in light of Alphonsus Liguori's later adaptations of probabilism. If Liguori's reinterpretation allowed the resurgence of a *moderate* probabilism, then it is easy to presume that the earlier forms must necessarily have been extreme. Testing that contention is daunting because it involves so many authors, so many rare books, and so many pages of seventeenth-century Latin. Reconsidering the history of probabilism will undoubtedly be a long, slow task that will require the efforts of many scholars. Few of us can claim the energy of Caramuel, or even of Deman. Yet without disparaging Deman's achievement, perhaps it is time to trust more (as Caramuel would say) in the evidence of our own eyes, by returning to the original texts. Caramuel's example urges us to reconsider the complex legacy of our predecessors.

The Problem of Provisional Knowledge

One of the most striking characteristics of Caramuel's ethical theory (indeed, of probabilism in general) is its comfort with what might be called provisional moral knowledge. For Caramuel, a basic ethical task concerned the classification of moral problems and opinions. Which proposed courses of action were certain (and hence, obligatory)? Which were probable (and hence, adequate for security of conscience)? Caramuel and other probabilists assumed that there were many situations in which the agent would have to choose between opposed alternatives, either of which could be a responsible act under conditions of speculative uncertainty. Probabilism thus presumes that moral knowledge is often provisional, and focuses upon the attainment of an acceptable choice.

One need not subscribe to the *Dialexis*'s arguments about liberty's possession in the face of uncertain law to notice certain advantages in this acceptance of provisional knowledge. Suppose, for example, that the U.S. bishops' famous pastoral letter, *The Challenge of Peace: God's Promise and Our Response*, had spoken of pacifism and just war theory as *probable* options for individuals, rather than describing the two theories as complementary.[1] (The eclipse of probabilism, of course, would have required an explanation of the adjective *probable*, or perhaps the substitution of another word such as *acceptable, reasonable,* etc.) But whether or not one uses the term, the theory of probabilism does seem to explain quite effectively how both pacifism and just war theory can be reasonable options for responsible Christians. The two approaches, as many theologians have pointed out, are clearly opposed to one another. Each, however, can appeal to appropriate sources within the Christian tradition. In Caramuel's terms, one could say that each has solid arguments and authorities in its favor, and solid arguments and authorities in opposition. Both represent legitimate responses for Christians, who may choose between them on the basis of their own consciences. Probabilism can thus differentiate these approaches from other conceivable views (e.g., that war is a neutral instrument of government, available for use whenever it suits national convenience). Even when moral knowledge is incomplete, probabilism helps to separate the reasonable from the unreasonable. Perhaps someday Catholics will regard only pacifism, or only just war theory, as a legitimate option for individuals. But until that day, probabilism (or some modern equivalent) can distinguish these two very different evaluations of warfare from other theories that fail to meet the test of Christian responsibility.

Recognition that moral knowledge can be provisional as well as definitive might be a valuable lesson that the twenty-first century could draw from the seventeenth. In working with students, I notice that many of them expect all moral conclusions (and particularly, all Church teachings regarding morality) to be definitive. This attitude regards Christian ethics as an all-or-nothing proposition: either the Church has *the final answer* for a moral problem or it has nothing to say. (Perhaps this is true, in part, because central Church authorities now intervene in debates over moral questions with a frequency that would have been unimaginable in Caramuel's time.) Catholics today expect their Church to be able to resolve complicated moral problems, including those involving new technologies and new social or scientific questions, in very short order. Whether they agree or comply with such teachings, many people tend to assume that—like it or not—the Church has a definitive answer for any conceivable dilemma. In terms of our quest for moral knowledge, this might be called the age of instant ethical gratification. We anticipate that truth will emerge quickly and unambiguously, or that it will never emerge at all.

Ironically, in a period when experience has taught us that knowledge in many disciplines, especially the sciences, is provisional, ethics (including Christian ethics) is still expected to produce the single "right" answer rapidly, in clear, unequivocal terms. When it cannot do so, many conclude that such definite knowledge is permanently unattainable, and that all possible answers are equally good. We have either certainty or relativism. Probabilism, however, maintains that in the dark of night, not all cats are gray. Without denying the possibility of eventual resolution, it insists upon the value of provisional moral knowledge. These, it argues, are the reasonable conclusions, the reasonable courses of action, given what we know at the present time. These are the defensible pathways as we travel together through the twilight. Such a reminder of the necessity and the utility of provisional moral conclusions might prove very useful for our discipline as it struggles to respond to a rapidly changing world.

The Problem of God

Caramuel's theory of probabilism is ultimately grounded in a particular type of Christian hope, a trust that God is more interested in persons' conscientious attempt to fulfill divine law than in their success in carrying out the letter of that law. If a priest's poor knowledge of Latin leads him inadvertently to baptize his parishioners in the name of the Fatherland, the Daughter, and the Holy Spiritess, Caramuel's God understands what he intended to say. Like an ideal abbot who listens to the heart of the tone-deaf chorister and reads the intentions of the clumsy copyist, Caramuel's God is a God of understanding and mercy who sets the bar of moral law within human reach and asks only that persons act reasonably and responsibly when they are uncertain about its boundaries. God, as the Spanish theologian repeats *ad infinitum*, does not demand the impossible. The sacraments of the Church stand ready as a remedy for the failings and deficiencies of finite and sinful creatures. Caramuel finds no appeal in the image of a God who gives the grace to conform to divine commands only to a chosen few. Such a conception, from his perspective, denies the very nature of God. God does not prescribe the impossible because such an order cannot be squared with the divine character. God is not a tyrant. This theological conviction is the foundation for Caramuel's ethical theory.

Caramuel's theology also does much to explain his visceral reaction to clerical avarice in Germany and to Jansenism. From his perspective, these two very different phenomena have the same effect: They drive people away from the Church and, hence, away from the outstretched hand of divine mercy. God is reaching out to sinners. But if they fail to approach the sacraments because their priests demand offerings that they are in no position to make, because they are scandalized by clerical greed, or because their rigorist confessors impose impossible demands, then the channel of divine beneficence is narrowed. Both greedy clerics and Jansenists, from Caramuel's perspective, allow the unnecessary (money or ethical rigor) to impede the essential, the acceptance of divine grace, as mediated by the Church. In modern terms, one might compare Caramuel to an aid worker in a refugee camp who watches bureaucrats turn hungry people away because they do not have the proper papers. His anger is the anger of a believer who knows that, although divine assistance is available, myopic Christians with misplaced priorities are impeding access to the font.

Caramuel's God reaches out to the finite creature as well as the sinner, and comforts those who are struggling with circumstances that are less than ideal. From the Catholic ruler who must sacrifice the Church's property in the interests of its people, that God requires a logical choice—the lesser of two evils. It is inconceivable to the Spanish theologian that God could prefer Catholic intransigency to the loss of the German Church. Thus, one must not dismiss the advice that Caramuel gives to his prince as political expediency. Instead, it represents his conclusions regarding moral fidelity in a world where consequences matter and the choices of limited persons shape human welfare. Caramuel's advice arises from his faith that

God is a God of priorities whose grace envelops finitude in understanding, mercy, and the gift of courageous perseverance.

One cannot truly appreciate Caramuel's approach to probabilism without recognizing that it is, at root, founded upon such theological convictions. Scholars have explained probabilism in many ways, invoking, for example, the allure of novelty and intellectual excitement or (more sympathetically) a desire to serve the needs of a rapidly changing world.[2] But one misunderstands Caramuel if one dismisses his ethics as an attempt at social accommodation, motivated by a desire to make things "easier" for people. Although he was certainly an advocate of permitting recourse to the "more benign" opinion, this was not because benignity was an end in itself. Benign opinions reflect the charity of a merciful God who is all too aware of humanity's sinfulness and finitude. Just as Caramuel advised his emperor that the Christian prince should mirror divine justice by tolerating the tares to protect the wheat, Caramuel's ethical method calls the moral theologian to mirror divine mercy, which respects human freedom and reads the intentions of the heart. Caramuel's probabilism speaks of how human beings *should* behave, but it is grounded in a faith about how God *does* behave and the conviction that grace is more powerful than invincible ignorance.

Like his assumptions about the value of provisional knowledge, Caramuel's insistence that theological ethics builds upon a conception of God and God's dealings with humanity merits the serious attention of modern scholars. When one compares representatives of the various camps in contemporary moral theology, for example, it is relatively easy to chart differences in method, ecclesiology, and practical conclusions. Whether and how we differ in our conceptions of God is much less obvious. Yet it may be an important and even a necessary question, especially because moral theologians' presuppositions about God are sometimes unstated. It can be tempting to leave God to the systematicians. Relatively few of us have explicitly considered the questions that Germain Grisez raises in *The Way of the Lord Jesus*, volume 1, chapter 18, where he concludes, "the alternatives to a populated hell are theologically unacceptable."[3] Yet if others were to respond to that assertion, their answers might prove more theologically revealing than explanations of method, or even conclusions regarding concrete moral issues. We might learn something very important from describing the nature of our hope and the God in whom we believe.

In a sense, consensus in vocabulary can mask important differences in theologies of God. All Christians (including specialists in Christian ethics) agree that God is merciful. Disagreement centers around the scope of that mercy, and the range of Christian opinions on the subject is certainly broader today than it was in Caramuel's time. One must not underestimate the contemporary appeal of a narrow view of divine mercy, which anticipates the salvation of a remnant plucked from the *massa damnata*. The enduring influence of that conception is evident in many places today, not least within popular literature. But those of us who entertain a broader hope regarding the extension of divine mercy should explain how that hope shapes both our method and our practical conclusions. How does the beneficence of God reach creatures who are not only sinful but also finite, who often stumble rather than stride toward a good that they perceive in a distorted mirror, through actions that embody their limitations as well as their faith? The answer will not emerge from a return to probabilism. It will come from the same trust in a generous grace that made probabilism an attractive ethical theory.

Caramuel, his colleagues, and his adversaries argued about divine mercy in terms of competing scriptural images: the easy yoke and the narrow gate. In this, their claims illustrate an unresolved tension in Christian ethics that arises from the scriptures themselves. Each image embodies an understanding of the moral life that has exercised great influence upon Christian ethical imaginations. Each provides a cogent explanation of Christian practice. Yet their differences are quite striking. Small wonder that Christian ethicists have disagreed (and continue to disagree) regarding important questions of practice, when the Tradition offers them such diverse portraits of theological morality.

In a sense, one can argue that proponents of the narrow gate enjoy definite advantages over their counterparts, in terms of theoretical coherence, psychological attractiveness, and ecclesial reputation. First, it is relatively simple to reconcile the narrow gate and the easy yoke by interpreting their relationship chronologically. Those who accept the demands of the narrow gate eventually discover that divine grace has rendered the apparent burden an easy yoke after all. Augustine's conversion, with its extended struggle over chastity, leading to an eventual surrender and subsequent peace, offers an outstanding case in point. By choosing the narrow gate, one encounters the easy yoke; apparent stringency becomes actual mercy. This capacity to reconcile the contrasting images contributes to the strength of the narrow gate as a Christian ethical model.

On several levels, this approach also enjoys psychological advantages. The narrow gate appeals to our desires for a heroic form of discipleship that sacrifices without stint and embraces the cross with courage and fortitude. Christians inspired by the example of the martyrs and ascetics can find their own self-abnegation in the narrow gate. Fidelity to this model and its high standards also provides reassurance that one is different from the world, the weak, and those who have accommodated both. It represents a tangible reminder of one's own commitment and, hence, of one's connection with God. Finally, the narrow gate is psychologically satisfying because it conforms to our recognition of our own sins and of the world's sinfulness. We recognize that both fall far short of moral perfection. It is easy to imagine a God who looks down in sadness and righteous rage at a humanity so corrupt that only a very few can reach the narrow gate, much less pass through it. Given our sins, logic suggests that this is the most that one can logically desire, if one respects divine justice at all. Perhaps all of us have moments when we wonder if we are truly "sinners in the hands of an angry God."

Finally, the narrow gate has arguably enjoyed a better reputation than the easy yoke as a recognized model of Christian praxis. If, in theory, the Church has rejected both rigorism and laxism, history suggests that it has been far less anxious regarding the former than the latter. The club of Catholic laxists, after all, contains no self-appointed members. All moral theologians (including Caramuel) have been eager to condemn opinions that seem excessively benign, and to avoid any suspicion of permissiveness. It is easier to defend oneself from the charge of rigorism (by appealing, for example, to the witness of the martyrs or to the image of the cross) than to fend off an accusation of laxism. Raising the ethical bar provokes less controversy than lowering the ethical bar. For such stringency, the image of the narrow gate provides a theological justification. And the unwritten presumption of this model is that conformity with such standards will not "hurt anyone," even if the standards should ultimately prove erroneous. At most, Christian ethics is asking people to sacrifice for Jesus. The sacrificing heart will be sincere, even if the particular sacrifice should prove unnecessary.

The easy yoke, by contrast, enjoys fewer advantages as a Christian ethical model, not least because it is commonly misinterpreted as accommodation, worldliness, or even moral anemia. (Caramuel, who led ecclesiastics into battle, cared for plague victims, and died concealing the wounds of sackcloth under his ordinary clothing, would have scoffed at the notion that his theory encouraged a wimpish form of discipleship.[4]) It is easy to misconstrue the easy yoke unless one recognizes it, first and foremost, as a confession of trust in divine generosity. For this model, God's love for all, and desire to save all, is the first theological key for ethical analysis. The second key is God's recognition of human limitations. God does not demand the impossible, as Caramuel and Liguori and so many others have insisted. From a consciousness of the convergence between the salvific will of God and the divine awareness of human frailty, this approach draws conclusions about invincible ignorance and provisional moral knowledge. One could describe this approach, in one sense, as a theology of God that, secondarily, gives rise to an ethical model. It is a theory of divine mercy that grounds an assessment of human moral choices.

The primary fear of those who adopt the easy yoke model is not that persons will fail to recognize moral truth. God's understanding of the human condition explains the mitigating character of invincible ignorance, and this approach trusts that God sees the heart. Nor is this model's prime concern that people will reject Christianity because its ethical standards are too high. Rigorism can indeed become an impediment to evangelization, according to this view, but that is not the core of the problem. Instead, these theologians fear that those who are already responding to God's call under the influence of grace will be deterred by the imposition of unnecessary demands, so that the Christian community mediates rejection instead of mercy. Their anxiety is that those who are attempting to cope with circumstances of limitation will turn to the Church for help, only to be rebuked for infidelity and counseled to embrace what their consciences tell them is the greater evil in the name of heroic sacrifice. That is why Caramuel warns leaders, both civil and ecclesiastical, that power is given for edification rather than destruction. The awareness that Christian moralists can become ethical efficiency experts rather than evangelists motivates Caramuel (and others like him) to be on guard against human impediments to grace. Do not make Christ a liar, Caramuel warns in the *Apologema*, by imposing unnecessary burdens that contradict the promise of divine beneficence.[5]

The legacy of Juan Caramuel's reflections about probabilism, therefore, is a reminder of unfinished business for contemporary moral theology. Caramuel's example suggests the need for renewed investigation of our seventeenth-century past, and for reflection on the role and value of provisional moral knowledge. It also reminds us of the importance of articulating what is at stake in ethical debates, especially regarding our theological foundations. Remembering Caramuel's theory of probabilism, therefore, is not solely an antiquarian concern, for at one level, all questions about the past reflect assumptions about the present. Caramuel's ultimate bequest to us is a task rather than an answer. One suspects that he, as an advocate of probabilism and the gradual development of moral knowledge, would be cheered at this result. No theologian would be in a better position than Juan Caramuel to sympathize with successors who used his legacy to strike out in a new direction. As Caramuel wrote in reference to Aristotle and the other classical philosophers: "Their teaching is a most illuminating torch, which disperses the shadows . . . Nevertheless, we do not follow this light, but continue on another [road]. . . ."

Notes

Abbreviations

assert. = *assertum*
BR = *In D. Benedicti Regulam Commentarius Historicus Scholasticus Moralis Iudicialis Politicus*
cap. = *caput*
disp. = *disputatio*
DNC = *Dialexis de Non-Certitudine*
Ep. = *Epistola*
fund. = *fundamentum*
PL = *Sacri Romani Imperii Pacis Licitae Demonstratae, Variis Olim Consiliis Agitatae, . . .*
q. = *quaestio*
resol. = *resolutio*
RR = *Rationalis et Realis Philosophia*
TMF = *Theologia Moralis Fundamentalis*
TR = *Theologia Regularis: Hoc est in SS. Basili, Augustini, Benedicti, Francisci, &c Regulas Commentarii*
tract. = *tractatus*

Preface

1. Juan Caramuel, *Apologema pro Antiquissima et Universalissima Doctrina de Probabilitate. Contra Novam, Singularem, Improbabilemque D. Prosperi Fagnani Opinationem* (Lyon: Anisson, 1663).

2. Prospero Fagnani, *Commentaria in Primum Librum Decretalium,* . . . (Venice: Paul Balleonius, 1709), *De constit.*, *cap.* 5, *Ne innitaris*, pp. 25–91.

3. Alphonsus Liguori, *Theologia Moralis*, rev. ed., ed. Leonard Gaudé (Rome: Typographia Vaticana, 1907), vol. 2, p. 143: "Magnus rigoristarum princeps."

4. See Th. Deman, "Probabilisme," *Dictionnaire de théologie catholique* (Paris: Letouzey et Ané, 1936), vol. 13, col. 417. Deman cites the word from a work of the Jansenist leader Antoine Arnauld.

5. See Deman, cols. 463–70; Louis Vereecke's unpublished lecture notes on the history of moral theology, "Storia della teologia morale moderna" (Rome: Academia Alfonsiana, n.d.), Vol. 2, "Storia della teologia morale in Spagna nel xvio secolo e origine delle 'institutiones morales,'" 77–84; M. W. F. Stone, "Scrupulosity and Conscience: Probabilism in Early Modern Scholastic Ethics," in *Contexts of Conscience in Early Modern Europe, 1500–1700,* ed. Harald E. Braun and Edward Vallance (New York: Palgrave Macmillan, 2004), 6–10; M. W. F. Stone and T. Van Houdt, "Probabilism and Its Methods: Leonardus Lessius and His Contribution to the Development of Jesuit Casuistry," *Ephemerides Theologicae Lovaniensis* 75 (1999), 370–75; Jean Delumeau, *L'aveu et le pardon: Les difficultés de la confession xiii²-xviii² siècle* (Paris: Fayard, 1990), 133–38; Albert R. Jonsen and Stephen Toulmin, *The Abuse of Casuistry: A History of Moral Reasoning* (Berkeley: University of California Press, 1988), 164–67; and John Mahoney, *The Making of Moral Theology: A Study of the Roman Catholic Tradition* (Oxford: University Press, 1987; Oxford: Clarendon Press, 1989), 135–43.

6. Julián Velarde Lombraña, *Juan Caramuel, vida y obra* (Oviedo, Spain: Pentalfa Ediciones, 1989), 200–202, 217–18, 240–44; Alessandro Catalano, "Juan Caramuel Lobkowicz (1606–1682) e la riconquista delle coscienze in Boemia," *Römische historische Mitteilungen* 44 (2002), 339–92; Dino Pastine, *Juan Caramuel: Probabilismo ed enciclopedia* (Florence: La Nuova Italia Editrice, 1975), 94, 101–103.

7. Velarde Lombraña, 255; Pastine, *Probabilismo,* 116.

8. Velarde Lombraña, 263.

9. Velarde Lombraña includes a catalogue of Caramuel's published works and unpublished manuscripts (381–415).

10. Ibid., 376.

11. Liguori, 1:286: "laxorum . . . principe."

12. See Franz Heinrich Reusch, *Der Index der Verbotenen Bücher: Ein Beitrag zur Kirchen- und Literaturgeschichte* (1885; reprint, Aalen: Scientia Verlag, 1967), 2:502.

13. See, for example, the discussion in Delumeau, *L'aveu,* 134–35.

Chapter 1

1. Vereecke, vol. 3, "Storia della teologia morale nel XVII secolo: La crisi della teologia morale," (Rome: Academia Alfonsiana, n.d.), 39.

2. Ibid., 3:42–43. See also Servais Pinckaers, *The Sources of Christian Ethics,* trans. Mary Thomas Noble (Washington, DC: Catholic University of America Press, 1995), 260–66. However, Caramuel did not follow Azor's approach.

3. For a discussion of the various genres, see Albert R. Jonsen and Stephen Toulmin, *The Abuse of Casuistry: A History of Moral Reasoning* (Berkeley: University of California Press, 1988), 139–42, 152–56.

4. See, for example, *Theologia Moralis Fundamentalis* (1652; reprint, St. Louis: Manuscripta, microfilms of rare and out-of-print books, list 37, no. 3), *fund.* II, sect. 5, no. 273 (p. 137); *fund.* 3, nos. 105–67 (pp. 48–80); *fund.* 5, sects. 2–4, nos. 173–176 (pp. 83–84). Subsequent references to this work will use the abbreviation *TMF* and the edition date (1652), (1656), (1675–76). I have not consulted the 1657 edition.

5. See Jean Delumeau, "Prescription and Reality," in *Conscience and Casuistry in Early Modern Europe*, ed. Edmund Leites (Cambridge: Cambridge University Press, 1988), 147.

6. Jonsen and Toulmin, 144.

7. See Heinrich Denziger, *Enchiridion Symbolorum: Definitionum et Declarationum de rebus Fidei et Morum* (hereafter *Enchiridion*), 33rd ed., ed. Adolf Schönmetzer (Freiburg, Germany: Herder, 1965), nos. 1679, 1709 (pp. 394, 402–403). On the discussion at Trent, see John Bossy, "The Social History of Confession in the Age of the Reformation," *Transactions of the Royal Historical Society*, 5th series, no. 25 (1975), 23.

8. *Enchiridion*, no. 1707 (p. 402).

9. See John Mahoney, *The Making of Moral Theology: A Study of the Roman Catholic Tradition* (Oxford: University Press, 1987; Oxford: Clarendon Press, 1989), 22–27; Jonsen and Toulmin, 143, 149–51; Louis Vereecke's unpublished lecture notes on the history of moral theology, "Storia della teologia morale moderna" (Rome: Academia Alfonsiana, n.d.), Vol. 2, "Storia della teologia morale in Spagna nel xvio secolo e origine delle 'institutiones morales,'"113–17; Vereecke 3:41–43, 46–48.

10. See Mahoney, 27–32.

11. See Jean Delumeau, *L'aveu et le pardon: Les difficultés de la confession xiii⁻ xviii⁻ siècle* (Paris: Fayard, 1990), 25–39 for the trajectory of this theme in the late medieval and early modern periods. Cf. Juan Caramuel, *Apologema pro Antiquissima et Universalissima Doctrina de Probabilitate. Contra Novam, Singularem, Improbabilemque D. Prosperi Fagnani Opinionem* (Lyon: Anisson, 1663), 151–52.

12. See M. W. F. Stone, "Scrupulosity and Conscience: Probabilism in Early Modern Scholastic Ethics," in *Contexts of Conscience in Early Modern Europe, 1500–1700,* ed. Harald E. Braun and Edward Vallance (New York: Palgrave Macmillan, 2004), 3–6.

13. See Jonsen and Toulmin, 165; and Th. Deman, "Probabilisme," *Dictionnaire de théologie catholique* (Paris: Letouzey et Ané, 1936), col. 426.

14. See Deman, cols. 422–23.

15. See Deman, cols. 421–30, on the prevalence of this approach in the Middle Ages.

16. See, for example, Dominic Prümmer, *Handbook of Moral Theology*, trans. Gerald Shelton (Cork, Ireland: Mercier Press, 1956), no. 152 (p. 65). Cf. the references to probabiliorism in Mahoney, 136; and Stone, "Scrupulosity," 7, 182, no. 6.

17. Those who endorsed the sufficiency of probable opinion identified various situations in which it did not apply, that is, circumstances that required the agent to follow the more probable or safer opinion. As we shall see, for example, Caramuel argues that a person cannot advocate one probable opinion if he or she has taken a vow to support the opposite view publicly. See *Apologema*, 55: *TMF* (1675–76) (Lyon: Anisson), *fund.* 11, no. 436 (p. 150). The casuistry of exceptions to the general rule authorizing appeal to probable opinion developed over time. See Jonsen and Toulmin, 170–71.

18. Notice, for example, Caramuel's favorite argument about the claim that the opinion of one doctor can render an opinion probable. Caramuel often points out that this claim is supported by more doctors, and thus is extrinsically more probable, than the opposite view. Hence, if the more probable opinion is actually binding, his opponents ought to adopt his position on the grounds of its authoritative support. This suggests that he believes that they are arguing for adherence to the more probable opinion, whether it favors law or liberty. See the *Dialexis de Non-Certitudine* (hereafter *DNC*) (Lyon: Anisson, 1675), "Dialexis," part 1, no. 292 (p. 117). Explanation of complex structure of this volume appears in chap. 6, note 1.

19. See Vereecke, 2:78; Deman, cols. 463–70; M. W. F. Stone and T. Van Houdt, "Probabilism and Its Methods: Leonardus Lessius and His Contribution to the Development of Jesuit Casuistry," *Ephemerides Theologicae Lovaniensis* 75 (1999), 371–75; and Mahoney, 135–43. Note, however, Stone's important discussion of the philosophical debates that preceded the development of probabilism in "The Origins of Probabilism in Late Scholastic Moral Thought: A Prolegomenon to Further Study," *Recherches de théologie et philosophie médiévales* 67 (2000): 114–57.

20. "Mihi videtur, quod si est opinio probabilis, licitum est eam sequi licet opposita probabilior sit." *Expositiones in Primam Secundae Divi Thomae*, 19.6, as cited in Stone and Van Houdt, 372; and Deman, col. 466.

21. Stone and Van Houdt, 375.

22. See Stone, 6–15; Stone and Van Houdt, 376–82; and Jonsen and Toulmin, 169–70.

23. See Deman, cols. 483–94.

24. Cited in Deman, col. 561 and Delumeau, *L'aveu*, 148.

25. See Deman, col. 566.

26. See Delumeau, *L'aveu*, 152; Giuseppe Cacciatore, *S. Alfonso de' Liguori e il Giansenismo* (Florence: Libreria Editrice Fiorentina, 1944); Deman, cols. 558, 580–88; Mahoney, 142–43; and Louis Vereecke, vol. 4, "Storia della teologia morale nel xviii secolo: In Italia ed in Germania: Concina e Sant'Alfonso de' Liguori—l'Aufklärung" (Rome: Academia Alfonsiana, n.d.), 112–22, 146–47.

27. See Cacciatore, 56–57; E. Amann, "Laxisme," in *Dictionnaire de théologie catholique* (Paris: Letouzey et Ané), vol. 19, cols. 41–54; Deman, cols. 513–23; Jonsen and Toulmin, 231–49; and Vereecke, 3:66–69, 87–91, 95–101, 135–46.

28. See Deman, cols. 501–9; 523–30; 537–47; Mahoney, 141–42; Marvin O'Connell, *Blaise Pascal: Reasons of the Heart* (Grand Rapids, MI: Eerdmans, 1997), 124–25, 139–40, 143, 153, 156; and Nigel Abercrombie, *The Origins of Jansenism* (Oxford: Clarendon Press, 1936), 210, 253–54.

29. See Dino Pastine, *Juan Caramuel: Probabilismo ed enciclopedia* (Florence: La Nuova Italia Editrice, 1975), 315–16, 318–19; and Julián Velarde Lombraña, *Juan Caramuel, vida y obra* (Oviedo, Spain: Pentalfa Ediciones, 1989), 328.

30. See Amann, cols. 41–42; Delumeau, *L'aveu*, 123, 143–44; and Vereecke, 3:148–60.

31. See Pastine, *Probabilismo*, 30–32, 35–37; Velarde Lombraña, 9–17, 212; and Vereecke, 2:78.

32. See Pastine, *Probabilismo*, 37–38.

33. *TMF* (1652), *fund.* 11, sect. 4, no. 271 (p. 136): "magno Viro." See Velarde Lombraña, 16.

34. Cf. Pastine, *Probabilismo*, 45; and Velarde Lombraña, 22, in reference to the date of Caramuel's early activities in Louvain (i.e., 1635 vs. 1632).

35. See Velarde Lombraña, 30, 32, 33; Pastine, *Probabilismo*, 50, 52–53: and Lucien Ceyssens, "Autour de Caramuel," *Bulletin de l'Institut historique belge de Rome* 33 (1961), 350.

36. See Claeys Bouuaert, *L'ancienne université de Louvain: Études et documents* (Louvain: Publications universitaires de Louvain, 1956), 128–154.

37. Cited in Bouuaert, *L'ancienne*, 153: "la chrétienté est divisée en 2 camps: la compagnie et les universités." Note that the University sent Cornelius Jansen, who had represented its interests at the Court of Madrid, to solicit the assistance of the Spanish universities against Jesuit pretensions (152). See also Jean Orcibal, "Un grand universitaire malgré lui: C. Jansénius d'Ypres," in *Facultas S. Theologiae Lovaniensis 1432–1797*, ed. J. M. Van Eijl (Leuven: University Press, 1977), 358–59.

38. On Baius, see Abercrombie, 87–92; and Lucien Ceyssens, "Les débuts du jansénisme et de l'antijansénisme à Louvain," in *Facultas S. Theologiae Lovaniensis 1432–1797*, ed. J. M. Van Eijl (Leuven: University Press, 1977), 385–86. Ceyssens notes that Baius's defense by his colleagues prompted a second condemnation in 1580 (386); on Lessius, see Bouuaert, *L'ancienne*, 131: "diamétralement opposée"; Ceyssens, "Les débuts," 386–87, 393.

39. Bouuaert, *L'ancienne*, 132.

40. See Cacciatore, 53–56; Abercrombie, 93. The chief proponents of the opposed positions were Molina and Bañez.

41. See Ceyssens, "Les débuts," 388–89, 395–96: *Enchiridion*, no. 1997 (p. 443).

42. See Ceyssens, "Autour," 352; Pastine, *Probabilismo*, 38, 52–53.

43. See the discussion of memorandum addressed to the privy council from the University cited in Bouuaert, *L'ancienne*, 147. See also Amann, col. 42.

44. Hugo Hurter *Nomenclator Literarius Theologicae Catholicae*, 3rd ed. (1910; reprint, New York, Burt Franklin, n.d.), vol. 4, col. 605: "Cum Liberto Fromond, ecclesiae s. Petri decano, de tute amplexanda opinionum probabilitate disputavit . . ." On Froidmont, see also Bouuaert, *L'ancienne*, 156; Orcibal, 351, 363, 371; and Ceyssens, "Les débuts," 390–91, 398, 413 no. 139, 414–17, 418, 425, 427, 428–30.

45. *Theologia Regularis: Hoc est in SS. Basili, Augustini, Benedicti, Francisci, &c Regulas Commentarii* (hereafter *TR*) (Frankfurt: Schonwetter, 1646), *disp.* 6, art. 3, nos. 59–64 (pp. 26–27). Note that this is a revised edition of a work originally published in 1638. Caramuel's *In Divi Benedicti Regulam* follows the same pattern: see *In D. Benedicti Regulam Commentarius Historicus Scholasticus Moralis Iudicialis Politicus* (hereafter *BR*) (Bruges, Belgium: Breyghels, 1640), *disp.* 6, art. 3, nos. 60–64 (pp. 27–29). For explicit references to Froidmont regarding this argument, cf. *Apologema*, 29, 63.

46. *Apologema*, 63.

47. See the chronological list in Velarde Lombraña, 381–83.

48. On Jansen's career at Louvain, see particularly Orcibal, 353, 354, 360, 366, 367.

49. See Orcibal, 366–68; Cacciatore, 56–59; Ceyssens, "Les debuts," 389–91; and Velarde Lombraña, 37–38. On the circumstances surrounding the publication in Belgium, see Ceyssens, 395–405. The book's distribution in France came in the following year. See Amann, col. 42; and Abercrombie, 193.

50. O'Connell asserts that the bull "contented itself with renewing the condemnation of Baius and complaining that any publication on the subject of grace and freedom contravened the strictures imposed by Paul V" (124).

51. *Const. "Cum occasione,"* issued May 31, 1653: "Aliqua Dei praecepta hominibus iustis volentibus et conantibus, secundum praesentes quas habent vires, sunt impossibilia; deest quoque illis gratia, qua possibilia fiant." In *Enchiridion*, no. 2001 (p. 445). See Cacciatore, 89; and O'Connell, 125.

52. As previously noted, Jansen had been involved in both. See Abercrombie, 125–26; Orcibal, 358–59; Bouuaert, *L'ancienne*, 144, 151–52; and Ceyssens, "Les debuts," 389.

53. See Abercrombie, 196.

54. See *TMF* (1652), *fund.* 46, sect. 2, no. 1035 (p. 467). See also Ceyssens "Autour," 336–37; Pastine, *Probabilismo*, 57; and Velarde Lombraña, 39.

55. Pastine, *Probabilismo*, 57–58; Velarde Lombraña, 39.

56. See Pastine, *Probabilismo*, 69; Velarde Lombraña, 44–79.

57. Pastine, *Probabilismo*, 72, 74; Velarde Lombraña, 114, 175–78.

58. Ceyssens, "Autour," 344, n. 3: "reformatione magna," "nimis reformati."

59. Pastine, *Probabilismo*, 75, 79–82; Velarde Lombraña, 114–15, 181–82.

60. This was the *Theologia Moralis* (not to be confused with his *TMF*), published in 1645. See Pastine, *Probabilismo*, 86, 88.

61. This was apparently in 1646 or 1647. See Pastine, *Probabilismo*, 94; Velarde Lombraña, 200–201.

62. Ernestus de Eusebiis [pseud.], *Judicium Theologicum super Quaestione, An Pax, Qualem Desiderant Protestantes Sit secundum Se Illicita?* (Ecclesiopolis: ad Insigne pietatis, 1648).

63. Pastine, *Probabilismo*, 95–96: Velarde Lombraña. 202–209.

64. Ceyssens, "Autour," 385. See Pastine, *Probabilismo*, 99–100; and Velarde Lombraña, 209–10.

65. "Egli era mio amico prima . . ." Cited in Ceyssens, "Autour," 386. See also Pastine, *Probabilismo*, 100; Velarde Lombraña, 210; and Alessandro Catalano, "Juan Caramuel Lobkowicz (1606–1682) e la riconquista delle coscienze in Boemia," *Römische historische Mitteilungen* 44 (2002), 347–48.

66. Ceyssens, "Autour," 388. See also Velarde Lombraña, 210.

67. For the text of Caramuel's letter, see Walter Friedensburg, "Regesten zur Deutschen Geschichte aus der Zeit des Pontifikats Innocenz X (1644–1655)," *Quellen und Forschungen aus italienischen Archiven und Bibliotheken* (1904), 169–72. On the circumstances behind it, see Catalano, 348–49.

68. Friedensberg, 171: "puto nihil in toto illo opere esse quod non sit probabile."

69. See *TMF* (1652), *fund.* II, sects. 7–8, nos. 275–77 (pp. 137–38).

70. Pastine, *Probabilismo*, 102–3; Velarde Lombraña, 240–42.

71. Pastine, *Probabilismo*, 109: "uno dei più significativi trattati seicenteschi sull'argomento."

72. Ibid., 113–15. See also Velarde Lombraña, 248–52.

73. Catalano, 370–82.

74. Pastine, *Probabilismo*, 113–15; Velarde Lombraña, 248–49, 251. On Caramuel's earlier trip to Rome in 1654, see Velarde Lombraña, 249, no. 152.

75. Velarde Lombraña, 255.

76. Ibid., 215–16, 263–64, 267.

77. Pastine, *Probabilismo*, 116–17; Velarde Lombraña, 263.

78. Pastine, *Probabilismo*, 120–21; Velarde Lombraña, 272, 278.

79. "Io credeva che il papa mi avesse vescovo ed ora trovo che mi ha fatto Auditore di Ruota." Cited in Pastine, *Probabilismo*, 122 and Velarde Lombraña, 280.

80. Cf. Ceyssens' interpretation ("Autour," 349–50) with the judgments of Pastine (*Probabilismo*, 120–23) and Velarde Lombraña (268–72).

81. Ceyssens, "Autour," 403–4. The document does not include a list of the propositions themselves.

82. For example, number 3 clearly refers to the reading of prohibited books; and number 4, to abstinence from meat.

83. Ceyssens, "Autour," 401–2.

84. *TMF* (1656) (Rome: B. Diversini, 1656): "*plurimis sententiis extremis laxis.*"

85. See Velarde Lombraña, who notes that this work is a response to the 1652 edition (271).

86. Ibid., 271, 328.

87. *Apologema,* 17: "Iansenistarum Princeps"; see also Velarde Lombraña, 34; Ceyssens, "Autour," 340; and Pastine, *Probabilismo,* 110.

88. *Apologema,* 17; Velarde Lombraña, 34, 244, 246.

89. *Apologema,* 14, 183. See also Velarde Lombraña, 245, 250.

90. In June of 1656, for example, the new vicar general of Mechlin wrote to the dean of the theological faculty at Louvain, requesting his help in an appeal to Rome. This letter, cited in Ceyssens ("Autour," 406–10), provides a history of the quarrel from the archdiocesan perspective. Cf. Velarde Lombraña, 250–52, 328.

91. One of the most noteworthy was the work of Irishman John Sinnigh, another student (and later professor) at Louvain who prepared the index for the *Augustinus* and played an important role in its defense. See Claeys Bouuaert, "Jean Sinnich: Professeur à Louvain et un des premiers défenseurs de Jansenius (1603–1666)," *Ephemerides Theologicae Lovanienses* 31 (1955), 406–17. Sinnigh's *Saul ExRex . . .* (Louvain, 1662) apparently attacked both Caramuel and Tamburini. See Velarde Lombraña, 248, 270, 328; Pastine, *Probabilismo,* 131–32.

92. See Velarde Lombraña, 249, 250, 251, 252.

93. In January of 1654, Chigi wrote to Caramuel to ask him for demonstration that the five condemned propositions reflected the thought of the *Augustinus* (Velarde Lombraña, 246–47). The decision of the Congregation's assessor regarding Caramuel's works was issued in September of that year (Ceyssens, "Autour," 403).

94. See Deman, cols. 502–3.

95. Ibid., col. 509.

96. In addition to Martínez de Prado, for example, these included Baron, Gonet, and Mercorus. See Deman, cols. 504–6.

97. Jonsen and Toulmin, 235; Amann, col. 46.

98. O'Connell, 124–128; Abercrombie, 235–44, 248–52.

99. The letters were published between January of 1656 and May of the following year. See Jonsen and Toulmin, 234–35; and O'Connell, 128–33, 137–48, 152–53.

100. Jonsen and Toulmin, 237.

101. Abercrombie, 252; O'Connell, 129; Jonsen and Toulmin, 235, 243–49.

102. See Jonsen and Toulmin, 248; however, Caramuel suffered more direct attacks in Pierre Nicole's notes to the Latin translation (Pastine, *Probabilismo,* 131).

103. See *Enchiridion,* no. 2070 (p. 455). For an explanation of the differences between attrition and contrition, and the significance of this distinction for Jansenism, see Delumeau, *L'aveu,* 57–78.

104. See *Enchiridion,* nos. 2090–95 (pp. 456–57).

105. See Pastine, *Probabilismo*, 133.

106. See Velarde Lombraña, 281, 286, 292, 326–27.

107. Ibid., 328, 330, 332.

108. Franz Heinrich Reusch, *Der Index der Verbotenen Bücher: Ein Beitrag zur Kirchen- und Literaturgeschichte* (1885; reprint, Aalen: Scientia Verlag, 1967), 2:502. Cf. *Apologema, 6.*

109. Velarde Lombraña, 332.

110. See Pastine, *Probabilismo*, 135.

111. See Velarde Lombraña, 295, 311.

112. See Pastine, *Probabilismo*, 135–36; Velarde Lombraña, 284–86, 288; and Maurizio Torrini, "Monsignor Juan Caramuel e l'Accademia napoletano degli Investiganti," in *Le meraviglie del probabile: Juan Caramuel 1606–1682: Atti del convegno internazionale di studi* (hereafter, *Le meraviglie*), ed. Paolo Pissavino (Vigevano: Commune di Vigevano, 1990), 29–33.

113. For a list of his publications during this period, see Velarde Lombraña, 386–87.

114. Pastine, *Probabilismo*, 139, 141; Velarde Lombraña. 326.

115. Pastine, *Probabilismo*, 143; Velarde Lombraña, 346–58.

116. See Pastine, *Probabilismo*, 144: Velarde Lombraña, 360. It is unclear to me whether the *Dialexis* ever circulated independently of the *TMF* (1675–76).

117. Velarde Lombraña, 371, 374. His last new book appeared in 1681, the year in which he also became completely blind.

118. Vereecke, 3:61; cf. Velarde Lombraña, who agrees in reference to the first group, but lists propositions 49 and 50 from the second group (332, 361).

119. *Enchiridion*, nos. 2044, 2045, 2054, 2055 (pp. 453, 454); nos. 2135, 2141, 2148, 2149, 2150 (pp. 461–64).

120. See, for example, *Enchiridion*, no. 2045 (p. 453).

121. For example, *Enchiridion*, nos. 2054, 2055 (p. 454).

122. I will cite the 1675–76 edition because it is the last; however, these arguments also appear in earlier editions.

123. *Enchiridion*, no. 2149 (p. 464): "saepe esset bona et aliquando obligatoria sub mortali." Note, however, that the *Enchiridion*'s notes identify the source as the Louvain censures, reflecting Caramuel's *Theologia Moralis* (1645) and *Theologia Intentionalis*, neither of which I have been able to consult.

124. *TMF* (1675–76), *fund.* 57, *q.* 6, art. 2, no. 2659 (*sic*, 2669) (p. 847): "esse mortaliter peccaminosam Doctores universi tenemus." The treatment here is identical to the discussion in *TMF* (1652), *fund.* 57, *q. incidens*, no. 1186 (p. 577).

125. *TMF* (1675–76), *fund.* 57, *q.* 3, no. 2654 (p. 841): "Si dicantur naturales actiones secundum se consideratae, nec bonae nec malae esse, & tota earundem malitia ab interdictione pendere, quod Scoto placuit, & hodie a doctissimis Viris defenditur, cessabit quaestio." Again, the citation in the 1652 version is identical, although the later version develops the arguments more extensively.

126. *Enchiridion,* no. 2148 (p. 463): "Tam clarum videtur, fornicationem secundum se nullam involvere malitiam, et solum esse malam, quia interdicta, ut contrarium omnino rationi dissonum videatur."

127. *TMF* (1675–76), *fund.* 56, *q.* 2, no. 2645 (p. 834): "Non inquiris, *An simplex fornicatio sit peccatum?* hoc enim a Deo, & Ecclesia doceris: sed inquiris tantummodo rationem illam fundamentalem, ob quam illa peccatum sit."

128. Ibid. Cf. the similar, but not identical description in *TMF* (1652), *fund.* 56, sect. 3, no. 1171 (p. 566).

129. *TMF* (1675–76), *fund.* 56, *q.* 2, no. 2645 (p. 835): "S. Thomam veneror."

130. Ibid.: "Et quarenti, Cur interdicta sit, dicam, . . . quia inter alia inconvenientia illegitimam & dissentaneam prolis educationem infert."

131. The major difference between the 1652 and 1675–76 versions is that, in the former, Caramuel makes no effort to answer his objections to the Thomist argument. Moreover, in the earlier version, Caramuel does express a hesitation (on strictly rational grounds) to call Thomas's opinion probable (though he acknowledges it as such, presumably by reason of Thomas's authority), precisely because of the objections against it. See *fund.* 56, sect. 3, no. 1171 (p. 566).

132. The footnotes to the *Enchiridion* cite two sources that I have been unable to consult: the original *Theologia Moralis* (1645) and the *Theologia Intentionalis* (1664). See *Enchiridion,* no. 2148, no. 1 (p. 463).

133. *Enchiridion* no. 2150 (p. 464): "Copula cum coniugata, consentiente marito, non est adulterium; adeoque sufficit in confessione dicere, se esse fornicatum."

134. *Apologema* 18: "Haec Theologis imponitur ex Epistola Archiepiscopi Mechliniensis Iansenistae. Producat ergo Theologos, qui hanc absurditatem delirant . . . Dixerunt Theologi in casu, maritum non posse . . . uxorem occidere, non posse accusare, non posse satisfactionem petere: at illos non committere adulterium, nec violare Decalogum, nemo dixit."

135. Amann, col. 70.

136. Pastine, *Probabilismo,* 145; Velarde Lombraña, 361. For background on the mission to Rome, see Claeys Bouuaert, "Précisions sur l'histoire de la députation envoyée à Rome, en 1677–1679, par la faculté de théologie de Louvain," *Revue d'histoire ecclésiastique* 56 (1961), 872–78.

137. Pastine, *Probabilismo,* 151; Velarde Lombraña, 376–77.

138. *Apologema,* 209: "Quidquid Caramuel docet, bene docet./Quidquid Caramuel dicit probabile, est probabile./Si alii aliter sentiunt, vel non legerunt, vel non penetrarunt Fundamenta Caramuelis." See Velarde Lombraña, 362–63.

139. Cited in Mahoney, 27.

140. *Rationalis et Realis Philosophia* (hereafter *RR*) (Louvain: Everard di Witte, 1642), *disp.* 18, no. 432 (p. 62): "Media hyeme sub luce maligna pervenis ad locum difficilem quem transire non audes, venit ex alia parte Petrus face lucidissima instructus. Presentia ipsius locum illuminat, & tollit omnes difficultates.

Transis, transit: nec quia luce illius uteris, illum sequeris, sed peragis iter contrarium. Sic saepe contingit nobis philosophantibus. Venimus ad locum obscurum & difficilem: invocantur Zeno, Plato, Aristoteles; eorum doctrina fax est illustrissima quae fugat tenebras; transimus securissimi, non tamen ideo lucem sequimur sed alio pergimus . . ." See also Velarde Lombraña, 82–83.

141. See, for example, *RR, disp.* 18, nos. 424–31 (pp. 59–62).

142. For Caramuel's general statement on the *iuniores,* see *TMF* (1652), *fund.* 8, nos. 197–99 (pp. 95–97).

143. *TMF* (1652), *fund.* 10, no. 204 (p. 98): "cognosco Homines eruditos, qui non audebunt dicere solem esse lucidum, nivem albam, picem nigram, ignem calidum, nisi alicuius veteris Philosophi testimonio iuventur." See also Velarde Lombraña, 290, 292.

144. *TMF* (1652), *fund.* 11, sect. 5, no. 273 (p. 137).

145. See Jean Robert Armogathe, "Probabilisme et Libre-Arbitre: La théologie morale de Caramuel y Lobkowitz," in *Le meraviglie del probabile: Juan Caramuel 1606–1682: Atti del convegno internazionale di studi* (hereafter, *Le meravigle*), ed. Paolo Pissavino (Vigevano: Commune di Vigevano, 1990), 37.

146. *TMF* (1652), *fund.* 17, *q.* 1, no. 436 (p. 188): " . . . qui nescit quid Calvinus aut Lutherus dicat . . . dicitur imperitus." Note that this is an area in which the later editions are significantly different from the original. Cf. *TMF* (1675–76), *fund.* 17, *q.* 3, no. 639 (p. 219). Evidently, this was one of the areas that aroused complaints against the first edition. See Ceyssens, "Autour," 403 (*Ad* 3).

147. Preface, no. 3: "à l'Antiquité, aux traditions des Saints & aux vieilles coutumes de l'Eglise," in *Oeuvres de messire Antoine Arnauld* (1779; reprint, Brussels: Culture et Civilisation, 1967), 27:75–76. See Armogathe, 36.

148. Prospero Fagnani, *Commentaria in Primum Librum Decretalium,* . . . (Venice: Paul Balleonius, 1709), nos. 60–69 (pp. 35–36).

149. See Velarde Lombraña, 160–61, 168, 314, 363–64.

150. I.e., *Sacri Romani Imperii Pacis Licitae Demonstratae, Variis Olim Consiliis Agitatae,* . . . (hereafter *PL*) (Frankfurt: Schönwetter, 1648), "Pax Licita," no. 237 (p. 165). See chapter 3, note 11 for an explanation of the structure of this work.

151. On Diana, see Jonsen and Toulmin, 156.

152. *Coordinati, seu Omnium Resolutionum Moralium* . . . , rev. ed. (1728; reprint, St. Louis: Manuscripta, list 97, reels 16–17), vol. 8, *tract.* 1. (pp. 1–18). Diana does, however, discuss the "single author" question (see *resol.* 14, p. 7).

153. See, for example, *BR, disp.* 6, art. 3, sects. 1, 7, nos. 60, 69 (pp. 27–28, 30); and *TMF* (1652), *fund.* 11, sect. 2, no. 270 (pp. 135–36).

154. For their dates, see Vereecke 3:59–65.

155. *TMF* (1652), *Ep.* 1, p. 757 (*sic* 755): "ab amicis monitus, sciam quid retinere debeam, quid alterare, quid firmare."

156. Ibid., *Ep.* to Diana, no. 8 (p. 25): "semper dico quod sentio: & si hodie videro lapsum hesternum, non illum proterve defendam, sed potius confidenter expungam."

157. Ibid., no. 7 (p. 23): "hoc est sinceritatem ut sex: veracitatem enim imprudentiam appellant." See Velarde Lombraña, 211. The opponent in question was
Adam Adami.

158. Consider, for example, his claim that "more benign [opinions] . . . *per accidens* are always more useful and more secure [*Benigniores . . . per accidens sunt
semper utiliores & securiores*]." The crucial element in this definition is *per accidens*. Caramuel argues that less stringent opinions are safer in practice because
people are more likely to follow them than their strict counterparts. One needs
to read the argument in its entirety to discover this, however. See *TMF* (1652),
fund. 11, sect. 2, no. 268 (pp. 134–35).

Chapter 2

1. Juan Caramuel, *Apologema pro Antiquissima et Universalissima Doctrina de
Probabilitate. Contra Novam, Singularem, Improbabilemque D. Prosperi Fagnani
Opinationem* (Lyon: Anisson, 1663), 63: "*Probabilitatum usus est res nova. Non
potest non condemnari apud Deum, qui relinquens viam tutam, insistit opinioni
probabili. Opiniones, quae dicuntur aut sunt probabiles apud nos, non erunt probabiles apud Deum.*"

2. The actual date of publication for the first edition of the *Theologia Regularis* was 1638. See Julián Velarde Lombraña, *Juan Caramuel, vida y obra* (Oviedo,
Spain: Pentalfa Ediciones, 1989), 382; Dino Pastine, *Juan Caramuel: Probabilismo ed enciclopedia* (Florence: La Nuova Italia Editrice, 1975), 53; *Apologema*,
63: "Ego impugnavi in *Theologia Regulari*, quam anno 1639. Brugis edidi . . .
uberius fortiusque in secunda & tertia eiusdem Operis editione."

3. *In D. Benedicti Regulam Commentarius Historicus Scholasticus Moralis Iudicialis Politicus* (hereafter *BR*) (Bruges, Belgium: Breyghels, 1640), disp. 6, art.
2, no. 57 (p. 26): "Est communis omnium Doctorum resolutio, quae asserit non
posse judicari temerarios & imprudentes qui operantur secundum opinionem
probabilem."

4. Ibid., no. 59 (p. 27): "communem Theologorum sententiam."

5. Ibid., art. 3, sect. 7, no. 69 (p. 30); sect. 1, no. 60 (p. 27).

6. Admittedly, the *Theologia Regularis* provides the earliest example of a tract
on probabilism. However, Caramuel tells us that he expanded the discussion in later
editions. Comparison of the *Benedicti Regulam* (which appeared two years after the
first edition of the *Regularis*) with the 1646 edition of the *Regularis* reveals that the
two are quite similar: in fact, the two texts are identical at many points. I have chosen
to use the *Benedicti Regulam* because Caramuel himself quotes it in the *TMF*
(1652), and because the *Regularis* contains some misprints that are not present
in the *Benedicti Regulam*. Accordingly, the present discussion will focus on the
Benedicti Regulam with occasional supplements from the *Regularis* (1646).

7. *Dialexis de Non-Certitudine* (hereafter *DNC*) (Lyon: Anisson, 1675), part 2, no. 302 (p. 120).

8. *Disputatio* 6 ("De opinioni probabili"), in fact, is preceded by a disputation on the intrinsic/extrinsic qualities of law.

9. *BR, disp. 6*, intro. no. 51 (p. 23): "non simus Angeli, sed homines."

10. Ibid.: "solidissima certissimaque fundamenta."

11. Ibid., art. 1, no. 52 (p. 23): "Doctorum authoritatibus & testimoniis."

12. Ibid. (pp. 23–24): "antagonistas torqueant"; "objectis satisfaciant"; "hostium objectis satisfaciant."

13. *Theologia Moralis Fundamentalis* (1652; reprint, St. Louis: Manuscripta, microfilms of rare and out-of-print books, list 37, no. 3), (intro), "Theologia Moralis Fundamenta," no. 40 (no page number): *"Fundamenta, quibus nostra Consilia & Resolutiones substruximus."* See the "Synopsis totius operis" that appears on the following page for an outline of the work as a whole.

14. *TMF, fund.* 11, sect. 1, no. 267 (p. 134): "locum non habet."

15. Ibid., sect. 1, no. 267 (p. 134); sect. 4, no. 271 (p. 136).

16. Ibid., sect. 4, no. 271 (p. 136).

17. This is my own formulation; Caramuel does not state this explicitly.

18. See *DNC,* "Quaestio," art. 1, no. 2 (no page number).

19. *TMF* (1652*), fund.* 11, sect. 4, nos. 271–72 (p. 136).

20. Ibid., sect. 4 (*sic* 5?), no. 273 (p. 137): "Similiter agitur in Theologia Morali, multae sunt hodie opiniones probabiles, quae heri tales non visae; & multae heri judicatae probabiles, quae re hodie melius examinata transiverunt in certas: videlicet aut certo falsas, aut certo versas."

21. Ibid., sect. 4, no. 272 (pp. 136–37).

22. *BR, disp.* 6, art. 1, no. 52 (p. 23): "De intrinseca probabilitate ne sunto judices, qui Theologiam non docti."

23. *TMF* (1652), *fund.* 11, sect. 4, no. 271 (p. 136): *"Viro indocto aut etiam non satis in aliqua facultate erudito, nulla illius facultatis opinio, est ab intrinseco probabilis, aut improbabilis."*

24. *BR, disp.* 6, art. 1, no. 53 (p. 24): "moraliter loquendo securior."

25. Ibid: "Aliquando vidi defendi Compluti, quatuor Doctorum opinionem esse probabilem."

26. Ibid.

27. Ibid. See also no. 56 (p. 26).

28. Ibid., no. 56 (p. 26): "omnes Doctores . . . moraliter aequales esse; ac ideo qui pondus rationum non percallent, possunt securissime confidere numero authorum."

29. Ibid.: "Verum istae non sunt supputationes metaphysicae, sed mere-morales, sufficientes tamen ad securitatem conscientiae."

30. Ibid., no. 53 (p. 24): "ex meis principiis authores non sunt reducendi ad computum arithmeticum, sed ad geometricam analogiam."

31. Ibid.

32. The reason for this claim is the presumption that the more recent author has discovered something hidden from his predecessors (no. 55, p. 25).

33. *TMF* (1652), *fund.* 11, sect. 6, no. 274 (p. 137).

34. On Manrique (or Manríquez), see Pastine, *Probabilismo*, 38; and Velarde Lombraña, 16.

35. *TMF* (1652), *fund.* 11, sect. 4, no. 271 (p. 136): "*ab annis triginta doceo, & habeo mei ingenii experientiam publico testimonio firmatam; & tamen hanc opinionem non intelligo . . . ergo sive sit D. Thomae, sive alterius, mihi ab intrinseco est improbabilis.*" (The ellipsis in this citation contains Caramuel's own interpolated identification of the philosophical argument to which his teacher was referring.)

36. *BR, disp.* 6, art. 2, no. 59 (p. 27): "tenemur sequi probabiliorem opinionem. Atqui sententia illa quae docet sufficere minus-probabilem, est probabilior: ergo tenemur asserere & sentire non peccare eos qui sequuntur partem minus probabilem."

37. Ibid.: "solidiora fundamenta, atque rationes nobiliores"; "multo majori numero authores." See *TMF* (1652*), fund.* 11, sect. 3 (p. 136). Here Caramuel remarks that he regards this position as morally certain.

38. Cf. *Apologema*, 15–16, 186–87.

39. See *TMF* (1652), *fund.* 11, sect. 2, nos. 268 (p. 134–35).

40. Caramuel attributes the first position to Navarrus (i.e., Azpilcueta) and the second to Diana. See *TMF* (1652), *Ep.* to Diana, no. 7 (p. 24).

41. Again, Caramuel does believe that there are limits to the freedom to use probable opinions. Presumably, for example, he would hold that a person who had taken a vow to follow the stricter view would not be free to adopt the opposite opinion.

42. *TMF* (1652), sect. 2, no. 268 (p. 134).: "quis spondebit mihi, me sine distractione Horas Canonicas recitaturum? Ergo praevideo periculum, non ortum ab opinione severiore, sed a propria fragilitate; periculum tamen quod severiorem opinionem comitatur, & adesse benigniori non potest. Ergo benignior, esti supponatur esse minus probabilis, est securior & tutior."

43. *BR, disp.* 6, art. 3, sect. 7, no. 72 (p. 30): "Est ruina religionis fingere obligationes ubi non sunt."

44. Ibid., no. 69 (p. 30).

45. Ibid., sect. 4, no. 66 (p. 29): "communiter in talibus casibus reperiuntur."

46. Ibid.

47. *Theologia Regularis: Hoc est in SS. Basili, Augustini, Benedicti, Francisci, &c Regulas Commentarii* (hereafter *TR*) (Frankfurt: Schonwetter, 1646), *disp.* 6, art. 3, sect. 4, no. 66 (p. 27): "*Ab eo tempore quo Ioannis Sancii, Dianae, & Caramuelis opera evulgata, Praelati non sumus Praelati.*"

48. Ibid: "vel est posse jubere dispotice, bona mala, obligatoria non obligatoria, apta inepta, utilia nociva, & hoc pro abitrio: aut est posse facere ut subditi satisfaciant suis obligationibus.

Si existimes Praelati authoritatem consistere in eo quod possit cogere subditos, ut faciant etiam illa quae mala, nociva, perniciosa, aut ut verbo dicam, illa ad quae non tenentur, Praelatum cum Tyranno confundis."

49. Jean Delumeau, *L'aveu et le pardon: Les difficultés de la confession xiiie-xviiie siècle* (Paris: Fayard, 1990), 25: "De saint Thomas d'Aquin à saint Alphonse de Liguori, nombreux furent les conseils de bienveillance donnés aux confesseurs par des directeurs de conscience qui savaient d'expérience ce dont ils parlaient."

50. *TMF* (1652), *cap.* 6, prologue, no. 1029 (p. 463): "'*Iugum meum suave est, & onus meum leve,*' dixit Dominus; ubi *Iugi* nomine Decalogum, & *Oneris* nomine reliqua praecepta intellexit: at illum & haec hodie multi tam severe, aut etiam crudeliter interpretantur, ut vel debeant ab orbe literario proscribi; aut debeamus fateri jugum Dei amarissimum esse, & onus ejus gravissimum, & insupportabile. Hanc ego ob causam sumo calamum, ut ostendam hic semper & ubicunque etiam sententias veras anteponendas falsis, seu videantur benignae, seu severae." Cf. Delumeau, *L'aveu*, 134–35.

51. See Delumeau, *L'aveu*, 79–90.

52. *BR, disp.* 6, art. 3, sect. 1, no. 60 (p. 27).

53. *Apologema*, 29, 63.

54. *BR, disp.* 6, art. 3, sect. 2, no. 61 (p. 28): "viam tutam." The reference to probable opinion as "safer" concerns the benign opinions that are safer *per accidens*.

55. Ibid.: "te liberet a culpa veniali aut mortali, si juxta illam exacte operis."

56. Ibid.: art. 3, sect. 1, no. 60 (p. 27): "*O felix Ecclesia primitiva quae non laborabat tot Doctorum sententiis!*"

57. Ibid. As an illustration, Caramuel mentions Dionysius the Areopagite's interpretation of a gospel passage.

58. Ibid., (pp. 27–28): "Dicere quod probabiles opiniones sint labores atque morbi Ecclesiae militantis, est error manifestus; sunt enim indices facilioris excellentiorisque salutis. Non inde Ecclesia infelix, quod Doctores opinentur passim, sed & inde felicior, quod benignius & facilius suos possit Lauream empyream promovere. Damnarentur plurimi, quos sententiae probabilitas salvat. Ergo & inde Ecclesia Catholica felicior debet dici, quod exuberet sanctissimis & doctissimis viris, qui introduxerunt benignas opiniones." I have chosen to translate *salutis* as *salvation* rather than *health*, because one does not speak of *easier health* in English. However, the reader should note the juxtaposition of the claim that probable opinions represent a disease of the Church on earth, with the contention that such opinions are a sign of that Church's health.

59. *BR, disp.* 2, art. 2, no. 21 (p. 10): "nego autem posse moralem malitiam intelligi sine praecepto: unde (seu id possibile sit, seu non) si tollerentur omnes

leges, nihil remaneret quod posset asseri malum moraliter." This appears within Caramuel's discussion of natural law. Cf. *TMF* (1652), *fund.* II, sect. 7, no. 275 (p. 137).

60. See, for example, *BR, disp.* 2, art. 2, no. 22 (p. 10).

61. Caramuel acknowledges that sometimes persons fail to recognize the existence of law through their own negligence. Thus he emphasizes that "ignorantia vincibilis non excusat a culpa" (*BR, disp.* 6, art. 3, sect. 8. no. 75 [p. 31]).

62. *Apologema*, 40–45.

63. *BR, disp.* 6, art. 3, sect. 8, no. 74 (p. 31): "non dependet a futuris Authorum Doctorumve resolutionibus."

64. Ibid.

65. Ibid., art. 3, sect. 3, no. 62 (p. 28): "*non omnes sententiae quae sunt probabiles apud nos, erunt probabiles apud Deum.*"

66. Ibid., no. 63 (p. 28).

67. Ibid.

68. Ibid., no. 64 (p. 29): "revera sit probabilis"; "non sufficere ut excusemur apud Deum."

69. Ibid.: "cum Angelus non sim, sed homo . . ." In the *Apologema* (141–48), Caramuel argues that angels too use probable opinion, but that claim does not appear in the *Benedicti Regulam.*

70. *TR* (1646), *disp.* 6, art. 3, no. 64, (p. 27): "non venerat in mentem meam"; "qui asseret Deum impossibilia jubere, & ignorantiam invincibilem non excusare a peccato."

71. See, for example, *Apologema*, 7–11.

72. See *TMF* (1652), *fund.* II, sects. 1–8, nos. 266–77 (pp. 133–38).

73. Ibid., *Ep.* to Diana, no. 7 (p. 23): "Ingenium Dianae viri quidem doctissimi, veneror: ejus industria multas opiniones evasisse probabiles, quae antea non errant . . . *Si jam sunt probabiles, quae antea non errant; jam non peccant, qui eas sequuntur, licet ante peccaverint.*"

74. Prospero Fagnani, *Commentaria in Primum Librum Decretalium*, . . . (Venice: Paul Balleonius, 1709), no. 332 (p. 70): "Quod si verum est, jam opiniones probabiles sunt supra legem Dei, & naturae."

75. See *Apologema*, 43.

76. See Fagnani, no. 401 (p. 85): "Infelix ergo fuit Ecclesia, quae hujusmodi laboravit ignorantia per quindecim saecula, si nunc dicenda est felix est multitudine opinantium." Cf. *Apologema*, 31.

77. This, of course, is quite distinct from the descriptions of those who have studied Caramuel's views extensively, such as Pastine and Velarde Lombraña.

78. The *Apologema* is listed as appearing on disk 12 of the Garden of Archimedes' series, *Historical Mathematics on CD-rom.* See http://www2.math.unifi.it/~archimede/archimede_inglese/CD_rom/informazioni1.html (accessed June 7, 2005).

79. *TMF,* Manuscripta, list 37, no. 3.

80. Th. Deman, "Probabilisme," *Dictionnaire de théologie catholique* (Paris: Letouzey et Ané, 1936), col. 492: "il n'y a que des opinions, point de certitudes."

81. Ibid., col. 530.

82. Ibid., col. 493: "l'enfant terrible des doctrines nouvelles de la probabilité"; col. 494: "sans le jugement quelque peu derange du personnage."

83. Delumeau, *L'aveu,* 121: "tous les casuists laxistes sur le modèle de Caramuel, personnage remuant, impéteux, . . . , parfois bouffon." Note that these adjectives appear in Deman, cols. 492–93.

84. Albert R. Jonsen and Stephen Toulmin, *The Abuse of Casuistry: A History of Moral Reasoning* (Berkeley: University of California Press, 1988), 156.

85. Notably, Pastine, Velarde Lombraña, and Jean Robert Armogathe, "Probabilisme et Libre-Arbitre: La théologie morale de Caramuel y Lobkowitz," in *Le meraviglie del probabile: Juan Caramuel 1606–1682: Atti del convegno internazionale di studi* (hereafter, *Le meraviglie*), ed. Paolo Pissavino (Vigevano: Commune di Vigevano, 1990).

86. And sometimes Daniel Concina. See Giuseppe Cacciatore, *S. Alfonso de' Liguori e il Giansenismo* (Florence: Libreria Editrice Fiorentina, 1944), 347.

87. James Franklin, *The Science of Conjecture: Evidence and Probability before Pascal* (Baltimore: Johns Hopkins University Press, 2001), 88–94.

88. The reader should compare his or her reading of the *TR* to my own interpretation of the *BR* (recalling that the texts resemble one another closely). See Franklin, pp. 89–91. This exercise should demonstrate that two commentators might come to a very different reading of the same words. Franklin regards Caramuel's references to numbers as prescriptive.

89. Franklin here confuses *TR* with *BR.* The works are distinct, although (virtually) identical discussions of probable opinion appear within each.

90. Franklin, 90.

91. Eligius Bassaeus, *Flores Totius Theologiae Practicae* (Antwerp: 1643), 204. On Bassaeus, see Hugo Hurter *Nomenclator Literarius Theologicae Catholicae,* 3rd ed. (1910; reprint, New York, Burt Franklin, n.d.), 4:305. I am grateful to Brother Anthony Logalbo, O.F.M., of the St. Bonaventure University Library, for confirming the presence of this passage within a later edition of Bassaeus's text.

92. The text appears in the edition of the *TR* that I consulted (i.e., 1646). Franklin seems to have used the 1651 edition (see Franklin 410, n. 91).

93. Many of the innovations of 1656 edition are repeated in the 1675–76 edition. I will cite the passages as they appear in the later edition. *TMF* (1675–76), *fund.* ii, intro. no. 437 (p. 150): "si sit opinio probabilis, secundum quam sine damno (nempe, meo, aut meorum) possum abstinere a damno proximi, illam tenebor sequi."

94. Ibid.: "quae probabiles circumstantias inducat, vi quarum debitum negetur."

95. Ibid. In another example, Caramuel distinguishes the probability of the view that the Virgin Mary might have been conceived with original sin from obligation not to defend such a view publicly (as a result of current Church prohibition). The obligation is certain, although the opposed theological views are both probable.

96. Ibid, sect. 6, no. 44 (p. 154): "Interim quidquid de ista subtilitate sit, tu illam sententiam sequere, quae docet, *quatuor Authorum opinionem esse satis probabilem.*"

97. Ibid., nos. 449–50 (p. 154): "Hic vir indoctus solet esse felicior: quia potest clausis oculis quatuor Scriptoribus credere: at doctus debet esse oculatior: sunt enim Authores, qui numerum non addunt, vel quod exscribunt potius, quam scribunt & cum caeteris saltant, quod non raro contingit: vel iussi hanc vel illam opinionem tuentur: & tunc consideranda est iubentis doctrina & authoritas, ut de probabilitate sententiae iudicemus.

"Iterum vir indoctus solet esse felicior: quia doctus in dubiis rationes & fundamenta debebit examinare: indoctus vero non debebit: laicus enim, qui suum Confessarium, aut aliquem Virum probum & doctum consuluit & interrogat, an haec vel illa sit opinio secura? potest illi credere, & iuxta eius directionem gubernari."

98. Ibid., sect. 9, no. 454 (p. 156): "quoniam contra rationem evidentem suffragia Scriptorum non obtinent."

99. Ibid.: "cessat enim extrinseca probabilitas in eo, qui demonstrationis vires percipit; non autem in illo, qui rationem esse fortem iudicat, at eandem esse certam, evidentem; & indubitatam non iudicat. Quamobrem si Petrus contra Ioannem argumentetur probaturus Ioannis esse sententiam improbabilem, tenebitur dare rationes evidentes & demonstrativas. Et quid, si illas Petrus evidentes affirmet, Ioannes autem graves quidem & fortes, non autem evidentes asserat? debebit Petrus ad Authores recurrere, & ostendere Ioannis sententiam non fulciri Virorum illustrium suffragiis."

Chapter 3

1. See Prospero Fagnani, *Commentaria in Primum Librum Decretalium*, . . . (Venice: Paul Balleonius, 1709), no. 336 (p. 71).

2. Ibid: "Jure ambigi posse, si Religioso mulierem a se turpiter cognitam occidere haud liceat, quando factum vulgat. Caramuel *ibid.* §7, pag. 551."

3. See *Theologia Moralis Fundamentalis* (1652; reprint, St. Louis: Manuscripta, microfilms of rare and out-of-print books, list 37, no. 3), (1652), *fund.* 55, sect. 3, no. 1140 (pp. 542–43).

4. Ibid., sect. 4, no. 1141 (pp. 543–44).

5. See Albert R. Jonsen and Stephen Toulmin, *The Abuse of Casuistry: A History of Moral Reasoning* (Berkeley: University of California Press, 1988), 216–27.

6. *TMF* (1652), *fund.* 55, sect. 6, no. 1149 (p. 549).

7. Ibid., sect. 7, no. 115, p. 551: "Legisti hanc doctinam, & inquiris, *An homo religiosus, qui fragilitati cedens foeminam vilem cognovit, quae honori ducens se prostituisse viro tanto, rem enarrat, & eumdem infamat, possit illam occidere?*"

8. Ibid.: "Tu rem accurate perpende."

9. *TMF* (1675–76), *fund.* 55, art. 6, no. 2590, 2591 (p. 809): "ominino falsum & improbabile"; "Non posse hominem occidere alium ob solius honoris defensionem."

10. Ibid., nos. 2590–91 (pp. 809–10).

11. The structure of the text renders citation difficult. There are three major sections to the work, which I will refer to in the notes as the "Prodromus," "Syndromus," and "Pax Licita." Page numbers begin again with each section. Some sections, but not all, have margin numbers or letters; and the margin numbers in the "Syndromus" begin with 437, suggesting that it was intended to appear after rather than before the "Pax Licita," as it does in my copy. There may well have been variant versions of the text. I will identify the citations by section, margin numbers (if available), and page numbers.

12. Richard S. Dunn, *The Age of Religious Wars, 1559–1715,* 2nd ed. (New York: W. W. Norton, 1979), 89–90.

13. Ibid., 90. Westphalia added toleration for Calvinism, which had been excluded from the Peace of Augsburg. Anabaptists continued to suffer persecution.

14. Ibid., 82–91.

15. See Robert Birely, *The Jesuits and the Thirty Years War: Kings, Courts, and Confessors* (Cambridge: Cambridge University Press, 2003), 249. Note that some earlier settlements with the Protestants had included only temporary concessions (pp. 160–61).

16. I have taken the term *militant* from Birely (248). On the history of Wangnereck's text, see Birely (218, 248–50) and Ludwig Steinberger, *Die Jesuiten und die Friedensfrage in der Zeit von Prager Frieden bis zum Nürnberger Friedensexekutionshauptrezess 1635–1650* (Freiburg: Herdesche, 1906), 63–75.

17. Birely, 249.

18. See Birely, 255–56, 261–62.

19. On the history and contents of the volume, see Birely, 251; Steinberger, 78–84, 125–29; Alessandro Catalano, "Juan Caramuel Lobkowicz (1606–1682) e la riconquista delle coscienze in Boemia," *Römische historische Mitteilungen* 44 (2002), 347–49. The text apparently circulated in manuscript form before it was printed (Catalano, 347). Unfortunately, I have been able to consult only one edition (1648).

20. On the questions from Anselm Casimir, see *Sacri Romani Imperii Pacis Licitae Demonstratae, Variis Olim Consiliis Agitatae,* . . . (hereafter *PL*) (Frankfurt: Schönwetter, 1648), "Syndromus," no. 437 (p. 1). Birely (249) suggests that Casimir (who died in 1647) was, in fact, the "main force" behind the publication of Wangnereck's book.

21. *PL*, "Pax Licita," no. 81 (p. 59): "sub illud tempus Moralem Theologiam non fuisse tam cultam, quam nunc; nec opinionum probabilium vim tam bene examinatam."

22. Cf. *In D. Benedicti Regulam Commentarius Historicus Scholasticus Moralis Iudicialis Politicus* (hereafter *BR*) (Bruges, Belgium: Breyghels, 1640), *disp.* 6, art. 3, sect. 1, no. 60 (p. 27); and Juan Caramuel, *Apologema pro Antiquissima et Universalissima Doctrina de Probabilitate. Contra Novam, Singularem, Improbabilemque D. Prosperi Fagnani Opinationem* (Lyon: Anisson, 1663), 97.

23. See *Apologema*, 106.

24. *PL*, see the initial preface to the reader (p. 10); "Pax Licita," pp. 3–5.

25. *PL*, initial preface, p. 10: "Totus liber Hypotheticus est."

26. *PL*, "Syndromus," no. 453, section without a margin number (pp. 11–12, 42). Note that only the first twelve pages of the Syndromus have margin numbers.

27. *PL*, "Prodromus," margin letter L (p. 26). The margin indicators in this section are letters rather than numbers.

28. *PL*, intro. to the "Prodromus," margin letter A (p. 19); "Pax Licita," no. 5 (p. 9).

29. See Lucien Ceyssens, "Autour de Caramuel," *Bulletin de l'Institut historique belge de Rome* 33 (1961), 384–89; Walter Friedensburg, "Regesten zur Deutschen Geschichte aus der Zeit des Pontifikats Innocenz X (1644–1655)," *Quellen und Forschungen aus italienischen Archiven und Bibliotheken* (1904), 169–72.

30. Nonetheless, Wangnereck faced serious consequences from his own order regarding his various writings on concessions to Protestants. See Birely, 219, 222–23, 253–61.

31. *PL*, "Syndromus," p. 41.

32. See *PL*, the initial preface, p. 14.

33. Apparently the text initially circulated without Caramuel's name. See Alessandro Catalano, "Juan Caramuel Lobkowicz (1606–1682) e la riconquista delle coscienze in Boemia," *Römische historische Mitteilungen* 44 (2002), 347.

34. On Chigi and Wangnereck, see Ceyssens, "Autour," 381; and Dino Pastine, *Juan Caramuel: Probabilismo ed enciclopedia* (Florence: La Nuova Italia Editrice, 1975), 95.

35. See Ceyssens, "Autour," 384–85; for its use in later volumes, see, for example, *TMF* (1652), *fund.* 11, sects. 7–8, nos. 275–77 (pp. 137–38).

36. Wangnereck's responsibility for the text was not revealed until 1663. See Birely, 249. See Steinberger (p. 128, n. 3) on the idea that Caramuel believed that a single writer was responsible for Wangnereck's text and for the *Anti-Caramuel* (actually composed by Adam Adami).

37. See *PL*, "Prodromus," margin letter E (p. 22); "Syndromus," no. 490 (p. 4).

38. *PL*, "Pax Licita," no. 99 (pp. 70–71): "quam non amat."

39. Ibid., no. 164 (pp. 117–18).

40. On Wangnereck's background, see Birely, 216.

41. *PL*, "Pax Licita," no. 100 (p. 72): "a nobis sine Deo, nec a Deo sine nobis."

42. *PL*, "Prodromus," margin letter O (p. 29): "*tametsi Thoma, Bernardo, vel etiam Augustino aequalis*"; "*controversia ista est politica & practica; pendet ab oculis, pendet ab auribus, pendet a manibus . . .*"

43. *PL*, "Pax Licita," no. 191 (p. 138): "victorias garrit, triumphos promittit, & . . . impedivit concordiam quam desiderat tota Germania."

44. Ibid., no. 180 (p. 128): "Credo meis oculis . . . Iacturas video; triumphos despero; Pacem suadeo, & multa Protestantibus necessario concedenda protestor."

45. See *PL*, the initial synopsis, p. 9.

46. *PL*, "Pax Licita," no. 49 (*sic*), (p. 135): "non sit lex humana aut divina, cuius Imperator relinquere viam tutam & securam & ingredi securiorem tutioremque teneatur . . . Probabilitatis communi doctrinae constemus; & inveniemus sufficere Caesari habere conscientiam securam tutamque . . . sufficere probabilitatem; nec probabilioritatem requiri."

47. Caramuel believes that Ernestus has essentially conceded that the legitimacy of the treaty is probable. See *PL*, "Pax Licita," no. 241 (p. 168).

48. Ibid., no. 237 (p. 165): "Sic aliqui nostrae sententiae defensores, qui ut declinent invidiam, eam probabilem vocant, quia praxin respiciunt, quae est mera probabilitate contenta. At nos, qui non practicis solum, sed & speculativis scribimus, Ernesti sententiam concludimus esse improbabilem ab intrinseco; quia caret rationibus quae sint alicuius momenti: concludimus eamdem esse improbabilem ab extrinseco, quia caret authoribus . . ."

49. Ibid., no. 242 (p. 168): "Illa sententia est evidenter vera, cuius opposita est improbabilis . . . Ernesti sententia improbabilis est: ergo nostra, quae illi opponitur, censenda est evidens."

50. Ibid., no. 436 (p. 300): "*evidenter veram*," . . . "*evidenter falsam*."

51. See *TMF* (1652), *fund*. II, sect. 8, no. 277 (p. 138). Caramuel says that he has taken this argument from the *Pax Licita* (*Definitio* 14, num. 1, p. 4). However, my edition of the volume contains no initial section of definitions.

52. *PL*, "Pax Licita," no. 356 (pp. 238–39).

53. Ibid., no. 239 (pp. 167): "*positive in ea consentire & cooperari*." On Becan, see Birely, 37–40. Note, moreover, the similarities between Becan's arguments and Caramuel's regarding the lesser of two evils (Birely, 39–40).

54. *PL*, "Pax Licita," no. 239 (p. 166).

55. See *PL*, the initial preface, pp. 11–15; "Prodromus," margin letter E (p. 22); "Pax Licita," no. 239 (p. 166).

56. *PL*, "Syndromus," pp. 14–20, 45; "Pax Licita," no. 158 (pp. 114–15).

57. *PL*, "Pax Licita," no. 236 (p. 165).

58. *PL*, "Syndromus," (p. 45). I have not listed all the precedents cited by Caramuel.

59. Ibid.

60. Ibid., nos. 438–39 (p. 2): "ignorantes & stupidos homines"; "monstrosae . . . resolutiones."

61. Ibid., no. 438: "sufficit hanc sententiam ab uno aut altero proferri, ut probabilis esse dicatur. Quod si servandae fidei obligatio mere probabilis sit, nulla erit securitas in ejusmodi pactis. At nos . . . tenemus enim Fidem non esse servandam Haereticis forte a duobus tribusve idiotis dictum, forte a nullo: at trium pluriumve idotarum sententiam esse probabilem . . . negamus."

62. Ibid.: "Opinionem unius Idiota esse probabilem, improbabile est."

63. See *PL*, "Pax Licita," no. 243 (pp. 169–70). Note that on the previous pages at number 242, Caramuel provides a slightly longer list of Ernestus's objections (pp. 168–69).

64. *PL*, "Prodromus," no number (p. 17): "Tota controversia . . ."

65. Ibid., margin letter C (p. 20): "E duobus malis, quorum utrum vitari non potest . . . minus est eligendum; errabitque, qui malit permittere majus, aut utrumque."

66. Ibid., margin letter E (p. 22).

67. *PL*, "Pax Licita," no. 373 (p. 261): "Hoc dictat naturalis ratio; hoc sine licentia hominis facere potes; id quocumque homine contradicente; non enim Pontifici, non Caesari, non Regi, dedit authoritatem Deus ut valide tibi praecipiat vitam potius perdere, quam pallium."

68. Ibid., nos. 28, 33 (pp. 26, 29).

69. Ibid., nos. 243–44, 252 (pp. 170, 174–75).

70. *PL*, "Prodromus," margin letter C (p. 20): "aut sarcinas in mare proiicere, aut Petri navim in Germania perire."

71. *PL*, "Pax Licita," no. 335 (p. 221): "existimo mortaliter peccaturum fuisse Caesarem, si maluisset perire Germaniam, quam Paci Religionis subscribere."

72. Ibid., nos. 13, 228, 229 (pp. 17–18, 161). Note that, according to Birely, Becan had offered this same analogy a quarter-century earlier regarding concessions to the Lower Austrian estates (p. 40).

73. *PL*, "Pax Licita," no. 15 (p. 19): "pereant igitur ipsa, ne pereamus."

74. Ibid., nos. 133–35 (pp. 163–65).

75. Ibid., no. 16 (pp. 20–21).

76. Ibid., no. 189 (p. 137).

77. Ibid., no. 185 (p. 131): "sicut Deus mala permittit ob majus bonum, aut ne sequatur majus malum . . ."

78. Birely, 40; note, for example, his claim never to have seen or heard of a single theologian who would deny the principle. See *PL*, "Prodromus," margin letter E (p. 22). See also "Syndromus," no. 440 (p. 4).

79. *PL*, "Syndromus," no. 440 (p. 4). Note that Caramuel describes Baianism and Jansenism as a single heresy.

80. See, for example, *PL*, "Pax Licita," nos. 257, 325 (pp. 174, 112 [*sic*, 212]).

81. Ibid., no. 252 (p. 174): "Ajo teneri Principem punire Haereticos, quando punitio ipsa est Republicae utilior quam tolerantia; at si punitio esset pernitiosa Reipublicae, & tolerantia utilis, non solum non teneretur eos punire, sed teneretur tolerare."

82. Ibid., no. 136 (pp. 99–100).

83. Ibid., no. 105 (p. 80).

84. *PL,* "Prodromus," margin letter H (p. 24).

85. *PL,* "Pax Licita," no. 311 (p. 205). See also no. 139 (p. 101).

86. *PL,* "Prodromus," margin letter f (p. 23): "Princeps, qui temere exponit suos milites, & sine publicae utilitatis spe saltem probabili, aliquos perdit, reus est innocentis effusi sanguinis, & ad restitutionem, ad quam caeteri homicidae, tenetur. Temere exponit milites, qui bellum improbabile suscipit, cum pacem deberet. Dicitur bellum improbabile ratione causae, ratione effectus. Nempe ratione causae, cum injustum, nec ulla probabile ratione subnixum: ratione effectus, cum temerarium, & sine spe probabili Ecclesiae & Reipublicae authoritatem, securitatem, & utilitatem promovendi."

87. *PL,* "Syndromus," pp. 46–47.

88. *PL,* "Pax Licita," no. 201 (p. 144): "esse communia toti Imperio . . ."

89. Ibid., nos. 9, 90 (pp. 14, 64).

90. *PL,* "Syndromus," p. 46: "quod Deus hic vel ibi colatur: non quod Ecclesiastici sint divites aut pauperes . . ."; "Ecclesiam confundere cum muris."

91. *PL,* "Pax Licita," no. 140 (p. 102): "non enim Christus suum sanguinem fudit pro muris."

92. Ibid., no. 4 (p. 8): "Anne Mundi Redemptor, mortem obiit pro bonis Ecclesiasticis? Anne crucifixus, mortuus, & sepultus, descendit ad inferos, resurrexit a mortuis & adscendit in coelos, ut ditaret Ecclesias? Nego, nego. . . moriens pro animabus nos docuit, vel unam solam animam multis divitiis praeponendam."

93. Ibid., no. 30 (p. 27): "O pereat pecunia, quae has miserias invexit!"

94. Ibid., no. 179 (p. 127): "Non enim tanti bona terrena facio, ut eorumdem causa cum haereticis differere velim; nec scio cur non possit quis illis fundos aut pecunias concedere, ne concedere maiora cogantur."

95. *PL,* "Syndromus," p. 45.

96. *PL,* "Pax Licita," no. 249 (p. 173): "nihil . . . perniciosius Reipublicae, quam periurium & infidelitatem."

97. *PL,* "Syndromus," no. 441 (p. 5).

98. *PL,* "Pax Licita," no. 281 (p. 189).

99. *PL,* "Syndromus," nos. 442–43 (pp. 6–7).

100. *PL,* "Pax Licita," no. 238 (p. 96): "vera mendacia mendaci veritatis nomine condecorata."

101. Ibid., p. 95.

102. Ibid., no. 247 (p. 172): "Cum igitur Caesar sit imago Dei, & in saecularibus nomine Dei praesideat, debet esse summe fidelis; quoniam sine fiditate [*sic*]

non possunt res humanae subsistere; nec enim poterunt firmari Rerumpublicarum contractus, si Principes fide digni non sunt."

103. Ibid., no. 181 (p. 129).

104. Ibid, no. 184 (pp. 139–40): "Quid si Pontifex, defectu experientiae erraret, & non esse cur haeretici tolerarentur in Germania diceret? An deberemus omnes perire & permittere omnia haereticis, ne aliqua permittamus? Minime. Nati sumus in doctissimo saeculo; potentiam Dei esse insitam scimus, omnium & singulorum hominum potestatem limitatam supponimus; a Deo ipsis ad aedificationem concessam: & quando videmus superiorum mandata in destructionem vergere, cessat legis finis, cessat obligatio obediendi, nec volumus ob eorumdem velleitatem totam Religionem Catholicam in discrimen coniicere." Again, this text is taken from the 1648 edition.

105. Ibid., no. 13 (pp. 17–18).

106. See, for example, *PL,* "Pax Licita," nos. 198, 228 (pp. 142, 161).

107. See Pastine, *Probabilismo,* 102–3; Catalano, 351–52.

108. *TMF* (1652), *fund.* 3, sect. "generalis probatio," no. 102 (p. 50): "*Lutherana Religio non est vera; Non est vera Calviniana Religio: sed neque caeterae, quae a Romana damnantur: & tamen sola Romana est vera.*"

109. See, for example, *Apologema,* 13–14.

110. See *PL,* "Syndromus," no. 450 (p. 9–10); "Pax Licita," nos. 102, 181 (pp. 74, 129).

111. *PL,* "Pax Licita," no. 228 (p. 161): "Si indigemus pictura, pictorem quaerimus, non Christianum; si salute, medicum, nec a Iudaeo dedignamur: adeoque etiam poterit Respublica haereticos ad consilia adsumere, si vel hoc ad pacem publicam conducat, aut eos aptiores iudicaverit."

112. Ibid., nos. 13, 415 (pp. 18, 284); "Prodromus," margin letter MM (pp. 49–50).

113. *PL,* "Syndromus," p. 43.

114. Ibid.: "ad probabilem aliquam positionem reduci."

115. Ibid.: "Lutheranismi causa est quaedam irritatio & scandalum . . . Sed neque haec tam fortibus rationibus fundata, ut sublata irritatione & scandalo manere queat: sunt enim homines rationales ut nos . . ."

116. *PL,* "Pax Licita," no. 394 (p. 267).

117. Ibid. (p. 266): "per imprudentiam & avariatiam committi."

118. Ibid., no. 396 (p. 268): "Fluxerunt anni & anni; serpsit cancer; viximus in spe; & nescivimus aut noluimus adhibere remedium."

119. Ibid. (p. 269).

120. Ibid. (p. 268): "Dixi aliquando, plus Catholicae Ecclesiae adulatores nocuisse, & Haeresiarchas minus. Displicui meo Dianae; sed rem teneo, & pace optimi amici oculis crediturus sum. Non detestantur Lutherani Clerum, sed Cleri superbiam, avaritiam, & fastum."

121. Ibid. (p. 269): "*se mecum Catholicos esse posse, sed cum aliis non posse.*"

122. Ibid.

123. *PL,* "Prodromus," margin letters PP (p. 51).

124. *PL,* "Pax Licita," no. 396 (p. 270): "O nos miseros! A desiderio insatiabili pecuniarum invadimur; & quam putamus haeresin, plerumque avaritia pura est; plerumque monstrum ab avarita mera natum."

125. Ibid. (p. 269): "murmurantes Judaeos & ridentes Lutheranos"; "Obstupui: nec judicavi posse dici sine omnium Ecclesiasticorum ignominia tantam in Parrocho avaritiam, ut deberet trimum cadaver illud pedibus transfeuntium advolvi, ut congeretur pecunia."

126. Ibid. (pp. 269–70): "Video percellorque; & insolentia facinoris multa alia suggerit, quae frequentiora."

127. Ibid. (p. 271): "si videar acer, imputandum dolori est, quem a miseria illius insepulti cadaveris hodie concepi." The word *hodie* (which I have omitted in the translation) suggests that Caramuel is incorporating into the *Pax Licita* an account of the incident that he wrote at the time of the event itself.

128. Ibid. (p. 271).

129. A point emphasized by Dino Pastine's "Caramuel nel suo tempo," in *Le meraviglie,* 22. For the original comment, see Ceyssens, "Autour," 385.

130. See Catalano for an illustration of the way in which Caramuel's enemies in Bohemia used the book against him (371, 389–90).

Chapter 4

1. Pietro Palazzini, "Prospero Fagnani: Secretario della sacra congregazione del concilio e suoi editi ed inediti," in *La sacra congregazione del concilio, quarto centenario della fondazione, 1564–1964: studi e richerche* (Rome: Città del Vaticano, 1964), 361, 363, 364.

2. The argument at *Apologema* 73 could conceivably be a reference to Fagnani's lifestyle, but the text is too general to ground certain conclusions on this point.

3. Palazzini, 366.

4. The discussion of probability was reissued as a separate tract in 1665. See Th. Deman, "Probabilisme," *Dictionnaire de théologie catholique* (Paris: Letouzey et Ané, 1936), col. 510. Palazzini (369) mentions another separate publication in 1677, a year before Fagnani's death.

5. As Deman points out, Fagnani received permission to print the work several years before it actually appeared. Deman also notes that Fagnani mentions the work of Julius Mercorus, but asserts that his own treatise had been written before the Dominican's. See Deman, col. 509; Prospero Fagnani, *Commentaria in Primum Librum Decretalium,* . . . (Venice: Paul Balleonius, 1709), no. 108 (p. 41). Deman and Hurter observe that Mercorus's work was published in 1658, while Cacciatore (following Concina) asserts that it was written in 1658 but

published in 1660. See Deman, col. 504; Hugo Hurter *Nomenclator Literarius Theologicae Catholicae,* 3rd ed. (1910; reprint, New York, Burt Franklin, n.d.), vol. 4, col. 288; Giuseppe Cacciatore, *S. Alfonso de' Liguori e il Giansenismo* (Florence: Libreria Editrice Fiorentina, 1944), 351.

6. Fagnani, no. 43 (p. 34): "quam durum sit impetum fluminis sistere, & doctrinam hanc prurientem auribus Principum, & privatorum, ac fere omnium mentibus infixam convellere."

7. Ibid., no. 25 (p. 32). Fagnani distinguishes three grades of recourse to probable opinion and he rejects them all. This is a reference to the first grade.

8. Ibid., no. 14 (p. 31): "Utrum in omni materia sequi liceat quamcumque opinionem probabilem." "An in moralibus sequi liceat opinionem probabilem secundum se, praescindendo a quacumque probabilitate opinionis oppositae." "An ex duabus opinionibus oppositis aeque probabilibus liberum sit cuilibet sequi utramque . . ." "An sequi liceat opinionem minus probabilem, & minus tutam, relicta probabiliori, ac tutiori." "An authoritas unius Doctoris reddat opinionem probabilem."

9. Ibid., no. 15 (p. 31).

10. Ibid., no. 23 (p. 32).

11. Ibid.

12. Ibid., no. 23 (p. 32): "hoc saeculo introducta est . . ."

13. Ibid.: "cognoverunt judicium probabile non posse assumi pro regula recte operandi."

14. Ibid., no. 24 (p. 32): "Verum post multa saecula irrepsit alia doctrina, videlicet, ad rectitudinem operationis non requiri judicium certo . . . sed sufficere probabile judicium cum formidine partis oppositae."

15. Ibid., nos. 24–25 (p. 32): "statuerunt tres gradus probabilitatis."

16. Ibid., nos. 24–25: "laxiorem, & gravioribus difficultatibus, & periculis involutum."

17. Ibid.: "Et quia abyssys abyssum invocat, ab hoc secundo probabilitatis gradu Scholastici nostri saeculi processerunt ad tertium, disseminantes doctrinam novam, & anteactis saeculis inaditam . . ."

18. Ibid., no. 26 (p. 32).

19. Ibid., no. 28 (p. 32): "Mirum autem est, quam longe lateque hos gradus postea dilataverint."

20. See ibid., no. 41 (p. 33).

21. Ibid., no. 95 (p. 39).

22. Ibid., nos. 123–24, 256 (pp. 43, 59).

23. Note the prominence of advocates and judges in the initial examples that Fagnani mentions to highlight the dangers of probabilism. See, for example, nos. 28 and 31 (pp. 32–33).

24. Ibid., no. 332 (p. 70).

25. Cf. ibid., nos. 43, 336, 401 (pp. 34, 71, 85) with nos. 331, 332 (p. 70): "Author modernus."

26. Ibid., no. 335 (p. 70). See also the reference to Bassaeus and Caramuel at no. 43 (pp. 33–34). On Mercorus, see Deman, col. 504.

27. Fagnani, no. 336 (p. 71). On the history of this response, see Amann, cols. 48–49.

28. See E. Amann, "Laxisme," in *Dictionnaire de théologie catholique* (Paris: Letouzey et Ané), col. 48.

29. Juan Caramuel, *Apologema pro Antiquissima et Universalissima Doctrina de Probabilitate. Contra Novam, Singularem, Improbabilemque D. Prosperi Fagnani Opinationem* (Lyon: Anisson, 1663), 28.

30. Hurter, vol. 4, cols. 192–94. Page 4 of the *Apologema* refers to this work.

31. On Caramuel's references to Sfortia Pallavicino, see Sven K. Knebel, *Wille, Würfel und Warscheinlikchkeit: Das System der moralischen Notwendigkeit in der Jesuitenscholastik 1550–1700* (Hamburg: Felix Meiner, 2000): 111–12, n. 140. Döllinger and Reusch, however, indicate that the cardinal repudiated probabilism (which he had once supported) in the last years of his life (Ignaz von Döllinger and Heinrich Reusch, *Geschichte der Moralstreitigkeiten in der römische-katholischen Kirche seit dem sechzehnten Jahrhundert mit Beiträgen zur Geschichte und Charakteristik des Jesuitenordens* [Nördlingen, Germany: C. H. Beck, 1869], 1:52–54)

32. Hurter, vol. 4, col. 193.

33. The first letter is five pages in length, with an accompanying twenty-seven pages of notes. The second is thirteen pages, and the third, twelve. Epistle 4 is over one hundred pages long and is followed by various notes and appendices; *Apologema,* 184. Velarde Lombraña asserts that Caramuel originally intended to include nine letters, but does not mention his source for this information (Julián Velarde Lombraña, *Juan Caramuel, vida y obra* [Oviedo, Spain: Pentalfa Ediciones, 1989], 330).

34. Although the title page lists the publisher as Laurentius Anisson of Lyon, this friend of Caramuel's in fact sold the books prepared in Caramuel's printshop. See Antonio Cestaro, ed., *Juan Caramuel, vescovo di Satriano e Campagna (1657–1673): cultura e vita religiosa nella seconda metà del Seicento* (Salerno, Italy: Edisud, 1992), 124.

35. See the initial unnumbered page entitled "Totius operis argumentum."

36. Palazzini, 370–71.

37. *Apologema,* 5: "personam . . . veneror."

38. Ibid., 6: "materialiter . . . in invincibili ignorantia; 6–7: "Et quidem homini Canonistae non est inglorium Philosophicas & Theologicas subtilitates ignorasse . . ."

39. Ibid., 58: *"Materia de Probabilitate non potest tractari a Iuristis."*

40. Ibid., 59.

41. See, for example, *Apologema,* 198.

42. Ibid., 189.

43. Ibid., "Totius Op. Arg.": "Scommatibus, Iniuriis, Contumelias."

44. See, for example, *Apologema,* 198.

45. Ibid., 10, 92: "aeger & coecus"; "nimia lectione & scriptione."

46. See *Apologema,* 25–27, 183–84.

47. Fagnani, no. 335 (p. 70): "falsis, temerariis, & scandolosis . . . a Scriptoribus nostri temporis."

48. *Apologema,* 17: "ex illis multas esse evidenter veras; aliquas probabiles; aliquas, quae etiam mihi non placent."

49. Ibid., 17–18: "Praeterea, Lectorem meum monere volo, Theologos prudentissime ponere omnes circumstantias, quae possunt sub considerationem venire, & sic Casus debitis limitationibus definire: cum tamen D. Fagnanus, ut in illos concitet Lectorum odia, eorundem Resolutiones ponat universim, a limitationibus praecisas."

50. Ibid.

51. Ibid., 152–60, 181–82. (Note that errors in pagination mean that page 181 follows page 160).

52. Ibid., 160, 181.

53. Ibid., 160.

54. Ibid., 181.

55. Ibid., 183: "stricta"; "laxissimae."

56. See *Apologema,* 93, where Caramuel again invokes the example of Columbus.

57. Ibid., 95, 39.

58. Ibid., 151–52.

59. Ibid.: "*qui non vult nos tentari & gravari supra id quod possumus.*" Cited in *Apologema,* 152. The identification of the original appears on the previous page.

60. Note, for example, his references to Antonio Merenda, Julius Mercorus, and Luis Crespín de Borja (pp. 7, 23, 47, 52, 59, 185, 186, 199).

61. Fagnani mentions the document (in reference to Mercorus), but it does not play a significant role in his arguments either. See no. 334 (p. 70).

62. Note Caramuel's appeal to the constitutions of the "wisest and most learned [*sapientissimus, doctissimusque*]" Order of Preachers to refute Fagnani's call for greater stringency in moral teaching (*Apologema,* 72).

63. Ibid., 46: "*Tolle Thomam . . . & Romanam Ecclesiam debellabo.*"

64. Ibid., 46–47: "*Tolle,* inquam Ego, *Propositionem hanc,* Ad securitatem conscientiae in Fidei & morum materia sufficit Opinio probabilis, *Et non Ecclesiam modo, sed & Rempublicam totam Christianam (Ecclesiasticam, & saecularem) debellabis.*" Note that for the sake of clarity, I have reversed the italic and roman type in the translation.

65. Ibid., 95: "Fuit sane vivente D. Thoma nova. An ideo debuit reijci [*sic*]?"

66. Ibid., 95, 96–97.

67. Ibid., 95: "*condemnant moderni Thomistae in aliis Doctoribus: novitates in S. Thoma laudantur, & extolluntur, ut vides, quando in aliis Doctoribus vituperantur & detestantur.*"

68. Ibid., 96: "At Deus non dispensavit cum S. Thoma, ut ipse solus faceret, quod caeteris erat inhibitum."

69. Ibid.: 97: "Ergo *quod post Hieronymum, Augustinum, Gregorium, Ambrosium, D. Thomae: post D. Thomam Scoto, Ochamo, Durando, Cajetano, & aliis licuit, etiam hodie post omnes hos Ioanni Sancio, Thomae Sanchez, Suario, Vasquezio, Dianae, Mascurenhae, & etiam Caramueli licebit.*"

70. Ibid., 123–24.

71. Ibid., 126.

72. Ibid., 124: "alias . . . ut certas, alias ut probabiles."

73. Ibid., 124: "aemuli" might also be translated as rivals. In this passage, Caramuel distinguishes simple propositions from modal ones.

74. Ibid., 35–36, 126.

75. See *Enchiridion*, nos. 2015–17 (pp. 448–49). Cf. the much earlier decree of Sixtus IV, which prohibited the adherents of either position from accusing the other of heresy (nos. 1425–26 [p. 351]).

76. *Apologema,* 126.

77. Ibid., 128.

78. Ibid., 128–29.

79. Ibid., 127–28.

80. Ibid., 130: " . . . a peritis & imperitis legitur, & nullum errorem inducit: ergo neque tunc inducebat."

81. Ibid.

82. Ibid., 129, 135.

83. Ibid., 134.

84. Ibid., 135.

85. Ibid.: "*Utrum licite possit doceri Parisiis doctrina patris Thomae quantum ad omnes Conclusiones eius?*" "*Haec doctrina ubique recipitur tanquam probabiliter vera, & continens fidem & bonos mores, quia veritas non est dimittenda propter quamcumque poenam.*"

86. Ibid., 137.

87. Ibid., 7, 10, 11, 17.

88. Ibid., 11: ". . . una aut altera linea contentus est"; ". . . ut a pag. 95. num. 336 ad. pag. 103. inclus. per 17. columnas . . . legere Iansenistas cogamur." In my later edition of Fagnani's work, this extends from pages 71–77.

89. *Apologema,* 11–17.

90. Ibid., 18: "Doctorum Iansenistarum Censurae."

91. Ibid., 11.

92. Ibid., 15.

93. Ibid., 14, 183. The bull in question was *In eminenti*.

94. See *Apologema,* 28.

95. Ibid., 16: "videlicet . . . dominabantur Iansenistae." On the reputation of the faculty of Louvain in Rome a few years later, see Claeys Bouuaert, "Préci-

sions sur l'histoire de la députation envoyée à Rome, en 1677–1679, par la faculté de théologie de Louvain," *Revue d'histoire ecclésiastique* 56 (1961), 872–73.

96. Ibid., 17: "Sane omnes hi (Parrochi, Episcopi, Doctores) qui a D. Fagnano allegantur, sunt Iansenistae. . . ."

97. Claeys Bouuaert, "L'opposition de quelques évêques belges a la bulle 'In eminenti' (6 mars 1642) d'après des documents inédits," *Revue d'histoire ecclésiastique* 23 (1927), 802. Bouuaert notes that the faculty was divided in its response to the bull.

98. Bouuaert, "Jean Sinnich: Professeur à Louvain et un des premiers défenseurs de Jansenius (1603–1666)," *Ephemerides Theologicae Lovanienses* 31 (1955), 407. Sinnigh would later attack Caramuel directly in the *Saul Ex-Rex . . .* (Ibid., 416–17).

99. Bouuaert, "L'opposition," 802.

100. Ibid., 804.

101. Ibid., 805. Boonen apparently offered to publish the bull, provided that Rome would undertake a reexamination of the *Augustinus*. Bouuaert asserts that Boonen's response contains an elogy of Jansen. Orcibal points out that Jansen had been ordained at Mechlin (Jean Orcibal, "Un grand universitaire malgré lui: C. Jansénius d'Ypres," in *Facultas S. Theologiae Lovaniensis 1432–1797*, ed. J. M. Van Eijl [Leuven: University Press, 1977], 353).

102. Bouuaert, "L'opposition," 806.

103. Fagnani, no. 337 (pp. 73–74).

104. Bouuaert, "Précisions," 872–74, 876–77. The faculty actually proposed 116 propositions for condemnation. Claeys Bouuaert, "Autour de deux décrets du saint-office, celui du 2 mars 1679, condamnant 65 propositions de morale relâchée et celui du 7 décembre 1690, condamnant 31 propositions rigoristes," *Ephemerides Theologicae Lovanienses* 29 (1953), 429.

105. Bouuaert, *L'ancienne*, 271.

106. Ibid., 155–78. Note that the chapter entitled "Le jansénisme à l'université" extends to events that occurred in the eighteenth century.

107. Marvin O'Connell, *Blaise Pascal: Reasons of the Heart* (Grand Rapids, MI: Eerdmans, 1997), 157–59.

108. *Apologema*, 63: "Eram Lovanii cum iam mortuo Iansenio Exsequutores Testamenti de clandestina eius Augustini Editione secretissime deliberabant. Et D. Libertus Fromondus inter huius novae doctrinae Asseclas Coriphaeus, ut viam superventuro aperiret errori; aut verius, ut illum, nihil simile Academiae Doctoribus praevidentibus, dissiminaret, has Propositiones . . . Quae considerata Authoris intentione, aequivalent huic, *Ad securitatem conscientiae non sufficit opinio probabilis . . .* conatus est in scholam protrudere."

109. Ibid., 189: "Haeresis Ianseniana, iterum iterumque suppressa, condemnata, proscripta, mutata larva in Orbem litterarium revertitur . . . Heri illa Religionem mentita, omnes Doctores Orthodoxos esse Pelagianos asseruit . . . At hodie mentita Pietatem . . . doctrinae laxae & temerariae Theologos universos accusat.

"Et quid quaeso praetendunt Ianseniani, cum se morum relaxatorum reformatores simulant . . . ? Obtinere, ut in Vulgi tribunali, ultima illa annulletur sententia, quam contra Iansenii pernitiosa deliria in supremo Romanae Ecclesiae tribunali per Innocentium X. Spiritus Sanctus pronunciavit."

110. See, for example, *Apologema* 3, 7, 63, 189, 191.

111. Ibid., 191: "Haec verba, *Peccant omnes, qui in materia conscientiae sequuntur opinionem probabilem,* dialecti Iansenianae sunt, & complectuntur omnes haereses, quas anno 1653 . . . Apostolica Sedes . . . condemnavit. Qui enim hanc Propositionem reijcit [*sic*], totam haeresim Iansenianam condemnat: &, qui Iansenianus est, hanc ipsam negare non potest."

112. Fagnani, of course, cites the censures of the priests of Paris and Rouen— censures that were the eventual result of the *Provincial Letters.* Since Caramuel refers to the priests who wrote against Jerónimo de Mascarenhas and himself, it is reasonable to presume that he knew something about the circumstances behind these events. See Fagnani, no. 336 (pp. 71–72); *Apologema,* 11.

113. *Apologema,* 3: "sub vitae strictioris specie . . ."

114. Cf. Amann, cols. 41–42. One should note, however, that what would become the Jansenist party certainly existed prior to the publication of the *Augustinus.*

115. *Apologema,* 7: "Fundamentum & basis Haereseos Ianseniane est."

116. Fagnani, no. 115 (p. 42): "non modo . . . possibile, sed etiam facile."

117. *Apologema,* 10: "Lepidissima sane responsio! scribat igitur *Moralium Certitudinum Librum* D. Fagnanus, & cessabit contentio."

118. Ibid.: "hallucinationes."

119. Ibid.

120. Ibid., 1.

121. Ibid., 189: "catena haereseos Iansenianae."

122. Ibid.

123. Ibid., 190: "consistit in libertate a coactione non autem in libertate a necessitate." For a helpful summary of the *Augustinus,* see Abercrombie, 125–58.

124. *Apologema,* 190. Caramuel acknowledges elsewhere in the text that the Jansenists are referring to ignorance of divine and natural law, not human law (see 13).

125. Ibid., 190: "Ergo Via, quae ducit ad vitam tam est arcta, ut nullas probabiles opiniones admittat.
"Ergo non excusatur apud Deum, qui in praxi iuxta sententiarum probabilium benignitatem operatur."

126. Ibid., 191: *"Deus praeciperet impossibilia; nam praeciperet, ut sciat, quae scire non potest."*

127. Ibid., 192.

128. Ibid., 21.

129. Ibid., 190: "sententiarum probabilium benignitatem."

130. See Palazzini, 371.

Chapter 5

1. Juan Caramuel, *Apologema pro Antiquissima et Universalissima Doctrina de Probabilitate. Contra Novam, Singularem, Improbabilemque D. Prosperi Fagnani Opinationem* (Lyon: Anisson, 1663), 93.

2. *In D. Benedicti Regulam Commentarius Historicus Scholasticus Moralis Iudicialis Politicus* (hereafter *BR*) (Bruges, Belgium: Breyghels, 1640), *disp.* 6. art. 3, sect. 1, no. 60 (p. 27).

3. Prospero Fagnani, *Commentaria in Primum Librum Decretalium*, . . . (Venice: Paul Balleonius, 1709), no. 15 (p. 31): "ad fidem, aut mores non pertinet."

4. Ibid.

5. See, for example, his first major question at no. 44 (p. 34): "Quaero igitur primo, an in moralibus sequi liceat opinionem probabilem secundum se . . ." Notice that the reference to *faith* has disappeared.

6. See, for example, *Apologema,* 60, 62, 64, 69–70.

7. Ibid., 96.

8. Ibid., 71–72.

9. Fagnani, nos. 24–26 (p. 32).

10. *Apologema,* p. 106.

11. Ibid., 141–48.

12. Ibid., 97: "Pronuncio Naturae Humanae statum, & laudabilem probabilium opinionum usum coaetaneos esse."

13. Ibid., 97–98.

14. Ibid., 97–105.

15. Ibid., 105: "Ergo etiam hodie, qui faciat illud quod materialiter est peccatum mortale, si probabilibus rationibus ductus, esse veniale putet, committet peccatum quod formaliter & quoad Deum non nisi veniale sit. Ergo etiam hodie, qui faciat illud, quod materialiter est culpa lethalis, si tamen probabiliter iudicet esse nullum peccatum, nullum committit peccatum."

16. Ibid., 107: "Cum ergo sub Deo iusto homines non habeant obligationem, aut supra mentis vires intelligendi, aut supra corporis vires operandi, praeceptis Divinis satisfacient si illa humano modo intelligant, & humano modo exsequantur."

17. Ibid., 141–48. The discussion of probable opinion among the angels draws upon an interpretation of Daniel that posits angelic disagreement about whether the exiled people of Israel should be returned to their homeland.

18. Ibid., 107–9.

19. Ibid., 111: "suis militibus proposuit singularem & novam sententiam in materia fidei & morum."

20. Ibid., 113–14.

21. Ibid., 114–15.

22. Ibid., 116, 122.

23. See ibid., 76–87. The explicit focus of this section is actually on the negative consequences of repudiating probabilism for the reputation of Church leaders.

24. Ibid. On the development of papal power over marriage, see John Noonan, *Power to Dissolve: Lawyers and Marriages in the Courts of the Roman Curia* (Cambridge, MA: Belknap, 1972), especially 129–36.

25. *Apologema*, 86: "cur non licebit caeteris?"

26. Ibid., 93: "Pontificum Bullas pie defenditur."

27. Ibid.: "An ne illae, quae hodie cum applausu, aut etiam veneratione leguntur, . . . reiectae a prudentibus sunt, quando erant novae?"

28. Ibid., 94.

29. Ibid., 93.

30. Fagnani, no. 401 (p. 85): "Et haec via non ad lauream Empyrei, ut putat Caramuel, sed ex divino oraculo ad inferna deducit."

31. Ibid., no. 41 (p. 33): "perniciem animarum."

32. See, for example, Diana, *Coordinati, seu Omnium Resolutionum Moralium* . . . , rev. ed. (1728; reprint, St. Louis: Manuscripta, list 97, reels 16–17), *tract.* 1, *resols.* 1–6, 17–28 (pp. 1–4, 8–15).

33. Fagnani, no. 304 (p. 67): "Unde in foro animae judex sequi cogitur judicium rei . . ." For the various cases, see nos. 31–39, 293–310 (pp. 32–33, 65–68).

34. *Apologema*, 65.

35. Ibid., 47, 65, 66.

36. Ibid.

37. In *Theologia Moralis Fundamentalis* (Lyon: Anisson, 1675–76), Caramuel attributes the first position to Bishop Malderus of Antwerp, and the second, to Diana and others. See *fund.* 55, nota 2, *q.* "De medicis," no. 2564 (p. 800). This later statement of the case makes it clear that the person did not give any sign of penitence before he became insensate.

38. *Apologema*, 62.

39. Ibid., 11–12. This is one of the propositions condemned by the priests of Paris and Rouen.

40. Ibid., 12: "sacrilegam confessionem"; "indigere instructione."

41. Ibid., 66–67.

42. Ibid., 67: "quis enim Superior persuadere subditis discolis poterit, ea, quae praecipit, esse semper certo aut probabilius necessaria aut utilia?"

43. Ibid., 73: "si non fecit, nos scandalizat, nam aliter vivit, quam docet"; "senem optimum."

44. Ibid., 73–74.

45. Ibid., 151–52.

46. Ibid., 152.

47. Ibid., 74: "tota Gallia turbabitur."

48. Ibid.: "Germaniam, Bohemiam, Hungariam, Belgium."

49. Ibid., 151–52. See Fagnani, no. 43 (pp. 33–34).

50. Ibid., 33.

51. Ibid., 34: "*Indubitata & Certa.*"

52. Ibid., 94, 96. See also page 40.

53. Ibid., 34: "*quae pro se habet rationes fortes, nullam autem demonstrativam: quae contra se habet rationes fortes, nullam autem demonstrativam.*"

54. Ibid., 94: "inter noctem & diem; inter manifestam falsitatem, & manifestam veritatem medio, quod *Probabilitatem* appellamus. Hoc Veritatis lumen S. Ioanni in Apocalypsi sua videtur ostendi, sub libri septem sigillis clausi specie. Quandiu nullum sigillum aperitur, ambulamus in tenebris, & veritatem penitus ignoramus. Cum septimum, aut Demonstratio naturalis, aut Fides Divina in hac vita, aut in altera visio beatifica recludit, Veritatem infallibiliter assequimur, exuimurque omni errandi formidine. Quando autem aliqua referantur, & aliqua non referantur, tenebrae & luces in nostro intellectu confligunt, & per probabiles semitas conducimur ad veritatem." For a use of this biblical image (borrowed from Antonio de Escobar) in outlining the discipline of moral theology, see *TMF* (1652), "Prooemium de sigillis et clavibus theologiae moralis," nos. 30–39 (44–48).

55. *Apologema*, 34.

56. Ibid.

57. Ibid., 52.

58. Ibid., 35.

59. Ibid., 55, 61. As we have seen, these receive more extensive attention in the later editions of *TMF*. See the conclusion to chapter 2.

60. Ibid., 55: ". . . quando superior intra limites suae iurisdictionis praecipit, quod probabile est, tenetur subditus obedire; nam qui obedientiam promisit; omnia, quae sunt necessaria, ut gubernetur, compromisit. Et nisi subditus cedat iure sequendi opinionem, quam velit, quis Superior poterit gubernare? Vix lex ulla universalis & communis subsisteret; semper aut fere subditus posset dicere, etiam oppositum videri probabile; aut etiam, si velit, probabilius: & tota turbaretur Ecclesia, tota Respublica, omnes Communitates."

61. *BR, disp.* 6, art. 3, sect. 4, nos. 65–66 (p. 29).

62. *Coordinati, tract.* 1, "de opinione probabili," *resol.* 2, §1.

63. Ibid., §2.

64. *Apologema*, 55: "Unde, cum debeam favere proximo in extremo periculo constituto quantum possim, & melius sit infantem habere minus probabilem baptismum, quam nullum; in casu, quo non habeam materiam certam, nec probabiliorem, debebo uti materia etiam minus probabili." Note, however, that Caramuel presumes that the minister should use the certain or more probable matter, were it available. His practical conclusion is not different from Diana's; it is simply a difference in emphasis.

65. Ibid., 39: "ex circumstantiis adiacentibus & extrinsecis."

66. Ibid., 38: " . . . lex non obligat hos, quibus non est imposita: & ubi nulla

est lex, non datur ulla (formalis aut materialis) praevaricatio. Lex autem (Divina aut humana ea fit) non imponitur his, quibus non est sufficienter intimata & proposita . . . Et lex, de qua apud doctos hinc inde probabiliter disputatur, An sit? invincibiliter & insuperabiliter ignoratur."

67. Ibid., 38–39.

68. Ibid., 190.

69. Fagnani, no. 332 (p. 70): "Author Modernus non erubuit sua epistola disseminare hanc propositionem, videlicet, Opiniones probabiles efficere, ut quod olim peccatum erat, modo amplius non sit." (Although Caramuel is not mentioned by name, the context of the discussion makes it clear that he is the "modern author" in question.)

70. Blaise Pascal, *Les provinciales: Écrits des curés de Paris. Pierre Nicole et Jean Racine lettres. Le père Daniel résponse aux provinciales*, ed. Jean Steinman (Paris: Librairie Armand Colin, 1962), 95: "Et de là vient que le docte Caramuel, dans la lettre où il adresse à Diana sa *Thèologie fondamentale*, dit que ce grand *Diana a rendu plusieurs opinions probables qui ne l'étaient pas auparavant, quae antea non erant: et qu'ainsi on ne pèche plus en les suivant, au lieu qu'on péchait auparavant: jam non peccant, licet ante peccaverint.*"

71. *Apologema*, 40: "nam non omnes sciunt, quid Probabilitas authentica sit, secundum suum Metaphysicum conceptum considerata."

72. Ibid., 40: "nuda Authorum nomina"; "contra certitudinem, non datur Probabilitas."

73. Ibid.

74. Ibid., 42: "oves ovem."

75. Ibid., 44: "valde difficilis"; "saepe impossibilis."

76. Ibid., 44: "quatuor authores esse doctos ut 8. & Petrum esse doctum ut centum."

77. Ibid.

78. Ibid., 37.

79. Ibid., 36: "ex affectu & praeiudicio pendet."

80. Ibid., 37: "*non semper est perceptibilis & cognoscibilis.*"

81. Ibid.: "nam Prudentiae sigillo omnes insigniuntur, & aeque bonae sunt, ut gloriam aeternam emamus."

82. Ibid., 40–41: "Sed unde sciam, utrum habeat illa rationem gravem? si illa ratio proponatur, & ego sim bonus Theologus, habeamque ingenium & doctrinam sufficientia, ut illam ponderem & examinem, & in sinceritatis libram esse gravem percipiam, illa Opinio erit mihi probabilis ab intrinseco."

83. *TMF* (1652), *fund.* 11, sect. 4, no. 272 (pp. 136–37).

84. *TMF* (1675–76), *fund.* 11, sect. 6, no. 450 (p. 154): "quia doctus in dubiis rationes & fundamenta debebit examinare, indoctus vero non debebit."

85. Ibid.: "felicior." See also Pastine's discussion of Caramuel's views on the responsibilities of superiors (Dino Pastine, *Juan Caramuel: Probabilismo ed enciclopedia* [Florence: La Nuova Italia Editrice, 1975], pp. 281, 285–86).

86. *Apologema*, 41: "Sed quid, si vel ratio, cui opinio insistit, non proponatur?"

87. Ibid., 41–42.

88. Ibid., 43–44: "Hinc patet Authores, qui pro aliqua opinione citantur; non dare illi probabilitatem, sed testificari expresse aut implicite illam esse probabilem. Unde, ut alia via, sed quae in idem recidet, utriusque probabilitatis differentiam exponam, dicam: *Opinio probabilis ab intrinseco illa est, quam ratione gravi fulciri video: probabilis authentice & ab extrinseco, quam tametsi ratione gravi fulciri non videam, gravi fulciri a Viro aut Viris doctissimis audio.*" Emphases added in the English translation.

89. Ibid., 45: "Unde placere non est formalis nec efficiens causa suavitatis sed effectus."

90. Ibid.: "Ergo illa melior ratio, quae pluribus Viris doctis placet. At loquendo a priori, non dant docti rationi bonitatem, sed hanc ratio praehabet . . ."

91. Ibid.: "Ergo Authorum pluralitas non dat probabilioritatem Opinioni: sed illam ab intrinseco probabiliorem esse consensu suo testificatur. Ergo probabilioritas authentica ad probabilioritatem intrinsecam reduci debet."

92. *TMF* (1652), *Ep.* to Diana, no. 7 (p. 23); *BR, disp.* 6, art. 3, sect. 1, no. 60 (p. 28): "Damnarentur plurimi, quos sententiae probabilitas salvat."

93. *TMF* (1652), *fund.* 55, sect. 6, no. 1145 (p. 547): "opinionem Dianae non reddi probabilem, si antea non erat."

94. In Caramuel's terms, he or she may be guilty of *hypothetical malice*, but not of lawbreaking, since the presence of invincible ignorance indicates that the law is insufficiently promulgated.

95. That is, from acting without sufficient grounds for security of conscience to acting with sufficient grounds for security of conscience.

Chapter 6

1. The structure of the *Dialexis* poses considerable challenges for citation. After the censures and dedicatory epistles, the text begins with an index. The first section is the "Quaestio Prooemialis," followed by a "Prodromus" and the "Dialexis" proper. Finally, the "Syndromus" includes a collection of letters to and from Caramuel regarding the text's arguments. Some sections do not have page numbers, and marginal enumeration begins again at the "Prodromus." Accordingly, my references to the text will begin with the title of the section—"Index," "Quaestio," "Prodromus," "Dialexis—or to a specific *epistola*, including its number, followed by whatever other placement information is available.

2. *Dialexis de Non-Certitudine* (hereafter *DNC*) (Lyon: Anisson, 1675), *Ep.* 10, no. 949 (p. 323): "nondum in lucem missam suffocare conati."

3. *DNC, Ep.* 1, no. 745 (p. 253); *Ep.* 2, no. 832 (p. 272).

4. See Caramuel's reference to them in the heading for *Epistola* 3 (p. 273).

5. See *DNC, Ep.* 2, nos. 832, 750 (pp. 272, 254). See Caramuel's comments that appear in the bottom margin of page 254.

6. See also his comments to Francisco Verde in *DNC, Ep.* 11, no. 954: "Invidiae insolentiam & audaciam praevideo" (p. 325).

7. Note the comments of Vincent Baron, as cited in Franz Heinrich Reusch, *Der Index der Verbotenen Bücher: Ein Beitrag zur Kirchen- und Literaturgeschichte* (1885; reprint, Aalen: Scientia Verlag, 1967), 2:502.

8. *DNC,* "Index," (no page numbers): "Index capitum et articulorum"; "Non hic (Lector Candide & Erudite) Novas Doctrinas Curiositati Ingeniosae propino, sed Communes, Antiquasque clarius dilucidatas; quas Universi Veteres & Iuniores Scriptores supponunt; quas admittunt omnes, & exercent in praxi, tametsi illas ipsas obscurioribus verbis tradiderunt."

9. *DNC,* "Dialexis," part 2, art. 6, no. 614 (p. 217): "semper habui, & Lectoribus, ubi occasio postulavit, tradidi."

10. That is, in *Theologia Moralis Fundamentalis* (Lyon, Anisson, 1675–76).

11. *DNC,* "Dialexis," part 2, no. 302 (p. 120): "non repeto, quae in nostra Fundamentali Theologia *a num.* 435 edisserui; te enim illa iam legisse suppono: ibi enim communem doctrinam *de Probabilitate* dilucido, nunc promoveo superatis nonnullis intercurrentibus difficultatibus."

12. Ibid., art. 1, no. 303 (p. 120): "Ante diem hunc existimo Rationem illam formalem, quae conscientias hominum securas reddit, non fuisse inventam."

13. Ibid.: "putabamus enim esse Probabilitatem, cum tamen non sit Probabilitas, sed aliud quid distinctum, quod aeque Probabilitatem ac Certitudinem concomitatur."

14. Ibid: "doctrinam de actibus humanis . . . in qua ego hucusque cum caeteris adlucinabar."

15. Ibid., "Prodromus," no. 1 (p. 1): "Et quid si novam traderem? Non est mala nova, si vera."

16. Ibid., "Dialexis," part 2, art. 14, nos. 679–703 (pp. 235–44). Of course, Caramuel anticipates some of these arguments in earlier sections of the text.

17. Ibid., "Totius Operis Assertiones Praecipue" (this page appears between the "Index" and the "Quaestio"): "Ratio formalis, quae reddit Conscientias securas in praxi, non est Sententiae, quam sustinemus, Certitudo; non eiusdem maior, aequalis, aut minor Probabilitas, sed mera Contrariae Non-Certitudo."

18. Ibid., *Prodromus,"* *cap.* 1, "certitudo," no. 47 (p. 34): "multa enim non sunt certo vera, quae tamen incerta non sunt. Quae enim sunt certo falsa, non debent *incerta* vocari."

19. Ibid., "Dialexis," part 2, art. 1, no. 304 (p. 120): "Ergo haec ratio, in qua ponitur conscientiae securitas, erit aliquid Certitudini & Probabilitati commune."

20. Ibid., part 2, art. 4 (*resp. obj.* 2) no. 402 (p. 146).

21. Ibid., part 2, art. 1, no. 304 (p. 120).

22. On this attack, see Th. Deman, "Probabilisme," *Dictionnaire de théologie catholique* (Paris: Letouzey et Ané, 1936), col. 506.

23. *DNC*, "Prodromus," art. 7, no. 107 (p. 59): "tametsi enim de plerisque notionibus particularibus disputetur, generales & universales infallibiles sunt."

24. Ibid., art. 5, no. 94 (p. 52).

25. Ibid.,"Dialexis," part 2, art. 1, no. 340 (p. 131): "*quod necessario verum est: quod de absoluta Dei potentia aliter se habere non potest.*"

26. Ibid. The reference to the Second Table appears in Caramuel's interpretation of Bernard. See no. 347 (p. 133).

27. Ibid., part 2, art. 1, no. 340 (p. 131).

28. Ibid., nos. 340, 341, 343 (pp. 130–32).

29. Ibid., no. 340 (p. 131): "*non autem possum dicere*, fortassis aliter se habet, *quia non habeo rationem, qua possim hanc ipsam suspicionem fundare.*" Note that for clarity in the text, I have made the original roman type italic and vice versa.

30. Ibid., no. 342 (p. 132): "*gravi aliqua (particulari aut generali) ratione fulcitur.*"

31. Ibid.

32. Ibid., no. 344 (p. 132).

33. In the *Apologema*, Caramuel typically refers to this as the distinction between fear of the object and fear of the act (Juan Caramuel, *Apologema pro Antiquissima et Universalissima Doctrina de Probabilitate. Contra Novam, Singularem, Improbabilemque D. Prosperi Fagnani Opinationem* [Lyon: Anisson, 1663]).

34. *DNC*, "Dialexis," part 2, art. 1, no. 346 (p. 133): "*Eum, qui praeceptum metaphysice, physice, aut moraliter certum violat, committere peccatum certum est . . . Eum, qui operatur contra praeceptum, quod nec metaphysice, nec physice, nec moraliter est certum, nullo modo peccare, certum est.*"

35. Ibid., part 2, art. 1, no. 305 (p. 120): "Homo sane in suae est libertatis possessione certissima: & tam essentialis ipsi est abitrii libertas, ut qui eam negare audeat, insanus censendus sit . . ."

36. Ibid., part 2, art. 11, no. 658 (p. 230).

37. Ibid., part 1, no. 294 (p. 118).

38. Ibid., "Quaestio," art. 3, no. 13 (no page number).

39. Ibid., "Dialexis," part 2, art. 1, no. 306 (p. 120): "*Licitum dicitur, quod nulla lege prohibitum est.*"

40. Ibid., "Prodromus," *cap.* 3, art. 9, no. 116 (p. 63); Ibid., *cap.* 1, "peccatum," no. 35 (p. 28). Note Caramuel's distinction here between philosophical and theological malice.

41. Ibid., *cap.* 2, art. 5, no. 93 (p. 51).

42. See, for example, ibid., "Prodromus," *cap.* 4, no. 249 (p. 105): "manutendus est, qui possidet."

43. Ibid., "Dialexis," part 2, art. 1, nos. 308, 321 (pp. 121, 125).

44. Ibid., no. 328 (p. 127): "sententiam de peccato mortali, hoc est de morte aeterna."

45. Ibid., no. 331 (p. 128): "Nam omnis res censetur libera, nisi servitus & obligatio probentur."

46. Prospero Fagnani, *Commentaria in Primum Librum Decretalium*, . . . (Venice: Paul Balleonius, 1709), nos. 191–211 (pp. 49–52).

47. *DNC*, "Prodromus," *cap.* 4, no. 249 (p. 105): "*In poenis benignior est interpretatio facienda.*"

48. Ibid., no. 251: "*Semel Deo dicatum, non est ad usus humanos ulterius transferendum.*"

49. Ibid., *cap.* 4, no. 200 (p. 93).

50. Ibid., *cap.* 2, art. 9, no. 113 (p. 62).

51. Ibid., *cap.* 1, "peccatum" (margin number missing) (p. 29).

52. Ibid., *cap.* 2, art. 1, no. 64 (p. 42): "Lex nondum lata, aut nondum intimata, non est vera & actualis lex. Quam ob rem illa, quam invincibiliter ignoro, mihi non est sufficienter intimata, nec respectu mei est vera & actualis lex."

53. Ibid., *cap.* 2, art. 5, no. 81 (p. 47).

54. Ibid., *cap.* 2, art. 6, no. 102 (p. 56).

55. See, for example, ibid., "Quaestio," art. 4, no. 30 (no page number).

56. Ibid., "Dialexis," part 2, art. 14, *assert.* 9, no. 698 (p. 241): "lex, si non ligat, non existit; &, nisi cognoscatur non ligat;" "Ergo lex, quae non cognoscitur, nec formaliter, nec materialiter violari poterit."

57. Ibid., part 2, *assert.* 10, no. 700 (p. 242). In the *Apologema*, Caramuel also speaks of *hypothetical malice*; however, he does not explore the question of material sins (*Apologema*, 38–39).

58. See ibid., "Quaestio" art. 4, no. 31.

59. Ibid., "Dialexis," part 2, art. 1, no. 348 (p. 134).

60. Ibid., "Prodromus," *cap.* 4, nos. 232–33 (p. 102).

61. Ibid., "Dialexis," part 2, art. 14, *asserts.* 2, 3, nos. 682–83 (pp. 236).

62. Ibid., *assert.* 3, nos. 687–88 (pp. 238–39).

63. Ibid., *assert.* 5, no. 690 (p. 239).

64. Ibid., *assert.* 2, no. 682 (p. 236).

65. Ibid., part 2, art. 1, no. 350 (p. 134): "*libertatis possessione*"; art. 14, *assert.* 1, no. 681 (p. 235).

66. See ibid., *Ep.* 2, margin notes (p. 254). I have not summarized all of Caramuel's correspondents' objections or his responses to them.

67. Ibid., *Ep.* 2, no. 749 (p. 254): "Nescio an aliis evenerit, quod contingit mihi. Cum primum perlegissem doctrinam Illustrissimi Domini difficillima apparuit propositio tertiae Conclusionis. *Licitum est actionem quamcumque elicere, quae certo interdicta non sit* . . . Ex hac sententia plurima sequuntur absurda."

68. Ibid., nos. 750–56 (pp. 254–56). Note San Pedro's own analysis within the letter.

69. See the notes at the bottom of page 254 (ibid., *Ep.* 2).

70. Ibid., "Dialexis," part 2, art. 3, no. 386 (p. 143).

71. Ibid., part 2, art. 4, *resp. obj.* 3, no. 409 (p. 148).

72. Ibid.

73. Ibid., nos. 418–19 (p. 151).

74. Ibid., nos. 418–20 (pp. 151–52).

75. Ibid., no. 421 (p. 152): "Quia non scio contrarium. Quia Deus mihi iubet, *innocentiam praesumere, ubi culpa non probatur.*"

76. Ibid.

77. Ibid., no. 425 (p. 153): "possessione suae innocentiae."

78. Ibid., *Ep.* 2, no. 780 (p. 261).

79. Ibid., "Dialexis," part 2, art. 3, no. 387 (p. 143).

80. Ibid., part 2, art. 14, *assert.* 1, no. 680 (p. 235): "nullus Doctor asseruit."

81. Ibid., part 2, art. 6, no. 457 (p. 163): "antiquissimam & communissimam . . . "expresse in hanc unam veritatem conspirant."

82. See 1 Corinthians 10:25. Note, however, that Paul's text emphasizes respect for one's neighbor's conscience, not noncertitude.

83. *DNC,* "Dialexis," part 2, art. 6, nos. 458–60 (pp. 164–65).

84. Ibid., part 2, art. 4, no. 438 (p. 157).

85. Ibid., art. 6, no. 462 (p. 166): "*tene certum & dimitte incertum.*"

86. Ibid., no. 464 (p. 167): "turbant Theologiam."

87. Ibid., no. 462 (p. 165): "*Poenitentiam dare possumus, securitatem dare non possumus.*"

88. Ibid., no. 462 (p. 166): "*nam si scirem tibi* (absolutionem) *nihil prodesse, non tibi darem.*" Note that the parentheses mark Caramuel's interpolation into his quotation from Augustine.

89. Ibid., no. 463 (p. 166): "Videtur S. Pater his verbis totam hanc meam Dialexim expressisse." Note that this is a reference to the entire passage from Augustine.

90. Ibid.: "rigorose aut benigne."

91. Ibid., part 2, art. 6, no. 472 (p. 170).

92. Ibid., no. 466 (p. 167): "*nolenti dare, quam volenti negare,*" that is, in light of the catechumen's previously expressed desires.

93. Ibid., nos. 463–64 (p. 166–67).

94. Ibid., no. 467 (p. 168).

95. Ibid., no. 469 (p. 169).

96. Ibid., nos. 533–35 (p. 193).

97. Ibid., nos. 614–15 (pp. 217–18): "si forte . . . ut inter Theologos numerer." Article 6 of the "Dialexis" extends from no. 457 to 617 (pp. 163–218).

98. Ibid., part 2, art. 14, *assert.* 1, no. 680 (p. 235): "multis annis ante nos"; "*Opinio, quae tollit obligationem aliquid faciendi vel omittendi, . . . probabilis est, etsi nulla ratione positiva fulciatur, dummodo solvat omnia argumenta contrariorum.*"

99. Ibid., part 2, art. 6, no. 526 (p. 191): "plus dicit . . . quam nos in Apologemate."

100. Ibid.

101. See ibid., *Epistola* 13 (no margin number) (p. 339).

102. Ibid., "Dialexis," part 2, art. 14, *assert.* 1, no. 680 (p. 235).

103. Caramuel explicitly refers to his argument in the *Apologema* at this point (ibid., art. 4, *resp. obj.* 4, no. 430 [p. 154]).

104. Ibid., no. 429 (p. 154): "At haec objectio Nos non tangit: non enim de fide Orthodoxa differimus; sed de alia materia . . . quae tametsi gravissima, sine haereseos periculo in partem utramque disputatur."

105. Ibid.: "plausibiles . . . & probabiles."

106. Ibid., part 2, art. 4, nos. 432–33 (p. 155). No. 433: "nihil novum, nihil mirum sub Sole."

107. Ibid., part 1, no. 291 (p. 117): "Imperium impossibilia praecipientis iniustum & tyrannicum est: non ergo Deus supra humanae mentis Vires intelligere iubet, nec supra aliarum potentiarum vires agere."

108. See also ibid., "Prodromus," *cap.* 2, art. 5, no. 97 (p. 53).

109. Ibid., "Quaestio," art. 4, no. 30: "*Quando Ego mendacia, & falsa testimonia interdico, nil prorsus jubeo, quod vires humanas excedat. Sermonem tuum ita ab ore tuo prodire iubeo, ut cordi tuo, menti tuae, consentiat . . . Erit tibi huic praecepto obedire perfacile; non enim aliquid supra vires humani intellectus indico.*"

110. Ibid., art. 5, nos. 32–25.

111. Ibid., no. 32.

112. Ibid., "Dialexis," part 2, art. 14, *assert.* 9, no. 699 (p. 241).

113. Ibid., "Prodromus," *cap.* 4, nos. 200–2 (p. 93). No. 202: "vel iubet facere, quod possumus; vel iubendo monet, ut petamus quae nobis desunt; &, si petamus, dat nobis omnia necessaria, ut possimus: immo etiam frequenter etsi illa non petamus."

114. Ibid.: "*Deum* a dando dici."

115. In ibid., "Prodromus," *cap.* 3, art. 7, no. 181 (p. 87), Caramuel states: "Nec contra hanc consequentiam est Alexander VIII. nam agit de Authore gravi, & de sententia certo probabili: & Doctor iunior, ubi, singularis esse vult, & tueri opinionatem, quam universi reprobant: nec censeri debet Author gravis: nec eius authoritas est certo probabilis: non enim singulares sententias, prudentes Viri scribunt, ut illas sequamur, sed ut illas discutiamus & perpendamus." Since Alexander VIII did not become pope until seven years after Caramuel's death, this is presumably a reference to the theologian's former patron, and to the condemnations of 1665–66. Proposition 27 in the first group states: "Si liber sit alicuius iunioris et moderni, debet opinio censeri probabilis, dum non constet, reiectam esse a Sede Apostolica tamquam improbabilem" (*Enchiridion*, no. 2047 [p. 453]).

116. Ibid., "Prodromus," *cap.* 3, art. 7, no. 181 (p. 87): "*Resolutio unius Doctoris positis limitationibus, quas adhibent Theologi. . . est probabilis.*"

117. Ibid., "Dialexis," part 2, art. 1, no. 303 (p. 120): "in arena"; "per quadraginta aut plures annos." The *Theologia Regularis* first appeared slightly less than forty years before the *Dialexis* was published.

Afterword

1. See par. 74 in *Catholic Social Thought: The Documentary Heritage*, ed. David O'Brien and Thomas Shannon (Maryknoll, NY: Orbis, 1992), 509.

2. See, for example, Th. Deman, "Probabilisme," *Dictionnaire de théologie catholique* (Paris: Letouzey et Ané, 1936), cols. 494–97; Albert R. Jonsen and Stephen Toulmin, *The Abuse of Casuistry: A History of Moral Reasoning* (Berkeley: University of California Press, 1988), 171; and Jean Delumeau, "Prescription and Reality," in *Conscience and Casuistry in Early Modern Europe*, ed. Edmund Leites (Cambridge: Cambridge University Press, 1988), 138–39. Note, however, the important comments of Stone on probabilism as a response to the recognition of human finitude and sinfulness (M. W. F. Stone, "Scrupulosity and Conscience: Probabilism in Early Modern Scholastic Ethics," in *Contexts of Conscience in Early Modern Europe, 1500–1700,* ed. Harald E. Braun and Edward Vallance [New York: Palgrave Macmillan, 2004] 3).

3. Germain Grisez, *The Way of the Lord Jesus*, vol. 1, *Christian Moral Principles* (Chicago: Franciscan Herald Press, 1983), 447.

4. On his death, see Dino Pastine, *Juan Caramuel: Probabilismo ed enciclopedia* (Florence: La Nuova Italia Editrice, 1975), 151.

5. Juan Caramuel, *Apologema pro Antiquissima et Universalissima Doctrina de Probabilitate. Contra Novam, Singularem, Improbabilemque D. Prosperi Fagnani Opinationem* (Lyon: Anisson, 1663), 72.

Index